READING COLOSSIANS, EPHESIANS, AND 2 THESSALONIANS

READING THE NEW TESTAMENT SERIES

Reading Corinthians
by Charles H. Talbert

Reading John
by Charles H. Talbert

Reading Luke
by Charles H. Talbert

Reading Matthew
by David Garland

Bonnie Thurston

READING COLOSSIANS, EPHESIANS, AND 2 THESSALONIANS

A LITERARY AND THEOLOGICAL COMMENTARY

CROSSROAD • NEW YORK

1995

The Crossroad Publishing Company
370 Lexington Avenue, New York, NY 10017

Printed in the United States of America

Library of Congress Cataloging-in-Publication Data

Thurston, Bonnie Bowman.
Reading Colossians, Ephesians, and 2 Thessalonians : a literary
and theological commentary / Bonnie Thurston.
p.   cm. — (Reading the New Testament series)
ISBN 0-8245-1475-0
1. Bible. N.T. Colossians—Commentaries. 2. Bible. N.T.
Ephesians—Commentaries. 3. Bible. N.T. Thessalonians—
Commentaries. I. Title. II. Series.
BS2715.3.T48   1995
227—dc20   94-48659
                                                    CIP

In gratitude for
the Jesuit Tradition of Education
and
My Colleagues at Wheeling Jesuit College, 1985–1995

CONTENTS

EDITOR'S FOREWORD

"Reading the New Testament" is a commentary series that aims to present cutting-edge research in popular form that is accessible to upper-level undergraduates, seminarians, seminary educated pastors, and educated laypeople, as well as to graduate students and professors. The volumes in this series do not follow the word-by-word, phrase-by-phrase, verse-by-verse method of traditional commentaries. Rather they are concerned to understand large thought units and their relationship to an author's thought as a whole. The focus is on a close reading of the final form of the text. The aim is to make one feel at home in the biblical text itself. The approach of these volumes involves a concern both for *how* an author communicates and *what* the religious point of the text is. Care is taken to relate both the *how* and the *what* of the text to its milieu: Christian (New Testament and noncanonical), Jewish (scriptural and postbiblical), and Greco-Roman. This enables both the communication strategies and the religious message of the text to be clarified over against a range of historical and cultural possibilities. Moreover, a section of commentary on a large thought unit will often contain a brief excursus on some topic raised by the material in the unit, sometimes sketching Old Testament, postbiblical Jewish, Greco-Roman, New Testament, and noncanonical Christian views on the subject. Throughout, the basic concern is to treat the New Testament texts as religious documents whose religious message needs to be set forth with compelling clarity. All other concerns are subordinated to this. It is the hope of all participants in this project that our efforts at exposition will enable the New Testament to be understood better and communicated more competently.

Charles H. Talbert, General Editor

AUTHOR'S PREFACE

In view of the literature already in print, anyone undertaking commentaries of Colossians and Ephesians is likely either to be highly egotistical or very naïve. I hope I am not the first, but, alas, I am rather too old to be accused of the second! Had it not been for the initial encouragement and assurance of Charles Talbert, and for his wise advice and editorial assistance throughout the project, this work would not have been completed. I am also grateful for the editorial assistance offered by Crossroad, and especially the work of Lynn Schmitt.

Most of the final research and writing was done during a sabbatical granted me by Wheeling Jesuit College in 1993. I am grateful to the college and to St. George's College, Jerusalem (where I was visiting scholar from January to May, 1993), and the Ecole Biblique in Jerusalem, both of which granted me access to their very fine libraries. Other materials were cheerfully located by Wheeling Jesuit College interlibrary loan librarian, Mary Gasiorowski, to whom I owe both professional and personal debts of gratitude.

My friend and colleague Debra Hull read parts of the manuscript and endured many cups of cafeteria coffee during discussions of this work. I could produce no finished work without the careful proofreading of George Miller. Fr. James O'Brien, S.J. maintained constant interest in the state of the project and routinely encourages my work and discipleship. For these friends, and especially for my students, I am most grateful.

A note on the book itself seems in order. For each epistle in the volume I have provided an introduction, commentary on the text, and bibliography. Each bibliography covers the entire section preceding it and notes works used in the writing of that section. Primary sources are noted in the text, and when reference to a fuller discussion of an idea does not occur in the bibliography, it appears as a reference in the text. Quotations from the apostolic fathers are from the Kirsopp Lake edition. I have relied heavily on F. Rienecker and C. L. Rogers, *A Linguistic Key to the Greek New Testament* (Grand Rapids: Zondervan, 1976–1980) and J. H. Moulten and

G. Milligan, *The Vocabulary of the Greek Testament* (Grand Rapids: Eerdmans, 1949). In writing the commentary on Ephesians, I benefited from the sermons on Ephesians by my late husband, the Rev. Dr. Burton B. Thurston, Sr.

Finally, readers requiring more technical information may wish to consult further commentaries. G. B. Caird's *Paul's Letters from Prison* (Oxford: Oxford University Press, 1991) treats both Colossians and Ephesians well. Students of Colossians will find Eduard Lohse's *A Commentary on the Epistles to the Colossians and Philemon* (Philadelphia: Fortress, 1971) and Petr Pokorny's *Colossians: A Commentary* (Peabody, Mass.: Hendrickson, 1991) of immense help. Markus Barth's two-volume commentary on Ephesians (ABC; New York: Doubleday, 1974) clearly sets the scholarly standard, and I have relied heavily on his scholarship. Finally, 2 Thessalonians has been illuminated by Robert Jewett, *The Thessalonian Correspondence* (Philadelphia: Fortress, 1986) and I. Howard Marshall, *1 and 2 Thessalonians* (Grand Rapids: Eerdmans, 1983).

It is my hope that this book will be of value to those who are both students of the New Testament and followers of the master whose life inspired it. I accept responsibility and beg pardon for any false readings. What is useful here is due to those who have taught and nurtured me in the faith. To them all I owe eternal gratitude.

Bonnie Thurston
16 August 1994

ABBREVIATIONS

(Abbreviations in italic type refer to book or journal titles; abbreviations in roman type refer to series or biblical versions.)

ABC	Anchor Bible Commentary
ABD	*Anchor Bible Dictionary*
AThANT	Abhandlungen zur Theologie des Alten und Neuen Testaments
ATR	*Anglican Theological Review*
BibT	*Bible Today*
Bib	*Biblica*
BibSac	*Bibliotheca Sacra*
BJRL	*Bulletin of the John Rylands Library*
CBQ	*Catholic Biblical Quarterly*
EQ	*Evangelical Quarterly*
ERT	*Evangelical Review of Theology*
ExpT	*Expository Times*
GTJ	*Grace Theological Journal*
HBC	Harper's Bible Commentary
HBD	*Harper's Bible Dictionary*
IBC	Interpreter's Bible Commentary
IBD	*Interpreter's Bible Dictionary*
ICC	International Critical Commentary
Interp	*Interpretation*
JB	*Jerusalem Bible*
JBL	*Journal of Biblical Literature*
JSNT	*Journal for the Study of the New Testament*
JTS	*Journal of Theological Studies*
KJV	King James Version
LXX	Septuagint
NAB	*New American Bible*
NCBC	New Century Bible Commentary
NIV	New International Version
NJBC	*New Jerome Biblical Commentary*

NovT	*Novum Testamentum*
NRSV	New Revised Standard Version
NTM	New Testament Message Series
NTS	*New Testament Studies*
RevExp	*Review and Expositor*
RGG	*Die Religion in Geschichte und Gegenwart*
RQ	*Restoration Quarterly*
RSV	Revised Standard Version
SBLDS	Society of Biblical Literature, Dissertation Series
StudEvan	Studia Evangelica
SWJT	*Southwest Journal of Theology*
TheoT	*Theology Today*
ZNTW	*Zeitschrift für die neutestamentliche Wissenchaft*

COLOSSIANS

INTRODUCTION

The City of Colossae

Colossae was in the southern part of ancient Phrygia (modern Turkey) near the south bank of the Lycus river about 120 miles east of Ephesus, eleven miles southeast of Laodicea and fifteen miles south southeast of Hierapolis. For the five centuries before the New Testament era, it was the principal city in the Lycus Valley, on the main trade route from Ephesus to the Euphrates, the Asian highway.

Colossae is mentioned by the ancient historians in connection with the armies of Xerxes and Cyrus of Persia. When Herodotus relates how Xerxes' army was stopped in its march on Greece, he speaks of Colossae as a "great city." A century later (4th century B.C.E.), Xenophon described it as "a populous city, both wealthy and large." In addition to its being a station and trade center on the Asian highway, the commercial importance of Colossae was due to its wool industry. Wool gathered from the sheep of the Lycus valley was woven and dyed a reddish purple; the product was known as "colossinum."

The importance of the city had declined by Roman times because Laodicea, the seat of Roman administration, and Hierapolis, known for its healing waters, had grown more prominent and prosperous. In the Christian era Strabo called Colossae a small town. The population in New Testament times was mainly indigenous Phrygian and Greek settlers. Josephus recorded that Antiochus III brought in several thousand Jews from Mesopotamia and Babylon in the second century B.C.E., and Cicero noted there were eleven thousand Jewish males in the city. So, if small, in Paul's day Colossae was cosmopolitan.

The religious environment was as varied as the population. Numismatic evidence suggests that the worship of Ephesian Artemis, the Laodicean Zeus and also Artemis was practiced. Other Greek gods as well as Egyptian Isis and Sarapis, the cult of Cybele, and Mithraism were in evidence. Judaism in the area was undoubtedly syncretistic; in fact from comparative study of Greek inscriptions, Ramsay decided that the Jewish communities of the region were characterized by religious laxity exceptional in the diaspora.

Sometime between 60 and 64 C.E. there was a powerful earthquake which destroyed cities in the region and led to the further decline of Colossae. It is speculated that the population of the city relocated at that time. The site remains unexcavated today, and in our reconstructions of life in Colossae we do not have helpful archaeological evidence like that uncovered at Ephesus.

The Church in Colossae

The author of the letter probably had not visited the city (2:1). The Christian community seems to have been the result of missionary work (possibly missionaries from Pisidian Antioch) in the Lycus valley which occurred during the years of Paul's Ephesian ministry, or between ca. 52 and 55 C.E. (see Acts 19). The church certainly existed by mid-century and was apparently founded by Epaphras (1:7–8; 4:12–13). Onesimus (and thus Philemon) lived in Colossae (4:9), and the letter is well studied in connection with the letter to Philemon. Several references to the heathen past of the recipients of this letter (for example, 1:21–22 and 2:13) suggest that the Christian population was largely Gentile, although, as noted above, Jews were certainly present.

The Question of Authenticity

The question of the authorship of Colossians engenders lively debate. "Proof positive" of authorship is not only objectively impossible, but also beyond the scope of this commentary. However, a brief review of the issues is instructive, so long as it does not distract us from the primary task of understanding the letter as we have it.

Arguments in favor of Pauline authorship include the fact that the letter mentions Paul's name and those of his friends and has a structure similar to that of uncontested letters. The early church fathers accepted

Colossians as authentic without debate. Its earliest New Testament attestation is in the letter to the Ephesians (see "The Relationship of Colossians and Ephesians" later in this volume). The earliest external reference to the letter occurs ca. 180 C.E. in Irenaeus (*Haer.* 3.14.1 quotes 4:4). Marcion used the letter, and it is included in the Muratorian canon. There was no serious question about authorship until the nineteenth century.

Modern inquiry into the vocabulary and style of the letter led to questions about authenticity. The first argument against Pauline authorship was developed by Mayerhoff (1838) on the basis of lexical, stylistic, grammatical, and theological differences. Some of this material is summarized in what follows.

In the Nestle text Colossians has 1,577 words, 10.6% of which are found also in the uncontested letters. It contains 34 words not found elsewhere in the New Testament and 87 not found in the authentic letters. While the vocabulary of Colossians would appear to be unusual, Philippians, about which there has been no question of authorship, has 1,629 words in Nestle, only 3.9% of which agree with the vocabulary of other uncontested letters. So the lexical evidence alone does not weigh heavily against the Pauline authorship of Colossians. Furthermore, the distinctive vocabulary of the letter may be due to the author's extensive use of traditional materials (hymns, confessions, vice and virtue lists, household codes) which are incorporated into the text, or may be due to the fact that he is quoting the arguments of the false teachers.

Comparing Colossians stylistically to genuine Pauline letters reveals other differences. Colossians is marked by long sentences with synonyms heaped together. It uses conjunctions less often and participial constructions and relative clauses more often than in the authentic letters. Colossians has a liturgical or hymnlike style in contrast to the Cynic–Stoic diatribe style of earlier writings. But again, these differences in style may be due to the situation addressed or to the fact that, because Paul is in prison, he has more time to write reflectively. Perhaps the amanuensis used to write the letter exerted more liberty in this instance. (Lohse has suggested the author is not a secretary, but an independent theologian of the Pauline stamp who lived in Ephesus.) Or perhaps the fact that Paul knew the church only at a distance prevented him from using the highly polemical style he used with churches he founded and knew well.

Efforts have been made to answer the authorship question with regard to literary dependence. Similarities with Philemon are used to argue for authenticity. On the other hand, literary dependence upon Romans,

1 and 2 Corinthians, Galatians, and 1 Thessalonians has been suggested without convincing effect. (It is argued from similar turns of phrase in these letters as well as from exact parallels that a later author constructed Colossians from material in the earlier letters. It seems equally likely to me, however, that Paul might well have repeated himself or fallen into customary or habitual turns of phrase in writing Colossians.)

Vocabulary, style, and dependency aside, it is true that certain key Pauline concepts (most notably righteousness and justification) seem to be absent from this letter. Furthermore, the theological viewpoint of the letter is different from that of earlier compositions. Here Christ is the true representative of God making visible what was before unseen. Christ is the head of a body that includes the whole cosmos. Again, in Colossians believers have experienced deliverance and their salvation is already established (cf. 1Cor 15). Paul has presented himself not only as a peerless apostle, but as one whose sufferings complete what is lacking in Christ (Col 1:24). Clearly the thinking in this letter is different from earlier letters. But some have argued that this is a natural development of Paul's thought at a later stage of his career.

With considerable reservation, I come down on the side of Pauline authorship and refer to Paul as the author in the commentary that follows. I grant that excellent scholars disagree with me, and I see the logic of many of their arguments. For our purposes in this work it is best not to be purloined by arguments about authorship, but to try to understand the letter as we have it from the pen of whoever it was who wrote it.

The Circumstances of the Writing

The Colossian church seems recently to have been established at the time of the writing of the letter. It may be that Philemon and Colossians were created as parallels and dictated and delivered at the same time. (Philemon 1:9 suggests the writer's imprisonment was recent.)

According to the text of Colossians, Epaphras brought Paul news of threats to the church's faith (1:7-8; 4:12-13). The Colossian Christians faced false teaching referred to in the letter as "philosophy" (2:8). The broad outlines of that teaching can be inferred from statements in chapter 2 and will be discussed in detail in that context. Those addressed by the letter were Gentiles and syncretistic Jews.

If the author is Paul, the letter is certainly written near the end of his life, between 57 and 60 C.E. The letter states that the author was in prison at the time of the writing (4:3), but the location of imprisonment is at issue and the text provides no clues. Ephesus is mentioned in the Marcionite prologue, and a later subscript reads "from Rome by Tychicus and Onesimus." The Roman tradition of imprisonment has always been strong. Read in connection with Philemon, however, Caesarea is also a possible location. Both Ephesus and Caesarea have proximity (that is, they are closer to Colossae than is Rome) and date in their favor.

However one decides where the letter originated, the crucial point is that false teaching has taken hold in the Christian community at Colossae, and the writer takes strong exception to it (2:28). Hoping to avoid or alleviate a crisis in the church, Paul sends the letter to Colossae via Tychicus and Onesimus (4:7-9).

The Structure of the Letter

Recent work on letter writing in the ancient world has added greatly to our understanding of the New Testament letters, and we shall have occasion to make reference to this scholarship in due course. For the moment, simply note that Colossians follows the general pattern of a letter in the first century. Its opening formula gives the name of the sender, those addressed, and a greeting (1:1-2). This is followed by a thanksgiving (1:3-8) and a prayer for the recipients (1:9-12). The body of the letter falls into two sections, one doctrinal (1:13-2:23) and one parenetic or hortatory (3:1-4:6), as is customary in Paul's uncontested writings. At the heart of the doctrinal section is a "Christ-hymn" (1:15-20) which forms the core of its argument, and a series of rhetorical questions (2:20-23) serves as a transition to the second, "practical" half of the letter. Colossians ends with messages to Paul's friends and co-workers (4:7-17) and closes with traditional formulas (4:18).

Colossians has sometimes been called polemical because of the material in 2:8-23. However, that section lacks the sharp tone of Galatians or 2 Corinthians, which are clearly polemical. By and large, Colossians is laudatory in tone, even when warning about present dangers. I agree with Victor Paul Furnish in the *Anchor Bible Dictionary* that Colossians is more "admonitory than argumentative"; it is, as he says, "a letter of exhortation and encouragement."

For purposes of exposition, I have divided the Colossian letter as follows:

F. F.Bruce, "Jews and Christians in the Lycus Valley," *BibSac* 141 (1984): 13-14.

M. S. Fukuchi, "The Letter of Paul to the Colossians," *Bible Today* 60 (1972): 762-76.

V. P. Furnish, "Colossians," *ABD* 1:1090-96.

E. Lohse, "Pauline Theology in the Letter to the Colossians," *NTS* 15 (1968-69): 211-20.

R. P. Martin, *Ephesians, Colossians, and Philemon* (Atlanta: John Knox Press, 1991).

E. Th. Mayerhoff, *Der Brief an die Kolosser* (Berlin, 1838).

B. Reicke, "The Historical Setting of Colossians," *RevExp* 70 (1973): 429-38.

E. P. Sanders, "Literary Dependence in Colossians," *JBL* 85 (1966): 28-45.

THE SALUTATION, THANKSGIVING, AND PRAYER

Colossians 1:1–12

The opening section of Paul's letter to the Colossians follows the standard conventions of hellenistic letters. The thanksgiving and prayer flow from a typical hellenistic salutation, and are so closely related structurally and thematically that they are hard to separate. The section begins and ends with giving thanks to the Father (vv. 3 and 12). Paul seems to have altered the Jewish practice of beginning and ending prayers with *beracha* (blessing). Instead, he begins and ends with *hodaya* (thanksgiving).

Within the inclusion formed by the *hodaya*, both the thanksgiving (vv. 3–8) and the prayer (vv. 9–12) begin with constant intercession for the Colossians (vv. 3 and 9). And at the center of each section is the idea of "bearing fruit and growing" (vv. 6 and 10). The close of the section is signaled not only by the return to a liturgical form (*hodaya* or thanksgiving to the Father) but also by the use of an "eschatological climax," in the reference to "the inheritance of the saints in light" (v. 12). This makes it possible for Paul to move smoothly into the cosmic language of 1:13–14, which introduces the crucial issue of the first half of the letter, the inclusive authority and universal power of Jesus Christ.

Salutation (1:1–2)

In beginning his letters, Paul maintains and elaborates the tripartite form of salutation–recipient–greeting that is characteristic of the salutations of hellenistic letters. In such letters in the papyri the greeting usually gives the name of the author in the nominative, the recipient in the dative, and then some form of the word "grace" (*chairein*). Paul follows this pattern in Colossians and also the hellenistic practice of indicating the relationship between the writer and recipients by means of the greeting. The opening verse of Colossians agrees almost verbatim with that of 1 Corinthians, but must be read in the Colossian context.

Paul is addressing himself to those who do not know him (2:1). In six other epistles (1 and 2 Corinthians, Galatians, Ephesians, 1 and 2 Timothy) Paul is introduced as an apostle "by the will of God," or words to that effect. Here he is setting forth the origin and authority of his apostleship to a church that he has not visited and one that has not questioned his authority. That he is sent "by the will of God" is, of course, a reference to the Damascus Road experience (see Acts 9, 22 and 26, and Galatians 1:11-17). Paul is telling the Colossians that his authority is equal to that of the apostles called by the earthly Jesus and of the Jerusalem church.

But the letter is not just from Paul; it also comes from "Timothy our brother." Paul indicates more than that he is not alone in his imprisonment or that Timothy is a "brother" not an "apostle," although he does share in the apostolic work as "God's servant in the gospel of Christ" (1 Thess 3:2). Timothy is the brother in Christ not only of Paul, but also of the Colossians. He was known in Asia Minor and thus could serve to corroborate Paul's authority and ideas there. Since the Colossians knew and accepted Timothy, with whom Paul is closely associated, Paul hopes they will be more favorably disposed toward him and the message he is sending.

It may also be the case that Timothy is the coauthor of the Colossian letter. He appears as co-sender with Paul not only of this letter but of 2 Corinthians, Philippians, 1 and 2 Thessalonians, and Philemon. Most senders of letters in antiquity used a professional letter writer or amanuensis, and Paul was no exception (see 1 Cor 16:21; Philm 19; 2 Thess 3:17; and Col 4:18). Perhaps Timothy served Paul in this capacity. What is not clear is the degree to which this secretary was a recorder or an editor or a substitute author. Sometimes, as in 1 and 2 Corinthians and 1 Thessalonians, the switch back and forth between singular and plural pronouns gives some hint about whether Paul is speaking alone or with coauthors. In Colossians there is also some help from the text. In Colossians 1:3-14, 28; 2:13-14; and 4:3 the first person plural pronoun is used. In 1:24-27, 29; 2:1-5; 4:3-4, 8-18 the first person singular pronoun is used. It may be pushing the evidence too far to suggest that Paul speaks alone in the first person singular passages and with his coauthor in the plural texts. However, Paul does affix the final greeting in his own hand, a traditional way of assuring the authenticity of the material. That is, in the hellenistic world, the sender of a letter added the closing in his or her own hand to guarantee the contents of the letter.

With regard to the recipients of a Pauline letter, there are three types of formulation which give a clue about what will follow. In ways that often reflect the situation of those addressed, Paul addresses letters to churches, to members of churches, and to individuals. "The saints" is the oldest self-designation of the church, and Paul addresses Christians as "saints" in Romans, 1 and 2 Corinthians, Ephesians, and Philippians, in short, in letters to all the churches except those in Galatia. Here, however, Paul addresses "the saints and faithful brethren" (*adelphois*, "brethren," in Greek would include both men and women). In view of the situation described in chapter 2, it is possible that Paul is addressing his remarks only to that part of the Colossian community that has remained faithful, to those who have unswervingly held to the "word of truth" brought by Epaphras (1:4–7). In any event, we must conclude that Paul approves of those he addresses, the steadfast "in Christ at Colossae." With that turn of phrase, Paul alludes to the two spheres of Christian life, the internal and mystical sphere of the Christian's life "in Christ," and the external and geographical sphere in which he or she lives day to day. Both are important, as the text of the letter will go on to explain.

"Grace and peace" is the standard greeting in hellenistic letters, but "grace" would have added theological import for Christian recipients of a Pauline letter (here see 1:6b). At the time when 1 Corinthians was written, "grace and peace" are understood by Paul to come from "God our Father and the Lord Jesus Christ," and this becomes his standard greeting. There is an anomaly in Colossians, however, because the letter does not have the usual addition "and our Lord Jesus Christ." Textual evidence reveals that later editors sometimes added the phrase to bring Colossians in line with other Pauline epistles, but the phrase does not appear in the best manuscripts. Perhaps because Christ is focal in the doctrinal part of the letter, indeed is central to the argument of the whole of the letter, Paul omits reference to him here. It would seem more logical, however, to introduce the Christ as soon as possible. Very simply, we do not know why the characteristic phrase is omitted from the salutation.

Colossians begins with the standard Pauline formulas. The recipients are introduced not only to the origin of his authority but to one they knew who could verify it (Timothy). Those who listened carefully would hear something of the direction the letter would take as Paul speaks to those who have remained faithful to the fullness of life in Christ.

Thanksgiving (1:3–8)

The verb "thank" in v. 3 (*eucharistoumen*) signals the thanksgiving portion of a hellenistic letter. Paul's thanksgivings (which appear in all the Pauline and deutero-Pauline letters except Galatians, 1 Timothy, and Titus) usually signal in some way what is to follow in the body of the letter, and this is the case in Colossians. The form is not just a convention but reveals what is uppermost in the writer's mind. Here the conventions of the thanksgiving not only reveal Paul's concerns as he addresses the church at Colossae but serve to establish friendly relations with them and to dispose them favorably toward his message.

In its simplest form, the thanksgiving expresses the thanks of the writer and the grounds for that gratitude. Characteristically, in Greek, the thanksgiving begins with the phrase "I give thanks to God," (*eucharistō tō theō*) and is followed by participial phrases and clauses subordinate to them. This grammatical form is followed in Colossians.

The thanksgiving begins and ends with the love (*agapē*) of the Colossians (vv. 4 and 8) and, although it is one long sentence in Greek, it falls logically into three sections. Verses 3–5 focus on the Colossian community, which Paul praises. Verse 6 shifts the focus to the whole church in an effort to stress the universality of Christian truth. And vv. 7–8 return to the Colossian situation as Paul reminds them of how they have received that truth.

The "we" of v. 3 includes Paul and Timothy, who constantly thank God for the Colossians (cf. 1:9). God is introduced in connection with the incarnation and is described as "the Father of Our Lord Jesus Christ," which foreshadows the focus on Christ in the body of the letter, emphasizes Christ's exalted state, and tells the Colossians in no uncertain terms who Jesus is. Paul and Timothy thank God, who was made known in Christ, for the faith, love, and hope of the Colossian Christians. This triad of Christian virtues also appears in 1 Thes 1:3 and 5:8 and in 1 Cor 13:13, so may already be a standard feature of Christian catechesis. Again, Paul stresses that their faith is in Jesus Christ. Faith in Christ implies belief in certain things, as Paul will make clear shortly.

Love is the "evidence" of that faith (see Gal. 5:6). *Agapē* was not a common word for love in pagan literature of the time but is the characteristic Christian usage. Here it signals the disinterested concern and active good will of the Colossians toward "all the saints," all believers in Jesus, not just those with whom they were in agreement or toward whom they were naturally favorably disposed. Their faith and love are sustained by the hope "laid up for you in heaven." "Laid up" (*apokeimenēn*) means "stored for future use." Its connotations include the custom (borrowed from the Persians) of hellenistic rulers of laying aside goods for faithful servants. The word is also used in connection with the Persian court book in which names of the faithful are recorded and with the "book of life" in Jewish apocalyptic. Mention of heaven introduces the whole question of the spiritual realm and its influence on human beings which will come to the fore later in this chapter and in 2:8–3:4.

They have "heard before" of this hope by means of the gospel, the "word of truth." The phrase is particularly suggestive. First, "the word of truth" is used appositively with "gospel." The "word of truth" is the sum total of the message connected with Jesus and all he has, does, and will accomplish. Second, "word of truth" suggests that there are also false words, and this, of course, prefigures Paul's concern in the letter that they not be made prey of false teaching. They had heard the truth "before," an allusion to the work of Epaphras, who taught prior to the false teachings that have appeared on the scene. Finally, "word" in the Johannine communities was another way of referring to Jesus (see John 1:14; 1 John 1:1–3). Perhaps here, again, as in vv. 3 and 4, allusion is made to Jesus Christ, the central concern of the first portion of the letter.

This word of truth is active not only in Colossians but "in the whole world," which for Paul would be the Roman Empire. Verse 6 enlarges the scope of the discussion and places the Colossian Christians in the context of the whole church. Paul uses the language of parables to set forth the characteristics of the true gospel. It bears fruit and it grows (see Mark 4:1–20 and parallels). "Fruit bearing" suggests outward activity and "growth" inward or spiritual development. The point for Paul is that the result of the true gospel is evident and observable. Its substance is the grace of God. In vv. 3–5 Paul has commended the faith of the Colossians. Here he has shifted focus to the whole church and the tests of true faith that are universal.

It is Epaphras from whom the Colossians have received this faith and from whom Paul has heard about it (vv. 7 and 8). Epaphras is one of their own. He, like others known to them, is beloved by Paul (see 4:7, 9, 14). But he is also a "fellow slave" (*syndoulou*), one having allegiance to a common master, and a servant (*diakonos*), one who participates in Paul's apostolic activity. Paul sets forth the authority of Epaphras, who has the apostolic word which the Colossians heard when they first believed. The implied contrast is with the teachers of "philosophy" (2:8) who have come on the scene later and are unknown to Paul.

The thanksgiving of the letter is entirely commendatory. There is no hint of a problem until 2:8. Perhaps this reflects an older and wiser Paul, one who learned from his experience with the Galatians. The opening section of this letter is part of Paul's effort to secure a favorable hearing from the Colossians. His praise for them begins and ends with their love, their practical acting out of the faith to which they have clung (1:6b). But the thanksgiving also serves to focus on Jesus Christ (vv. 3, 4, 7 and perhaps v. 5) because accurately understanding the work of Jesus will prevent their falling victim to false teaching with its attendant dangers. The thanksgiving is really about the continuing work of Christ as it outlines for the Colossians the characteristics of Paul's gospel. According to him, the gospel is the grace of God and the truth; it is universal, productive, and transmitted by human beings. The themes introduced in the thanksgiving are explicitly reiterated in the prayer for the community that follows.

Prayer (1:9–12)

In the prayers of his letters Paul usually intercedes for things mentioned in the thanksgiving, and this is the case in Colossians. Verse 9 follows closely from what preceded it (*dia touto*). The intercession is based on the good report Paul and Timothy have received (vv. 6–8); that report is the antecedent of "it" in v. 9. On the basis of what God has already done among the Colossians, Paul presumes to ask God to do more. The theme of constant prayer ("we have not ceased to pray for you") is picked up from v. 3 ("We always thank . . . when we pray for you").

The prayer itself has two petitions, one for fullness and one for power. In v. 9 Paul prays that they will be granted three theological virtues: knowledge of God's will, wisdom, and spiritual understanding. Those virtues result in practical consequences: a life worthy of the Lord, pleasing to the Lord, and bearing fruit and growing (v. 10). Verses 9 and 10 introduce the crucial Pauline assumption that theology is important because action proceeds from it. The second petition in v. 11 returns to theological virtues and the spiritual endowments the Colossians will need for practical activity. The prayer closes by pointing toward the final rewards of faithfulness.

The first petition begins by asking that they "be filled" (*plerōthete*). The word is a subtle introduction of the concept of "fullness" (*plerōma*), which will be crucial later in the letter (see 1:19 and 2:9). The three endowments with which Paul asks that they be filled—knowledge, wisdom, and understanding—are not original to him. The triad occurs in Exod 31:3; 35:31; Isa 11:2; Sir 1:19; and in the Qumran literature (1QS 4:4; 1QSb 5:21; 1QH 12:11ff., for example). In addition to their associations with Jewish wisdom tradition, the terms would be familiar to those whose background included the Greek religions, especially the mysteries and Gnosticism. One wonders if Paul is intentionally introducing the language of the false teachers in order to begin to refute it.

"Knowledge" (*epignōsin*) in the Hebrew Bible is always connected with practical obedience, and so serves to counter the heretical concept of knowledge that is speculative. "Wisdom" (*sophia*) for the Greeks implied mental excellence, but for the Jews "wisdom" connoted the ability to apply knowledge of God's will. Again, wisdom is understood as practical. "Understanding" (*synesei*) in this sense means "insight," the ability to put ideas together and draw conclusions, or to see the relationship between ideas.

Paul stresses these theological virtues because of their practical result; they will allow the Colossians to lead lives appropriate to the Christian faith they profess. For Paul, theological virtues are confirmed in practical living. Here he outlines four consequences of spiritual knowing: a life worthy of the Lord, pleasing to him, bearing fruit, and growing in knowledge (v. 10). The section begins with an infinitive of purpose (*peripatēsai*), whose Greek root means literally "walk." The Colossians are to conduct their daily walk, their lifestyle, in a way that is worthy of God. The word for "pleasing" (*areskeian*) is found in parallel literature with negative connotations; it means something like "brown-nosing," fawning to gain favor. But in this, its only use in the New Testament, Paul gives it positive content.

We have already encountered "bearing fruit" and "growing" in v. 6. The image of a vigorous plant with its health attested by fruit and new growth (that also promises continuance) is reintroduced. What the gospel is doing "in the whole world," Paul wants done in Colossae as well.

At the beginning of the second petition of the prayer Paul again introduces a word that will be crucial in the following argument. He prays that they may be "strengthened with all power" (v. 11). The root of both words is *dynamis,* in Hebrew tradition the chief characteristic of God, but also a concept that is crucial when Paul discusses Christ's authority over "the powers" (2:15). "All power" comes from God; forms of "all" (*pas*) occur eleven times in vv. 4–11 and twice in v. 11 to emphasize that fact. In the prayer Paul makes it clear that power belongs to God, who is glorious in might, and undoubtedly Paul hopes the Colossians will recall this as they consider his arguments later in the letter.

The Colossians are to be strengthened with power for endurance (*hypomonēn*) and patience (*makrothumian*), characteristic Pauline virtues which are frequently linked in eschatological contexts as necessary endowments for the end times (see 2 Cor 6:4ff. and 2 Tim 3:10). Endurance is the refusal to be daunted by hard times. Its root word means "to stay," "remain," "abide" or "last," and it characterizes the athlete in Heb 12:1 who runs the race with perseverance. In Paul the term appears in Rom 8:25 and 15:4, again, as an eschatological virtue. "Patience" connotes a more social virtue. It literally means being greater than anger and implies the refusal to be upset by perverse people, the sort of self-restraint that makes it possible to face opposition without retaliation, in other words, patience with people.

Both endurance and patience are to be exercised with "giving thanks to the Father" (v. 12). The idea of thanksgiving turns the whole petition away from simply grim long-suffering. It also signals the end of this section of the letter and the beginning of a new section. The letter proper begins with thanksgiving in v. 3, and its recurrence here signals a liturgical conclusion. This is borne out by the introduction of eschatological language in "the inheritance of the saints in light." "Inheritance" (*klērou*) is used in Exodus for the Promised Land, what is assigned or allotted, and in the LXX for the division of the land among the twelve tribes. The Christians in Colossae are being granted a new allotment. The light-and-dark imagery introduces cosmic language that prefigures Paul's description of Christ's defeat of "principalities and powers." The immediately following verses, vv. 13–14, give the reasons for thanksgiving (deliverance, redemption, and forgiveness), and they shall be treated shortly.

In the prayer, which constitutes a standard feature of hellenistic letters, Paul accomplishes a number of objectives. First, he keeps the themes raised in the thanksgiving at the fore. Second, he introduces two issues that will be crucial in what follows (fullness and power) and makes subtle reference to the false teachers he hopes to refute. Third, he places all the teaching that follows in the context of prayer to the all-powerful God. Finally, he continues the almost lock-step progression of ideas that was begun in the movement from the thanksgiving to the prayer sections of the letter. In Greek, vv. 9–20 form virtually one continuous thought. In v. 12, the last verse of the prayer, the attitude of thankfulness is introduced, so that the reasons for thankfulness can be set forth in vv. 13–14, which form the transition to the body of the letter in which Paul will set forth Christ as cosmic ruler and lord.

T. Y. Mullins, "Formulas in New Testament Epistles," *JBL* 91 (1972): 380–90.

_____, "Greeting as a New Testament Form," *JBL* 87 (1968): 418–26.

S. Olson, "Pauline Expressions of Confidence in His Addressees," *CBQ* 47 (1985): 282–95.

P. Pokorny, *Colossians* (Peabody, Mass.: Hendrickson, 1991).

J. T. Sanders, "The Transition from Opening Epistolary Thanksgiving to Body in the Letters of the Pauline Corpus," *JBL* 81 (1962): 348–62.

S. K. Stowers, *Letter Writing in Greco-Roman Antiquity* (Philadelphia: Westminster Press, 1986).

THE SUFFICIENCY OF CHRIST

Colossians 1:13-23

The whole argument of the letter hinges on Paul's ability to convince the Colossians that Jesus Christ is the ultimate authority and power in the universe. He alone is all-sufficient, and from that fact certain practical consequences follow. The error that Paul refutes in chapter 2 is related to the way the Colossian Christians viewed the person of Christ and his redemptive work. This section of the letter, then, is central to Paul's thinking.

Colossians 1:13-23 can be divided into three sections. In vv. 13-14 Paul outlines what God has accomplished through Christ; it describes the action. Verses 15-20, "the Christ-hymn," introduce the means by which God accomplished redemption and forgiveness; it describes the agent. And, finally, vv. 21-23 explain how the Colossians are affected and what they must do in response; it describes the effect. Verses 13 and 14 speak in terms of God ("he") and of "us" for whom "he" has acted. Verses 15-20 speak only of "he," Christ. And vv. 20-23 speak to "you," those effected. The fact that the writer and recipients figure in vv. 13-14 and vv. 21-23, but not in vv. 15-20, both support the three-part division of the text and suggest that vv. 15-20 are an insertion of some sort (about which, more shortly).

The context of the whole section is redemption (vv. 13-14) which is explained in terms of cosmological action (vv. 15-20) and given application in the specific Colossian situation (vv. 20-23).

H. W. House, "Doctrinal Issues in Colossians. Part I," *BibSac* 149 (1992): 45-59.
T. E. Pollard, "Colossians 1:12-20: A Reconsideration," *NTS* 27 (1981): 572-75.

The Action (1:13-14)

The verses that introduce the centrality of Jesus Christ to the plan of God are closely related to the thanksgiving prayers that precede them. In fact, Käsemann and other scholars see Col 1:12-20 as part of a baptismal liturgy. Paul "serves the best wine" at the beginning of the body of the letter; he states the enormity of what God has done as he enumerates the four reasons for his thankfulness: God has delivered, transferred, redeemed, and forgiven those who believe in the Christ.

The language of the Exodus dominates v. 13. As God had delivered Israel from slavery in Egypt, God now delivers from slavery to "darkness" (a New Testament metaphor for evil which, when personified, refers to Satan). In 1 Thess 1:10 Paul uses the same word for deliverance (*ryomai*) in reference to the final judgment. God's "rescue" is to be understood as cosmic and eternal. "Transferred" (*metesesen*) literally means "to remove from one place to another"; the term is used to describe the deportation of a large group of men to form a new colony (see Josephus, *Ant.* 12.129). Here the movement is between a "dominion" (*exousias*), literally "an authority," and a "kingdom" (*basileian*); it is from the authority of Satan to the rule of Christ.

It is easy to forget that the cosmology of the first century and that of our own time are very different indeed. We doubt the reality of what we cannot see, measure, or quantify. For persons in the first century, on the other hand, unseen realities were no less real; spiritual powers and forces had the same reality that temporal or political ones do in our day (thus Paul's interest in "principalities and powers" in chapter 2). The "dominion of darkness" and "the kingdom of his beloved Son" (a Semitism from early Jesus tradition?) had an immediacy and reality for the Colossians that may be lost on us. Therefore, it is even more important to notice how concrete Paul's language is when he describes these spiritual realms. In v. 13 he uses the language of rescue and deportation and in v. 14 that of economics. The "dominion of darkness" and the "kingdom of the beloved Son" are in opposition to one another; they are enemies in the competition for the lives and allegiance of human beings. (Those who view this section as part of a baptismal liturgy suggest the "beloved Son" language echoes that used of Jesus at his baptism. See Mark 1:11 and parallels.)

Verse 14 indicates that, while the transference is a spiritual one, its reality is no less crucial. The movement is accomplished in Christ (*en hō*), the same Christ in whom the Christians' real life is hidden (see 3:3). The idea of redemption is closely tied to those of inheritance (v. 12) and deliverance (v. 13). "Redemption" (*apolytrōsin*) literally means "complete release based on payment of a price, freedom through ransom" (the means by which prisoners or slaves were liberated). The same economic language stands behind "forgiveness" (*aphesin*), which means "to cancel" or "to remit" (as a debt).

Verses 13 and 14 are related both thematically and structurally. They set forth the reasons for the thankfulness expressed in v. 12. These reasons occur in two sets of parallel ideas: "delivered" and "transferred" (from one opposing power, that of darkness, to another, that of the beloved Son), and "redemption" and "forgiveness." Paul has also loaded the verses with ideas which serve to counter the rival claims that he will discuss in chapter 2. He notes that believers share the heavenly world, that God has rescued them from the Satanic realm, and that Christ alone redeems and forgives sin. Each claim represents an issue raised by the false teachers in Colossae.

Through Jesus Christ, God has delivered men and women from darkness to light (imagery that would appeal and be familiar to Greeks) and from slavery to freedom (imagery that would evoke the Exodus for Jewish hearers). In him they are transferred from the domination of Satan (darkness) to the benevolent rule of the Son (which, in v. 12 was described as "the inheritance of the saints in light"). The verdict "condemned" has changed to "forgiven" because of what Christ has done. This is the very heart of the issue in the Colossian letter (see 1:22; 2:12–14; 3:1). In the hymn that follows, Paul characterizes the One who has accomplished this liberation.

The Agent (1:15–20)

The "Christ-hymn" in Colossians is the first of the two primary focuses of scholarly attention in the letter—the second is the issue of Paul's opponents in 2:6–23. In fact, it has occasioned among the most comment of any passage in the New Testament. The critical literature on the hymn is voluminous and technical. An excellent brief survey of this material is presented in R. P. Martin in his NCBC volume on Colossians and Philemon. A full history of interpretation to the mid-60s can be found in H. J. Gabathuler, *Jesus Christus: Haupt der Kirche—Haupt der Welt* (AThANT; Zurich, 1965). The bibliography at the end of this section may be of help to those who wish to pursue the technical issues.

Debate has revolved around whether this material is an insertion, around whether the author wrote the hymn or used existing material, and around how the existing text is structured. (These issues are similar to those raised in connection with the other Pauline Christ-hymn, Phil 2:6–11.) The brief discussion that follows does not seek to contribute new material to the debate, but to summarize the existing literature and to suggest a reading of the hymn as it exists in the text and as it served Paul's purposes in the Colossian situation.

In his work *Agnostos Theos* (Berlin, 1913), E. Norden was the first to point out that the passage might be a hymn or liturgical text of some sort. He argued on the basis of the repetitions of words and the rhythm of the Greek that it is an insertion. His argument has been strengthened as scholars also noted the shift of pronouns from the surrounding material (vv. 13–14 are first person, vv. 15–20 are third person, and vv. 21–23 are second and first person) and the concentrated use of relative constructions, which are a mark of liturgical materials. The present consensus is that the passage is an insertion in the letter.

Accordingly, the question is raised whether the author wrote the hymn or used an existing one. It is noted that the words and ideas represented are rare in Paul. In fact, the hymn has the greatest concentration of words not found elsewhere in Paul, five *hapax legomena* and ten non-Pauline expressions. The conclusion has been drawn that the author employed an already existing hymn which he amended to stress ideas of crucial importance to him. The exact nature of the editing of the hymn is the subject of much debate, but most modern commentators accept that Paul added "the church" in v. 18a and "making peace by the blood of his cross" in v. 20.

Some scholars have felt this pre-Pauline hymn was marked with the Semitic stamp of the wisdom tradition, while others have argued that it has much in common with Gnostic redeemer-myth material. The phrase "firstborn from the dead" (v. 18b) suggests that the hymn was originally part of a Christian liturgical tradition. Käsemann suggests its context in the early church was baptismal, while Bornkamm argues it was eucharistic.

Another point of debate is the structure of the hymn. Where the hymn begins and ends is the first question. Both Col 1:15–20 and 1:12–20 are suggested as the parameters, with the former being the more common view (and the one adopted in this commentary). Within 1:15–20 it is clear that there are several nominal sentences beginning with "he" (vv. 15, 17, 18). In two of these, "he" is described as "firstborn" (vv. 15a,

18b), and this is followed by the phrase "for in him" (the *hoti* clauses in vv. 16, 19). Also noted is the incorporation of the formula "from . . . through . . . to," which also appears in Rom 11:33–35.

These repetitions have been used to divide the hymn into stanzas in a variety of ways. Two basic patterns have been set forth, and several others are suggested. First, E. Lohse has suggested that the hymn is divided into two strophes. Verses 15–18a deal with Christ and creation, and vv. 18b–20 deal with Christ and reconciliation. Second, following the work of E. Schweizer, R. P. Martin suggests a tripartite division in which vv. 15–16 discuss creation, vv. 17–18a its preservation, and vv. 18b–20 its redemption. A five-strophe metrical arrangement and a four-line pattern have been proposed but have not gained wide acceptance. Probably the most usual arrangement in the current literature is a bipartite one, which seems more natural and has in its favor the fact that closer parallelism between the two strophes can be demonstrated.

Whatever the divisions of the hymn, its purpose in Colossians is clear. Paul faced an error in the Colossian church that is related to the way Jesus Christ was viewed (see Col 2:6–23). The hymn serves as a christological statement establishing the preeminence and supremacy of Christ in creation. Paul wants to assure his readers that all powers are subject to Christ's lordship. In the hymn "all" appears eight times, "heaven and earth" twice.

In the discussion that follows, the hymn is treated in terms of the two crucial questions which it answers: What is the nature of the church's Lord? What is his relationship to the church, and, indeed, to the universe?

Christ's accomplishments are outlined in 1:13–14, so the hymn serves Paul well since it begins by describing Christ's nature in 1:15–17. The hymn characterizes the Christ in four ways: He is the image of the invisible God (v. 15a) and the firstborn of creation (v. 15b); in him all things were created (v. 16) and in him all things hold together (v. 17b).

The "beloved Son" of v. 13 is the antecedent of the pronoun "he" in v. 15. The connection between God and the Christ is assumed in the hymn and is the point at which it begins. The word "image" (*eikōn*) is suggestive. In Greek thought the "image" was understood to share in the reality of what it represented. Thus, Christ is not to be understood as a copy of God; Christ is God. In the words of the letter to the Hebrews, he bears "the exact imprint of God's very being" (1:3, NRSV). Behind the statement is not only the fact that the Christ stands with the creator above the creation and is, therefore, unique, but the conventional Jewish idea that the creator is also the redeemer (cf. v. 14). N. T. Wright has pointed out that this is the standard pattern of Jewish monotheistic confessions (see, for example, Pss 96:5; 146:5–6). Certainly all the biblical writers assume that God is spiritual and invisible. So in proclaiming Christ as "the image of the invisible God," the hymn draws on the traditions of both Greek and Hebrew religion to demonstrate how he participates in the nature of God.

It is in light of the Christ's relationship with God that his description as "firstborn of all creation" (v. 15b) is to be understood. In hellenistic Judaism the image of God was not only the original image of the rest of creation, but the Logos was also called "firstborn" (*prōtotokos*). Thus the whole wisdom tradition is introduced into the hymn.

Wisdom was not only personified as feminine (Prov 8; Ecclus 24; Wis 7; the Hebrew verb is feminine), but "created before all things" (Prov 8:22; Sir 1:4) and present with God from the beginning (Wis 9:9). Wisdom shares the divine throne (Wis 9:4; cf. Col 1:16) and, in a complication of genders, Philo calls her "the firstborn son." To say that the Christ is *prōtotokos,* then, is to speak of primacy of function as well as of priority in time. The reference is probably intended to be more to supremacy than temporality. The point is that Christ holds primacy over the orders of creation. (A full exploration of the wisdom tradition and Christology is found in James D. G. Dunn, *Christology in the Making* [Philadelphia: Westminster, 1980] and in Elizabeth Johnson's *She Who Is* [New York: Crossroad, 1992].)

Christ's primacy is of such importance that it is mentioned at three other points in the hymn. At the outset of v. 17 Christ is described as "before all things." The phrase uses the emphatic *autos* ("he, himself" would be a good translation) to speak of the absolute and universal priority of Christ. Verse 18 describes Christ as "the beginning" (*archai*), which, in a classic article, led C. F. Burney to suggest Col 1:16–18 was an elaborate exposition in the rabbinic manner of the first word of Genesis. Burney believes that the writer is demonstrating how, in every way, Christ is *reshith* (from Hebrew *rosh,* "head"). Probably in the context of the hymn *archai* means Christ was the origin, again stressing priority in power and time. Like "image" (*eikōn*), "beginning" (*archai*) is a designation of the Logos, which is another way the hymn is linked to the wisdom tradition. Proverbs 8:22 states, "The Lord created me [Wisdom] at the beginning of his work, the first of his acts of long ago" (NRSV).

Finally, in v. 18b Christ is described as "preeminent" (*prōteuon*), having the first or chief place. These statements of Christ's priority are of special interest to Paul because they serve to counter the false teaching he refutes later in the letter.

To return, then, to the characterizations of Christ in the first part of the hymn, the *hoti* clause which introduces v. 16 signals that the verse modifies the last clause of 15; it reveals more about Christ in creation. In and through and for him all things were created. The passive voice of the verb indicates that God is the creator. "In him" suggests that Christ is the locus of the work of creation, with the preposition being understood as instrumental as well as local. The creation is also "through Christ"; the preposition with the genitive makes Christ the instrument of creation. The hymn thus transfers Wisdom's role as agent of creation to the Christ (cf. John 1:3). The remainder of v. 16 indicates the extent of Christ's creation. All things, including all power and authority, whether temporal or eternal, visible or invisible, natural or supernatural, find their origin in Christ.

Finally, not only do all things find their origin in Christ; they all cohere or are held together in him (v. 17b). The term "hold together" (*syn-estēken*) is used by Platonic and Stoic philosophy to designate the wonderful unity of the whole world. Here the hymn plumbs Greek thought for a new idea; Christ is the principle of cohesion in the world. The Christ not only creates but sustains the creation.

The hymn to this point indicates that the redemption described in vv. 13–14 relates to the whole world through the Christ who is a present reality. Christ holds supremacy in both arenas of human reality, the heavenly (spiritual) and the earthly (material). This assertion is reinforced for the recipients of the letter in Colossae by the use of ideas that originate in both Greek and Hebrew thought. And the whole passage (vv. 15–17) sounds remarkably like the confessional statement in 1 Cor 8:6—"for us there is one God, the Father, from whom are all things and for whom we exist, and one Lord, Jesus Christ, through whom are all things and through whom we exist"—which is Paul's Christianization of the *Shema* (Deut 6:4).

With the preeminence and supremacy of Christ in creation established, the hymn turns to the question of the relationship of this Christ to the church and to the world. The second half of the hymn begins like the first with predications for Christ; he is the head of the body, the church; the beginning; and the firstborn from the dead (v. 18). The hymn goes on in vv. 19–20 to explain the soteriological significance of these statements.

As noted earlier, Paul probably added "the church" to the statement "he is the head of the body." The effect is to change a cosmological statement not only to an ecclesiological one but to a christological one. This is because in a variety of Greek sources (including Plato, the Stoics, and Philo) the universe is conceived of as a body ruled by a "head." The idea was that just as a human body needed the governance of a head, the universe needed a governing principle (like the Logos). "Head" (*kephalē*) here should be understood in terms of the Hebrew *rosh,* as "leader" rather than "source." (We already know from v. 16 that Christ is "source," since all things were created in and through him.) Paul takes this religious presupposition, expressed in a metaphor that compares the cosmos to a living being, and alters it slightly so that "body" is associated with the church (cf. Col 1:24). Unlike his use of the body metaphor in Rom 12 or 1 Cor 12, here Christ is the "head" of the church, again, underlining the lordship of Christ over all things.

Second, and continuing the structural parallelism with v. 15, Christ is "firstborn from the dead." As Christ was the firstborn of creation, now he signals the beginning of the New Creation and the first step in the general resurrection. The idea appears in Paul as early as 1 Thess 4:13–18. Occurring together, "beginning" and "firstborn" recall Gen 49:3 (in which both *prōtotokos* and *archai* appear in the LXX) and suggest that the firstborn is also the founder of a new people, an idea that Paul has set forth in Rom 8:20, where Christ is the "firstborn among many brethren."

As Christ was the "image of God" in v. 15a, he is described as the "fullness of God" in v. 19. The grammar of v. 19 is notoriously difficult, but it is well rendered in the RSV, which explains that the totality of divine power and saving grace of God were pleased to dwell in, or "settle down permanently" (*katoikēsai*) in, Christ. "Fullness" (*plerōma*) is a loaded term. Its nontechnical use in the ancient world suggested the "filling out" of something. But it was also used in the language of religious syncretism of late antiquity to designate the uppermost spiritual world, that closest to God. As filling the space between heaven and earth, it was a sort of intermediary between God and humans. The necessity for such mediation is precisely the sort of thing Paul argues against in 2:8ff. The hymn undercuts the necessity for an intermediary since it makes clear that the full nature of God rests exclusively in Christ. (That it is "pleased" to dwell there again suggests to some the baptismal language of Mark 1:11.) Once again the hymn is reinterpreting a well-known term, this time transferring it from ancient cosmology to soteriology.

Christ is ruler of the universe and the church and is the beginning of a new phase of creation. The enormity of God resides in him. The result of this is soteriological; Christ is able to reconcile to himself all things and to make peace by the blood of his cross (v. 20). That Christ reconciles to himself "all things" has raised a great issue in systematic theology about the nature of this universal reconciliation. The point here, however, must be understood in terms of the context "whether on earth or in heaven." Nothing in the universe stands outside the scope of Christ's reconciling work. Thus no alien or hostile power can stand against the church. (Recall that this is precisely Paul's point in Romans 8:38–39.) As all things were created in and through him (v. 16), all things are reconciled through him. The Creator is also the Redeemer (a standard Jewish understanding).

The language of v. 20 is clearly relational. "Reconcile" (*apokatallaxai*) means "to exchange hostility for friendship." In the Greek, the compound preposition suggests the return to a previous state. Christ restores the creation to its original relationship with God the Creator. Likewise, "making peace" (*eirēnopoiēsas*) uses a participle to describe the means of reconciliation. It is the same root used in Matt 5:9: "blessed are the peacemakers (*eirēnopoioi*) for they shall be called sons of God." (If the Christ-hymn tradition and the Matthean tradition were related, Col 1:20 would complete a most elaborate pun, since Christ has been called the "beloved Son" in v. 13.) Paul's addition "by the blood of the cross" makes the means of peacemaking vivid and places the hymn in the context of the historical realities of Christianity. By his own suffering and death on the cross, Jesus Christ has returned all things to proper relationship with God. Heaven and earth are brought back into the divinely created order. In contrast to Paul's earlier thinking on this matter (1 Cor 15, for example), the hymn suggests that reconciliation and peace occur not just at the end of time but have already been effected.

Paul has introduced the Christ-hymn at the outset of the letter because it presents an accurate (and cosmological) understanding of the Christ, and it closes with a proper soteriology in its depiction of what Christ accomplished. The hymn insists on Christ's identification with God, whose purpose in creation was to sum up all things in that Christ and to reconcile or return the whole creation to right relationship with the Divinity through him. What Paul is telling the Colossian church by means of the hymn is that it has all it needs in Christ. While the hymn may be a pre-Pauline insertion, its ideas suit precisely Paul's purposes here and are not in contradiction with what is known of Paul's thinking on these matters elsewhere.

The Effect (1:21–23)

The section of the letter dealing with the sufficiency of Christ (1:13–23) closes as it began by focusing on redemption; Paul applies the Christ-hymn to the recipients of the letter. The pattern that occurs in the thanksgiving of shifting the focus of attention from the Colossians specifically (1:3–5) to the "whole world" (1:6) and back to the Colossians (1:7–8) is repeated here as Paul explains their redemption (1:13–14), the universal means of that redemption (1:15–20), and its particular effect on them (1:21–23). Specifically, the passage opens and closes with the Colossians' personal relationship to the gospel (1:13–14 and 21–23). Hovering on the edge of parenesis, Paul shows the effect of Christ's reconciliation and peacemaking on them. Verses 21–22 allude back to the hymn and v. 23 echoes Paul's thought in the thanksgiving (1:3–8).

The general reconciliation of "all things" in v. 20 is brought sharply to bear on the Colossians by the emphatic positioning of "and you" at the beginning of v. 21. The cosmic reconciliation of the hymn has meaning for Paul primarily in the personal sphere. Thus he reminds the Colossians of what they were: estranged, hostile, evil. First, they were estranged from God, in a condition of alienation and continual lack of harmony. This was manifested in both their attitude and actions. They were "hostile in mind"; their intellect, itself, reflected their absence of relationship with God. In Paul's view this necessarily led to evil action, sinfulness in their daily walk. The Colossians' thinking and actions led them away from God.

That was "once" or then; this is "now" (v.21), after the New Age has been ushered in by Christ's death and resurrection (v. 18) and after they have heard and responded to the preaching of Epaphras (1:7). Their condition has changed precisely because of Christ's reconciliation "in his body of flesh by his death." With this one phrase, Paul demolishes the Christology of both Doceticism and Gnosticism. "In his body of flesh" brings into focus the personal and historical act of Jesus Christ. And "by his death" explains how reconciliation came about. Verse 22a applies the generality of v. 20 to the Colossians. (The thought is close to that in Rom 7:4 and 8:3.)

The second half of verse 22 is dominated by a characteristic of Paul's writing, mixed metaphors. (See for example 1 Cor 3:6–11 and Col 2:7.) The word "present" (*parastēsai*) has both cultic/sacrificial and legal connotations. One presents a sacrifice to God and an accused person before a judge. "Holy and blameless" sounds the language of the hellenistic synagogue and Temple sacrifice with its allusion to sacrifices, which were to be without spot or blemish. (See, for example, Exod. 12:5; Lev. 1:10; 3:1; 4:3.) "Blameless and irreproachable" suggest legal language, because to be blameless (*amōmous*) is to be acquitted of charges, and "irreproachable" (*anegklētous*) means literally "unaccused" or "not called to account." The point in either case is that Christ's death has made the Colossian Christians presentable to God.

However, as v. 23 (which contains numerous echoes of the thanksgiving in 1:3-8) makes clear, there are conditions for this presentation. They must "continue in the faith" and "not shift from the hope of the gospel." Paul calls for fidelity to the gospel heard from Epaphrus and sounds a note of warning in preparation for his discussion of false teaching in 2:6ff. The language of constancy here is the language of building. "Stable" (*tethemeliōmenoi*) implies laying the foundation of something; "steadfast" (*hedraioi*) refers to the firmness of a structure; and "not shifting" (*metakinoumenoi*) implies not moved from one place to another, not easily swayed. Their presentation as holy and blameless sacrifices or their verdict of "not guilty" depends upon their faithfulness to the gospel, the refusal to be swayed from its message as preached by Epaphras. These "living stones" are to maintain the firmness with which they first were built in the gospel.

And, so that there will be no mistake, Paul carefully defines the parameters of the gospel for them. It is the one taught when they first became Christian (cf. 1:5). It is now preached all over the world (cf. 1:6). (That is, it is universal in scope. Paul does not mean to suggest that all who have heard have responded to the gospel; his remark is anticipatory in nature.) Finally, the gospel is the one Paul (as an apostle of Christ Jesus; cf. 1:1) was called to preach. In short, Paul tells the Colossians that the gospel is apostolic and universal—the two basic criteria used in determining the canon of scripture.

This section of Colossians, which applies the Christ-hymn to the Colossian Christians, closes as it opened, with the insistence on a personal relationship to the gospel, theirs in v. 21 and Paul's in v. 23. Paul's relationship to the gospel is as its "minister" (*diakonos*) and thus the digression on his ministry (1:24-2:5) is introduced.

G. Bornkamm, "The Heresy of Colossians," in F. O. Francis and W. A. Meeks, *Conflict at Colossae* (Missoula: Scholars Press, 1975).

C. F. Burney, "Christ as ARXH of Creation," *JTS* 27 (1925/26): 160-77.

F. B. Craddock, "'All Things in Him': A Critical Note on Col. 1:15-20," *NTS* 12 (1965/66): 78-80.

P. Ellingsworth, "Colossians 1:15–20 and Its Context," *ExpT* 73 (1962): 252–53.

H. W. House, "Doctrinal Issues in Colossians. Part I," *BibSac* 149 (1992) 45–59.

_____, "The Doctrine of Christ in Colossians," *BibSac* 149 (180–192).

E. Käsemann, "A Primitive Christian Baptismal Liturgy," in *Essays on New Testament Themes* (Philadelphia: Fortress, 1964).

E. Lohse, *A Commentary on the Epistles to the Colossians and Philemon* (Philadelphia: Fortress, 1971).

R. P. Martin, *Colossians and Philemon* (Grand Rapids: Eerdmans, 1985).

_____, "An Early Christian Hymn (Col. 1:15–20)," *EQ* 36 (1964): 195–205.

_____, "Reconciliation and Forgiveness in the Letter to the Colossians," in *Reconciliation and Hope, ed.* R. J. Banks (Grand Rapids: Eerdmans, 1974) 104–24.

W. McCown, "The Hymnic Structure of Col. 1:15–20," *EQ* 51 (1979): 156–62.

P. D. Overfield, "Pleroma: A Study in Content and Context," *NTS* 25 (1979): 384–96.

A. G. Patzia, *Ephesians, Colossians, Philemon* (Peabody, Mass.: Hendrickson, 1990).

T. E. Pollard, "Colossians 1:12–20: A Reconsideration," *NTS* 27 (1981): 572–75.

J. M. Robinson, "A Formal Analysis of Colossians 1:15–20," JBL 76 (1957): 270–87.

B. Vawter, "The Colossian Hymn and the Principle of Redaction," *CBQ* 33 (1971): 62–81.

N. T. Wright, "Poetry and Theology in Col. 1:15–20," *NTS* 36 (1990): 444–68.

THE MINISTRY OF PAUL

Colossians 1:24-2:5

Colossians 1:24-2:5 is a digression triggered by Paul's personal remark at the end of 1:23; 2:6 could as easily follow from 1:23. However, the three subjects of this section—Paul's ministry, the nature of the gospel, and Paul's hope—all are raised in 1:23.

Furthermore, it is not unusual for Paul to discuss his own ministry at the beginning of a letter. He does so in 1 and 2 Corinthians, Galatians, Philippians, and 1 Thessalonians. Here Paul's statements function as an apology (in the classical sense) and an explanation. He is explaining to the Colossians why he is writing to them and why he has the authority to do so. For the first time in the letter, at 2:4, he raises the problem that has led him to make contact with them.

Perhaps the sufferings of his imprisonment put Paul's apostolic leadership in doubt. Imprisoned, he could not come to explain his position to them in person, so in the letter he justifies the sufferings brought on because of his ministry to the Gentiles and warns them against false teaching. The "now" of 1:24 should be understood both temporally (now, while Paul is in prison and the Colossians are threatened) and logically (now, on the basis of what Paul has just explained that Christ has done). Because of his relationship to Christ's gospel, it is possible for Paul to rejoice in suffering and to address the Colossian problem.

The passage follows the now familiar pattern in which Paul first focuses on the Colossians (1:24-26), then shifts to the wider context of the whole church (1:26-29), and finally returns to focus specifically on those to whom he is writing (cf. 1:3-8 and 1:13-23). Imagined geometrically, Paul is using a diamond-shaped approach to argument: a narrow focus at the beginning and end of sections as he speaks primarily to his recipients, and a wider, more universal focus in the center in which he relates their situation to that of the whole church and the world.

The discussion that follows treats the three main issues in the passage: Paul's understanding of his ministry, Paul's understanding of the "word of God," and Paul's hopes for the recipients.

Paul's Understanding of His Ministry

The passage reveals at least six significant revelations about Paul's understanding of the nature of his ministry. They shall be treated roughly in order of appearance in the text.

First, at least in his present circumstances, Paul's ministry has resulted in suffering and struggle (1:24, 29; 2:1). Reconciliation exacted of Christ a price in suffering, and the same is true for his apostle. The conditions of Paul's imprisonment would have led to suffering on many levels. He undoubtedly suffered physically. The only amenity a Roman prison offered was the cell or dungeon itself. Facing almost certain death, Paul's suffering was psychological, and in his concern for the churches and for the spread of the gospel, he suffered spiritually. And yet, he rejoices in his sufferings (not because of them, which would be masochism), sure that their outcome will be furtherance of the gospel cause (cf. Rom 5:3–5 and Phil 1:12–26).

Paul understands that his trials "complete what is lacking in Christ's afflictions for the sake of his body, that is, the church" (1:24). The phrase has occasioned much comment. Certainly in light of what Paul has been saying about the Christ thus far (and in general) it cannot mean that Christ's sacrifice was insufficient. It is generally understood that *hysterēma* ("lacking") does not imply need or deficiency, but what is lacking or remaining, and in any case *thlipseōn* ("affliction") is never used in the New Testament with reference to the suffering of Jesus.

Three general lines of interpretation of the phrase have been suggested. First, and least likely, is that Paul did, indeed, see his suffering as completing Christ's incomplete work. (But, at the very least, this is inconsistent with 1:13–14 and 1:22.) Second, interpreters have noted that Paul's suffering for the church has given him a deep sense of fellowship with Christ, and that mystical union benefits the church (cf. Phil 3:10). This seems more likely, though it raises questions of temporality and timing. The third, and to me most likely, interpretation points out that Jewish apocalyptic taught that before the end times, God's people would suffer. (We see Jesus teaching the same thing in Mark 13:1–27 and Matt 24:1–31, for example.) The key phrase is "for your sake," v. 24; Paul joins Jewish apocalyptic ideas and the notion of vicarious suffering and uses them for his own purposes. His reasoning proceeded as follows: Jesus died to save the church. The church must be enlarged and extended. Anyone suffering in that cause is, in some sense, fulfilling the work of Christ. (For a fuller survey of the issues connected with this verse, see Pokorny, pp. 96–102.)

In the second statement of his understanding of his ministry, Paul reminds his hearers of the claim he made at the outset (1:1) that his ministry is by God's commission; he "became a minister according to the divine office" (1:25). Paul's apostleship is not by human ingenuity but by God's direct call. What he preaches is not "man's gospel" but what came to him "through a revelation of Jesus Christ" (see Gal 1:12–24). His commission has made him a servant of the gospel (1:23), and now he speaks as well of his service to the church (1:25).

Third, Paul's call was not for his own glory or aggrandizement, but was "for your sake" (1:24) and "for you" (1:25; 2:1). Paul understands that God has called him to be a man for others. His ministry is for "every person"; the phrase is repeated three times in 1:28. (*Anthrōpon*, not *anēr*, is the inclusive term Paul uses, thus the translation should not be "every man.") Paul's apostleship leads him to strive on behalf of the Colossian Christians, of the Laodiceans, and even of persons he has not met (1:1–3).

Fourth, Paul understands that his basic task is "to make the word of God fully known" (1:25). The substance of that word is Jesus Christ. John and later Christians identified "word of God" with Jesus, but the origin of that thought is here in Col 1:25–27. Paul insists "him we proclaim" (1:28). In Christ the mystery of God is revealed (1:26–27; 2:2–3). The method of communication of Christ the word of God is also set forth; Paul spreads the message of Christ to every person by proclamation, warning, and teaching "in all wisdom" (1:28). "To proclaim" is "to announce." "To warn" (*nouthetountes*) is a pedagogical word which meant "to train" or "to discipline." Paul regularly used it for admonition, criticism, and correction (cf. 1 Thess 5:12 and 1 Cor 4:14ff.). "To teach" (*didaskontes*) means to define more clearly the substance of the proclamation. Paul's method—proclamation, warning, teaching—is precisely the method, and ordering principle, of the whole letter to the Colossians: 1:1–2:5 proclaims Christ; 2:6–23 warns against false teaching; 3:1–4:6 teaches about Christian living. Each section shows how Christ is perfectly and fully the wisdom of God. (Note that in 1:28 Paul shifts from "I" to "we." He includes his co-workers in his methods, but excludes the false teachers he is about to attack.)

Fifth, in his task of spreading the Word, Paul is energized and inspired by God (1:29). As Paul strives (*agōnizomenos* introduces an athletic metaphor appropriate to competition in the games), Christ supplies him with energy and inspiration. And finally, Paul's physical absence from those to whom he ministers does not imply any lack of concern for them. When he is "absent in body" he still rejoices in their order and firmness, military metaphors describing the qualities he is trying to encourage in Colossae and throughout the churches (2:5).

Paul's Understanding of "Word of God"

As noted above, for Paul, the word of God is Jesus Christ. Christ is focal: "Him we proclaim" (1:28). The whole letter is really focused on Christ. Verses 26 and 27 of chapter 1 fill out something of how God has gone about making that Christ known.

Jesus Christ was not an accident on the stage of human history but was part of the eternal plan of God. (The Ephesian letter will explicitly flesh out this point.) Jesus Christ, the word of God, is "the mystery hidden for ages and generations" (1:26). The term "mystery" is used extensively in the New Testament, twenty of the twenty-seven times in Pauline writings. The word would be familiar both to Jewish and Gentile Christians in Colossae. God's secret purpose for Israel's destiny is called a "mystery" in the LXX in Dan 2:28 and Wis 2:22. Those with experience in hellenistic religions would understand that the "mystery" needed for salvation was hidden. Now, Paul declares, in Jesus Christ the mystery is seen and fully revealed. God's mystery, Jesus Christ, has "now been made manifest to his saints" (1:26). God's secret plan is a person.

It is striking that these "saints" to whom Christ is revealed include the Gentiles. God's riches (a typically Pauline metaphor) and glory are shown in God's inclusion of the Gentiles. The hope of the gospel is not just for Jews but for Gentiles (see Rom 9:23–24). And Paul's very language here reflects that fact since he has chosen a vocabulary familiar to both communities.

Finally, Jesus Christ is not a historical character, albeit one from the recent past. That is, Jesus is not just someone who once lived and now is dead. Jesus Christ the word of God is "Christ in you, the hope of glory"

(1:27). Some have argued that "in you" should be translated "among you," as suggested by the parallel phrase "among the Gentiles." Certainly Paul means to stress the promise of the Messiah's presence among the Gentiles. But I think the phrase also properly belongs to Paul's "Christ-mysticism," his understanding that Christ indwells those who have been joined to him in baptism. Paul is reminding the Colossian Christians that the source of their ultimate hope is not a philosophy or a set of "rules of religious procedure" or a lifestyle, but a living Lord who is as close as their own breath.

Paul's Hopes for the Colossians

Paul has already said he and his colleagues want to "present everyone mature in Christ" (1:28). Christian perfection (*teleion*) is the goal (cf. Matt 5:28). At the close of the passage, Paul states in more specific terms what it is he hopes for the Colossians to have. Not surprisingly, 2:1–5 sounds the notes of the thanksgiving in 1:9–12.

"I want you to know" (2:1) emphasizes the importance of what is to follow. The general plan of salvation outlined in 1:26–28 has specific application to them. First, Paul wants them to know of his strivings for them. "Strive" (*agōna*) is from the same root from which we derive "agony" (and was introduced in 1:29). Those in Colossae and Laodicea and other places Paul has not visited who struggle for the faith are not alone; Paul shares their burdens and labors on their behalf. They have solidarity in their suffering for the gospel. He hopes that, by his strivings, the Colossians' hearts will be encouraged and that they will be knit together in love (2:2).

In spite of its translation and textual problems, 2:2 provides a recapitulation of 1:9–11. The word "encouraged" (*paraklēthōsin*) literally means "comforted." The paraclete is the one "called alongside" as advocate and helper. (The same root word appears in the Farewell Discourses in John.) Love (*agapē*) is always the principle that unites Christian congregations. Paul hopes that the church will be comforted from without (by his care for them and by the Comforter) and unified from within by their own behavior toward one another.

Furthermore, he wants them to realize "the riches of assured understanding and the knowledge of God's mystery, of Christ" who contains all the "treasures of wisdom and knowledge" (2:2b–3). All the powers associated with God are, again, attributed to Christ to stress his sufficiency. In Rom 11:33 knowledge and wisdom are the aspects of divinity seen in redemption. Here Paul uses the constellation understanding-knowledge-wisdom to hearken back to 1:9 (cf. Prov 2:3ff.). The two verses summarize all he has said to this point.

Understanding-knowledge-wisdom are not just attractive religious virtues. They directly counter false teaching. This is Paul's final hope for the Colossian church, "that no one may delude you with beguiling speech" (2:4). Paul's methodology included proclamation, warning, and teaching "in all wisdom" (1:28); that is, through the Christ who is Wisdom. The false teachers also have a "method." They "delude" (*paralogizetai*), that is, use seductively charming (and false) speech; and they "beguile" or use "pithy speech" (*pithanologia*), a legal reference to the persuasive power of a lawyer's arguments which help a criminal escape punishment. For the first time in the letter, Paul raises the issue of false teaching, admitting that the arguments of such teachers may sound plausible. He will go on to refute them in what follows. Here, he commends their "orderly arrangement" and "solid front" (2:5). Reference to their solidity and firmness of faith is undoubtedly intended to hearken back to the original teachings they heard from Epaphras. (Cf. 1:23.)

Conclusion

In the section of the letter on his ministry, Paul continues to make Jesus Christ the focus of attention as he both summarizes the thought about Christ to this point and shows its application to the Colossian situation.

Throughout the section, Paul uses what J. L Houlden calls "dual purpose vocabulary, terms like "mystery," "wisdom," "knowledge," and "understanding," which would have resonances for both the Jewish Christians and Greek Christians in Colossae. He is speaking of the Christ in terms of the religious aspirations of the Greeks and the scriptural traditions of the Jews. Everyone is included in the scope of the discussion.

Having established his credentials, Paul can proceed to speak to the situation in Colossae. At the outset of the letter he aligned himself with Epaphras, who was known to them and whom, presumably, they trusted. Now Paul has shown them he can "speak their languages," that he is suffering on their behalf, and that, although he has not met them personally, he is concerned for their welfare. As apostle to the Gentiles, he both cares for the church in Colossae and has the authority to intervene in their situation.

G. R. Beasley-Murray, "The Second Chapter of Colossians," *RevExp* 70 (1973): 469–79.

J. L. Houlden, *Paul's Letters from Prison* (Philadelphia: Westminster, 1970).

R. P. Martin, *Colossians and Philemon* (Grand Rapids: Eerdmans, 1981 [reissued 1985]).

P. Pokorny, *Colossians* (Peabody, Mass.: Hendrickson, 1991).

THE PROBLEM AT COLOSSAE

Colossians 2:6-23

Having argued for Christ's supremacy, and having explained his ministry, Paul turns to address directly the problem being faced by the Colossian Christians. The nature of this problem at Colossae constitutes the second great focus of scholarly attention in Colossians.

Since Paul has never visited Colossae, it would be irresponsible to speak of Paul's "opponents," and, in any case, this letter contains none of the vitriol reserved for such persons in 2 Corinthians or Galatians. Many commentators prefer to speak of the "Colossian heresy." The two terms the letter uses to describe the "rival teaching" are "philosophy" (2:8) and "forced piety" (2:23). Nominated by various scholars as possible sources of this teaching are sectarian Judaism, some form of syncretistic Judaism, wisdom speculation, Pythagorean philosophy, and incipient forms of Gnosticism, both Jewish and hellenistic. One scholar (M. D. Hooker) has suggested there were no false teachers. She believes that the Colossians were under pressure to conform to the religious practices of their neighbors, both Jewish and pagan. (An excellent treatment of the methodology appropriate for identifying Paul's opponents is found in J. Sumney, "Identifying Paul's Opponents," *JSNT* Supplement Series, 1990.)

Whatever the nature and source of the problem (and it is nearly impossible to define precisely since its precepts must be extracted from statements that are part of the polemic against it), Paul opposes it on the basis of his Christology. Christ is superior to any supernatural beings. His redemption of men and women makes any sort of legalism unnecessary. Correspondingly, Christianity is superior to any cult. Indeed, cosmic "principalities and powers" are captives in Christ's triumphal procession (2:15).

Paul appeals to apostolic tradition, arguing it to be more trustworthy than human tradition. He contrasts human tradition (*paradosin,* 2:8) and teaching (*didaskalias,* 2:22) with the apostolic tradition that the Colossians received (*parelabete,* 2:6) and were taught (*edidachthēte,* 2:7). Apostolic tradition is superior to what Paul thinks is a humanly made religion.

Rather than attempting to decide exactly what the rival teaching was and who promulgated it, the commentary that follows first will set forth Paul's exhortation and warning (2:6-8), then examine his objections to the teaching (2:8, 16-23), and, finally, set forth his answers to the rival teachers and his solution to the Colossian problem (2: 9-15). (In the text of the letter, Paul's "solution" [2:9-15] actually precedes the verses that contain the most information about the rival teaching [2:16-23].)

Paul's Exhortation and Warning (2:6–8)

Although logically 2:6 could as easily follow from 1:23 as 2:5, the purpose of the verse is clear: to set forth Jesus Christ as Lord and to contrast the "received" tradition (2:6) with "human tradition" (2:8).

Paul uses the technical language of the handing on of tradition that early Christianity borrowed from rabbinic Judaism (cf. 1 Thess 2:13; 1 Cor 11:23; 15:1; Gal 1:9). What has been received is, in effect, the earliest Christian confession, "Jesus Christ is Lord" (see 1 Cor 12:3; Rom 10:9). Having been taught this (2:7) from the "real authority" (i.e., Epaphras, who has Paul's apostolic approval), they are literally "to walk in him" (i.e., in Christ). The same word (*peripateite*) is used in 1:10 to describe the Christian's conduct of life.

Paul's exhortation is cast in a series of three participles which are mixed metaphors. The Colossian Christians are to be rooted, built up, and established. "To be rooted" (*errizōmenoi*) is to be firmly fixed. The same term was used in 1:6 and 10. Here the perfect passive suggests a present state that results from a past action. "Built up" (*epoikodomoumenoi*) is in the present tense, suggesting continuing action. That they are to be rooted and built up "in him" links the two. (The same mixed metaphor also occurs in 1 Cor 3:9.) "Established" (*bebaioumenoi*) introduces a legal term for "ratified and made binding." The Colossians are bound to the faith that they were taught and are encouraged to practice it with thanksgiving, the Pauline characteristic of a Christian life (cf. 1:3, 12; 3:15b, 16, 17; 1 Thess 5:13; and Phil 4:6).

There is a sharp contrast in vv. 7 and 8 between what they received and what is being pressed upon them. "See to it" (*blepete*) signals the beginning of the polemical argument against the rival teaching (cf. 1 Cor 8:9; 10:12; Gal 5:15; and Phil 3:2). In 2:8 Paul summarizes his objections to this rival teaching: it enslaves; it is hollow, deceptive philosophy; and its origins are human. Paul does not want them "made prey of" by such teaching. The word *sylagōgon* is unusual in the New Testament and means literally "kidnap." It is the language of a slave trading raid or of plundering and carrying off booty.

In a nutshell, Paul exhorts the Colossians to hold fast to the teaching they received about the lordship of Christ, and he warns them not to be taken captive by rival teaching of human origin. His objections to the latter are extensive and carefully presented.

Paul's Objections to the Rival Teaching (2:8, 16–23)

Although their arguments must be adduced from the polemic against them, the false teachers are systematically opposed by Paul. He objects to their type of teaching, to its origins and methods, and to the worship it enjoins. Most of this material occurs in one of the most obscure passages in the Pauline corpus, 2:16–23. The translation problems it presents, especially in vv. 18, 21, and 23, are notoriously difficult. In part this is because Paul apparently quotes the jargon he criticizes, jargon known to his recipients but with which we (and later Christians in the early church) are completely unfamiliar. In spite of its difficulties, the intention of the passage is clear and practical: to show how false ideas about Christ lead to aberrant practices.

Paul describes the rival teaching in Colossae as "philosophy and empty deceit" (2:8) and as "self-imposed piety" (NRSV, 2:23) or "self-imposed worship" (NIV, 2:23). Although this is the only use of "philosophy" in the New Testament, it had many meanings in the period. The Greeks used the term to describe the pursuit of knowledge and wisdom, and the Jews used it to describe sects within Judaism. Commentators on Colossians have linked philosophy to syncretistic Judaism because of the mention of circumcision, sabbaths, angels, and dietary laws; to the hellenistic mysteries because of the mention of visions; and to Gnosticism because of the angelology and asceticism in the passage. The fact is that we cannot know with certainty to whom Paul refers, but we do know that he disapproved; the philosophy is "empty deceit," and it enslaves people.

If "philosophy" is a puzzle for historians of religion, "self-imposed piety" (2:23) is a puzzle for translators, some of whom believe the author created the composite word. In Greek, *ethelothrēskia* joins *ethelo,* "self-appointed," and *thrēskia,* "religion" or "worship." The point is clear, Paul believes the worship of the rival teachers is their own invention or innovation and is, therefore, false.

This leads to a consideration of Paul's objection to the origins of the rival teaching; they are "according to human tradition, according to the elemental spirits of the universe" (2:8). Three times Paul scorns the rivals' origin as human, in the verse just quoted, in v.18 where he speaks of their "sensuous mind" (RSV) or "human way of thinking" (NRSV), and in v. 22 where he speaks of their human precepts and doctrines. The teaching that the Colossians have received from Epaphras is rooted in Christ Jesus; its source, therefore, is divine (1:15, 19; 2:9). The rivals, on the other hand, speak only from their own, human perspective.

Their human tradition, while not "according to Christ" (2:8), does however, have connections with the "universal spirits of the universe" (2:8, 20) to which, with Christ, the Colossian Christians have "died" (2:20). The word *stoicheion,* translated "universal (or elemental) spirits of the universe," is the source of much discussion by modern scholars. Etymologically it means "to be in a line" or "objects standing in a row"; its simplest definition is "a member of a series," "a component," or "an element." It was used in the hellenistic world to describe the alphabet, the elements of the physical world, fundamental principles, and the heavenly bodies, especially the signs of the zodiac. The general consensus is that in the New Testament it refers to spiritual forces (cf. Heb 5:12; 2 Pet 3:10), and this seems to be Paul's understanding (cf. Gal 4:3, 9). In Colossians the *stoicheia* are in opposition to Christ. They are powerful "spirit forces" capable of holding people prey and exercising tyranny over them. From Paul's perspective, they stand between God and humanity, and he is anxious to show that Christ has subdued them. (See the discussion below, especially that on 2:15.)

Paul also objects to the methods, we might say the practices, of the rival teaching. First, it is highly regulatory. It passes judgment with regard to dietary habits and religious observances (2:16), and it sets forth its rules in the imperative: "Do not handle. Do not taste. Do not touch" (2:21). Because each person's salvation is a gift, no Christian has the right to judge another (see Matt 7:1 and Jas 4:12–12). Furthermore, dietary laws were annulled by Christ himself (see Mark 7:18–23 and parallels). Paul objects to the legalism of the rival teaching, as well as to its insistence on "self-abasement" (2:18, 23).

Self-abasement (*tapeinophrosynē*), literally "humility," seems to carry the connotation of mortification. The word was used in connection with fasting, which in some contexts was a prelude to entrance into the heavens or spiritual realms. Paul not only thinks that such asceticism is unnecessary, he says it is "of no value in checking the indulgence of the flesh" (2:23). Even if it were required, it wouldn't work! Like the imperatives of 2:21 which are about food and drink (but also in the case of *apsē* refer to sexual activity, cf. 1 Cor 7:1), asceticism alone is not ultimately helpful. It does not affect the fundamental problem of humanity's "lower nature." Only regeneration by the Spirit affects human nature itself.

Finally, Paul finds fault with the worship or piety of the rival teaching. First, it requires the observance of festivals connected with "a new moon or a sabbath" (v. 16). As a good Jew, Paul would not object in principle to sacred days and seasons. In fact, the list here is fairly typical of Jewish piety (cf. Ezek 45:17; Hos 2:12), although astral calendars also figured in hellenistic religions and particularly astrology which was popular throughout the Empire, but especially in Asia Minor in the first century. The problem is not with religious holidays *per se.* The problem arises when one is judged on the basis of observing or ignoring those days, which, in any case, are "shadow" and not "reality" (2:17). For Paul, the Christian religion is not a matter of legalisms with regard to practices of any sort.

Furthermore, the Colossian Christians are not to be "disqualified" (*katabrabeuetō,* literally "robbed of a prize," "decided against"—in the sense of an unfavorable decision by a referee in sports—or "judged") by one who insists on "worship of angels, taking his stand on visions" (2:18). Several scholars believe that v. 18 contains the key to understanding the Colossian problem. The *crux interpretum* is whether "worship of angels" is to be translated as an objective or a subjective genitive. Recent literature tends to read it as a subjective genitive. Thus the phrase describes the worship in which the angels engage. What Paul objects to is not worship offered to the angels (in fact, it is exceedingly difficult to find evidence for worship of angels, for a cult of angel worship, in Judaism, Christianity, or paganism in the first century), but the worship *of* the angels. The false teachers advocate worshiping as the angels worship. They have seen this worship in visions.

The term translated "taking his stand on" confirms this reading. In the parallel literature "to take a stand" (*embateuōn*) meant literally "to enter a confined area." When it was used of a god entering a place consecrated to him, it was translated "to haunt." However, it was also found as a technical term for "initiation," "entering a mystery," and was used for humans when they entered a sacred place.

The rival teachers in Colossae engaged in visionary activity which they may have prepared for by asceticism. (The asceticisms of v. 21 would have been necessary preludes to the visions of v. 18.) They "enter heaven," behold the worship of the angels, and "return" to judge those who have not had their experience. They apparently believed dietary and cultic rules helped them have the visions that showed how angels worship. Again, the problem is judgment, relegating those who have not seen angelic worship to "second class" status. Understood in these terms, the problem at Colossae was not unlike that at Corinth where emphasis on supernatural gifts (like tongues) overshadowed the meaning of what Christ had done.

Although Paul's language in this section of Colossians is obscure, his message is not. He confronts a philosophy that taught asceticism, observance of special religious seasons, and entrance into the *plerōma* to view the worship of angels. It passed judgment on those who did not follow its teachings and seek out such experience. Paul objects, first, because these teachings are "not according to Christ" (2:8), and they do not hold fast to the head (2:19). Second, they are not enduring. Using Platonic language, in v. 17 he describes them as the "shadow" rather than the "reality" (the *sōma,* the word he uses for the church in 1:18 and 2:19). They are "an appearance" (2:22), not the "real thing" found in Christ. Furthermore, they refer "to things which all perish" (2:22), thus enforcing bondage to the transient. Third, and finally, the activities enjoined by the rival teachings are not effective (2:23). They are not only deceptive; they are useless. Excessive religiosity and the legalism of the rival teachings did not really promote the spiritual well-being of its adherents. On the contrary, it involved them in pride (2:18, *physioumenos,* "to be puffed up") and judgment (2:16, 18), un-Christlike attitudes, and dangerous spiritual sins. Truly Christlike behavior builds up the body of Christ, does not divide it into first- and second-class spiritual citizens. (In chapter 3 Paul takes up the practical ramifications of this point.)

The apostle Paul believes that Jesus Christ delivers believers from every form of legalism. Faith in Christ makes visionary experience unnecessary since "in him all the fullness of God was pleased to dwell" (1:19; cf. 2:9). Not surprisingly, Paul's solution to the Colossian problem and his answer to the rival teachers is the Christ who towers above any human tradition, spiritual experience, or cosmic power.

Paul's Answer to the Rival Teaching (2:9–15)

In order to answer a philosophy "according to human tradition, according to the elemental spirits of the universe" (2:8), Paul turns again to Christ. Verse 9 begins emphatically, "in him." In Christ the whole fullness of the deity dwells (1:19; 2:9), and in him the Colossian Christians have come to fullness (2:10) and put off the body of flesh (2:12). With Christ they have been buried in baptism, raised through faith, and made alive by forgiveness (2:12–13). Verses 9, 14, and 15 describe the accomplishments of Christ and vv. 10–13 the effect of those accomplishments on the Colossians. The brief prepositional phrases "in him" and "with him" provide linguistic keys to the progression of ideas. The whole section presumes 2:6, that they have received Christ Jesus as Lord; therefore, the rest follows logically.

Paul begins by reminding them of the crucial point made in 1:19, in Christ "the whole fullness of deity dwells bodily" (2:9). This sets the stage for his appeal and is fundamental to it as an explanation of why there is no need for multiple allegiances (the theme of the Christ-hymn in 1:15–20). The addition here of the word "bodily" (*sōmatikōs*) stresses the incarnate form of Jesus the Christ. The fullness of God is seen in the material world in a human person, thus excursions to the *plerōma* to view angels are unnecessary.

Playing on "fullness," Paul continues; in Christ the Colossian Christians, too, "have come to fullness of life" (2:10). Because of Christ's fullness, nothing is lacking in their relationship to God. Because Christ is "head of all rule and authority" (2:10; cf. 1:16 and Rom 13:1b), there is no need to look beyond him either for personal religion or for an understanding of the world. Practically, this results from their having been joined to Christ by "a circumcision made without hands" (2:12).

In spite of the difficulty of the verse, the point of 2:12 is to contrast physical, exterior circumcision with one that is spiritual and interior. The key phrase is "putting off the body of flesh." "Putting off" (*apekdyset*) signifies a clean break. The metaphor is that of taking off a set of clothes. Perhaps Paul has the baptismal act in mind, as converts were stripped before baptism and reclothed thereafter. He will use the same term again in 2:15, in which Christ "strips off" the principalities and powers, and in 3:9–10 in a parenetic context. "Body of flesh" signifies the whole sinful nature. (For a discussion of the terms "flesh" and "body," see J. A. T. Robinson, *The Body* [Philadelphia: Westminster, 1952].) Thus, true circumcision removes not just a small piece of flesh but the whole fleshly (prone to sin) nature. The idea is close to that in Gal 3:27: "For as many of you as were baptized into Christ have put on Christ." The point here is that baptism is true circumcision.

With Christ, the Colossians were buried in baptism and raised through faith (2:12). The argument assumes baptism by immersion as it compares the death and resurrection of Jesus to the physical acts of baptism, which is not only the symbol, but the means of grace. There is no need for any other spiritual experience. Baptism is sufficient for salvation.

The ideas in Col 2:12–15 share common elements with Rom 6:1–11, Gal 3:26–27, and Eph 2:1–10; this suggests they were part of the standard baptismal instruction of the early church. If that is the case, Paul is reminding the Colossians of what they have already been taught. However, there is a change. They have not only died and been buried with Christ in the baptismal grave and raised with him from it, they have been made alive or resurrected with him. Those "who were dead in trespasses and the uncircumcision of . . . flesh, God made alive together with him, having forgiven . . . all . . . trespasses" (2:13). Not only is resurrection the activity of God, but this resurrection to new life has already taken place in the life of the believer. Salvation has become present tense.

Verses 12 and 13 are central to the appeal of the letter. Because the fullness of God dwells in Christ (1:19; 2:9), the Colossian Christians are already filled (2:10). This occurred at their baptism, when God not only made them alive but forgave all their sins. To elaborate the meaning of that forgiveness, Paul draws three vivid pictures in 2:14–15. All the action in these verses is described in the aorist; it happened in the past, but its effect is continuing. (On the basis of parallelisms in the verses, it has been suggested that they represent another hymn fragment, but this view has not gained widespread acceptance.)

First, Christ "canceled the bond which stood against us" (2:14). The term *cheirographon* (the "bond") has engendered lively debate. Literally it means "written with the hand," but more technically it was used to describe a statement of obligation written by a debtor promising to pay what is due. So, in effect, it is a debt certificate, a "note." In the Colossian context the term has been interpreted in a variety of ways. The author of Ephesians apparently thought of it as the Law of Moses (Eph 2:15), but Irenaeus and Origin viewed it as a pact with Satan. It has been understood as an I.O.U. from humanity to God and also as a reference to the heavenly book kept by God regarding human sin (see Rev 5:1–5; *Apocalypse of Elijah, Odes Sol.* 23; *Gos. Truth* 19, 17). W. Carr has associated the *cheirographon* with the use of penitential *stelai*, an attested cultic aspect of Eastern religions in which people made public confessions of guilt on *stelai* set up in temple precincts. It has been linked to the notice nailed to the cross of Christ (Mark 15:26), and, on the basis of 2 Cor 5:21, has been identified as Christ's body itself.

Whatever the precise nature of the guilt list, Christ has cancelled it. *Exaleiphas* means "completely rubbed out," "wiped away," obliterated as writing on a wax tablet was obliterated. "Legal demands" (*tois dogmasin*), like those required by the rival teachers (cf. 2:16, 20, 21), are set aside, nailed to the cross. *Proselōsas* describes how Christ obliterated the *cheirographon*. He threw it away for good (*hērken ek tou mesou*, 2:14).

Christ has not only cancelled sin and set aside legal demands, he "disarmed the principalities and powers and made a public example of them" (2:15a). "Principalities and powers" occurred in the hymn at 1:16, which stated that they were created "through him [Christ] and for him." Astral religious beliefs taught that the principalities and powers controlled the course of the universe and the destinies of human beings (cf. Acts 7:42–43). The mystery cults and sympathetic magic of all sorts sought to bargain with or placate these cosmic powers. In contrast, the most ancient Christian sources taught that, by his death and resurrection, Jesus defeated the powers (see 1 Cor 15:24–25; Heb 10:12–13; 1 Pet 3:22).

Paul does not deny the existence of such powers (indeed, why address the issue if they didn't exist), but he asserts that Jesus has delivered his followers from them. In 2:15a, Paul states that Christ "disarmed" them. *Apekdysamenos* (one of six words that appear in the Pauline corpus only here in 2:14–15) introduces a double metaphor. First, it is a military term for disarming an enemy. Second, it is a term from court life, describing the process by which officials were publically stripped of honor. It is a picture not only of despoiling, but of undressing, thus linking the verse to 2:12 and 3:9–10.

The "public example" made of the principalities and powers culminates in their being led in triumphal procession (2:15b). "Triumph" (*thriambeusas*) is found in Greek only rarely before the Christian era and occurs in the New Testament only here and in 2 Cor 2:14. (For a full exposition of the term in 2 Corinthians, see S. Hafemann, *Suffering and Ministry in the Spirit* [Grand Rapids: Eerdmans, 1990].) It refers to the Roman practice of the triumphal procession in which a victor led his captives in a festal parade which also displayed the spoils of his victory. It constituted the highest honor Rome bestowed on its citizens, and the emphasis was not on the spoils so much as on the one who triumphed (who, as part of the ceremony, took off his old clothes and put on ceremonial dress), who was seen as an embodiment of good fortune. (Incidentally, since triumphal processions were held only in Rome some scholars view the term as evidence for a Roman origin of Colossians.)

The three metaphors provide picturesque and dramatic images of Christ's supremacy over the principalities and powers, indeed, over the *stoicheia,* or anything else that might try to stand between redeemed humanity and God. The Christ whom the Colossians received when they were baptized and of whom they were taught is omnipotent and all-sufficient. Through him God not only forgives sin, but blots out the acknowledgment of that sin. Thus, the necessity for ordinances ("legal demands," 2:14 or "regulations," 2:20) and visions (2:18) was also removed.

Conclusion

In Colossae Paul addressed a rival teaching he called "philosophy." The term was used in a religious sense to describe cultic requirements as a prelude to religious experience that led to supernatural knowledge. This combination of legalistic practice, visionary experience, and specialized knowledge suggests a syncretistic movement, whether Jewish or hellenistic is uncertain.

Paul tells the Colossian Christians that they should be untroubled by such teaching. Instead, they should hold fast to the apostolic gospel and to the Christ it proclaimed. They know (on the basis of 1:15-20) that this Christ is the fullness of God, Lord of creation, and the head of the church. Now, bringing his Christology to bear on their situation, Paul reminds them that Christ has made them alive to God and forgiven their sin. His lordship is here and now; all that is required has already been accomplished by him. The Colossians have no need of the *stoicheia* as mediators between themselves and God or of the principalities and powers under whose sway they might fear to fall. Christ has triumphed over them, and, through baptism with Christ, the Colossians share in his victory.

Apart from the scholarly activity that buzzes around it, Col 2:6-23 has profound implications for the contemporary church. It reminds us that God has removed the barrier of our sin and made it possible for us to be in relationship to God. That relationship is not dependent upon rules set down by human beings. Colossians argues against any "imposed spirituality" and also condemns judging others who do not practice Christianity "our way." Spiritual experiences are between us and God. What matters is faith in Jesus Christ the Lord in whom we, too, are to be rooted, built up, and established.

G.R. Beasley-Murray, "The Second Chapter of Colossians," *RevExp* 70 (1973): 469-79.

O. A. Blanchette, "Does the *Cheirographon* of Col. 2:14 Represent Christ Himself?" *CBQ* 23 (1961): 306-12.

G. Caird, *Paul's Letters from Prison* (Oxford: Oxford University Press, 1976).

W. Carr, *Angels and Principalities* (Cambridge: Cambridge University Press, 1981).

_____, "Two Notes on Colossians (Col. 2:14; Col. 2:18)," *JTS* 24 (1973): 492-500.

C. A. Evans, "The Colossian Mystics," *Bib* 63 (1982): 188-205.

F. Francis and W. Meeks (eds.), *Conflict at Colossae* (Missoula, Mont.: Scholars Press, 1975).

B. Hollenback, "Col. 2:23: Which Things Lead to the Fulfillment of the Flesh," *NTS* 25 (1979) 254-61.

M. Hooker, "Were There False Teachers in Colossae?" in *Christ and the Spirit in the New Testament*, ed. B. Lindars and S. Smalley (Cambridge: Cambridge University Press, 1973).

E. Lohse, *A Commentary on the Epistles to the Colossians and Philemon* (Philadelphia: Fortress Press, 1971).

_____, "Pauline Theology in the Letter to the Colossians," *NTS* 15 (1968-69): 211-20.

R. P. Martin, *Colossians and Philemon* (Grand Rapids: Eerdmans, 1985).

_____, *Ephesians, Colossians and Philemon* (Atlanta: John Knox Press, 1991).

_____, "Reconciliation and Forgiveness in the Letter to the Colossians," in *Reconciliation and Hope,* ed. R. Banks (Grand Rapids: Eerdmans, 1974).

G. MacGregor, "Principalities and Powers: The Cosmic Background of Paul's Thought," *NTS* 1 (1954-55): 17-28.

A. Patzia, *Ephesians, Colossians, Philemon* (Peabody, Mass.: Hendrickson, 1984).

P. Pokorny, *Colossians* (Peabody, Mass.: Hendrickson, 1991).

R. Yates, "Colossians 2:14: Metaphor of Forgiveness, " *Bib* 71 (1990): 248-59.

_____, "Colossians 2:15: Christ Triumphant," *NTS* 37 (1991): 573-91.

H. Weiss, "The Law in the Epistle to the Colossians," *CBQ* 34 (1972): 294-314.

THE PARENESIS

Colossians 3:1–4:6

Colossians exhibits the usual form of a Pauline letter. The practical, parenetic material follows the theoretical and theological. To use the language of Dibelius, parenesis grows from proclamation.

Both Greeks and Jews used parenesis in their teaching. Parenesis is exhortation to seek virtue and avoid vice; in form it gives advice or rules for proper thought and action that can be widely applied in various circumstances. Paul borrows the forms in which this advice is given from the literature of the hellenistic world, especially from the Stoics and Cynics. Apparently such instructional materials were collected and used before Paul and formed a standard Christian catechesis. The similarity to material in, for example, Hebrews, James, and 1 Peter suggests an oral common fund of such material. (See P. Carrington, *The Primitive Christian Catechism* [1940] and E. G. Selwyn, *The First Epistle of Peter* [London: Macmillan, 1947], Appendix II.)

Chapter 3, then, begins the ethical section of the letter and constitutes about a third of it. This practical instruction presupposes the christological material with which the letter opened, especially the Christian's sharing in the death and life of Christ (cf. 2:12 and 20). The indicative precedes the imperative just as the gift of the gospel is offered before its demands are made. Paul seems especially concerned that the moral condition of the Gentile converts (whose backgrounds probably did not include the strict morality of Judaism) reflect their belief in the Christ.

The parenetic material is very carefully organized. At the outset, the principle from which moral action arises is set forth in 3:1–4, which also forms a bridge from the previous section on false teaching. Then Paul presents the personal behavior required of Christians, first in the negative by setting forth the "don'ts" (3:5–11) and then in positive terms by enjoining the "do's" (3:12–17). The Christian's domestic and professional relationships are described in 3:18–4:1, and the section closes with final exhortations (4:2–6). Colossians 3:1–4:6 contains three forms of "borrowed," traditional materials, vice and virtue lists, a household code, and *topoi* (brief, pithy admonitions), and each will be discussed as it appears.

The Principle (3:1–4)

The transition from Christology to parenesis is introduced by a conditional prepositional phrase ("If you have been raised with Christ") to which the affirmative "we have" is assumed. Paul already has stated that the Colossian Christians have been raised with Christ (2:12), and he continues use of the baptismal imagery of 2:8–23. Because they have been baptized (died and raised with Christ), they must live their lives on the level of Christ's existence. "To seek" (*zēteite*) used in the present tense is continually or habitually to search or examine with the desire to possess. Ignoring the earthly rules presented by the rival teachers (2:21–22), they are to focus on "things above," the heavenly realm where Christ, high above any cosmic powers, sits with God. "Above" is to be understood practically not so much as a place as a quality of existence. (In his commentary E. Schweizer suggested "above" is where the Christian's future lies, thus linking the term to the eschatological language of 3:3–4.)

Paul, like Jesus in the Sermon on the Mount, is interested in human motivation. He realizes that "it's what inside that counts"; from within come the evil things which defile (see Mark 7: 14–23 and parallels). In Romans Paul spoke of being transformed by the renewal of the mind (Rom 12:2) and taught that "those who live according to the Spirit set their minds on (*phronousin*) the things of the Spirit. To set the mind on the flesh is death, but to set the mind on the Spirit is life and peace" (see Rom 8:5–11). Likewise in Colossians he counsels, "set your minds on (*phroneite*) things that are above" (3:2), because he realizes that the focus of attention of the interior life determines the exterior actions of a person. The first two verses of the parenesis, then, provide a direct link to the preceding material and the organizing principle for the first section of parenesis (things "earthly" in the "don'ts" in 3:5–11 and things "above" in the "do's" in 3: 12–17).

The baptismal image and the contrast between "earth" and "above" is continued in 3:3–4. "For" (*gar*), which opens 2:3, asserts that new life comes directly from baptism. The real life of Christians is the hidden life of inner transformation "in Christ." (Paul makes this point autobiographically in Phil 1:21 and Gal 2:20.) W. Barclay pointed out that when one died and was buried, the Greeks said she or he was "hidden in the earth." The Christian who has died the spiritual death of baptism is "hidden in Christ." A Christian's interior personal history follows the pattern of Christ's; he or she died, is hidden (in Christ), and is raised in glory.

That which is hidden (*kekryptai*) is concealed. (The hellenistic mystery teachers called their wisdom books *apokryphoi,* "hidden." Paul's recipients undoubtedly would have known this.) And so it is with authentic Christian life. (There is no place for boasting about spiritual experience; cf. 2:18.) What Christians really are is yet to appear (see 1 John 2:28 and 1 Pet 5:4). The reality of life may be hidden for the moment, but it "will appear" (*phanerōthē*), be made manifest, when Christ is fully manifested. The eschatological note is entirely characteristic of Paul's thought and the subtlety of its presentation should not blind us to its presence. Colossians 3:4 is a clear reference to eschatological glory.

Through their baptism, Christians in Colossae are completely identified with the Christ "above." Therefore, they must live as "above" people. The "principle" from which their actions must flow is a person, Jesus Christ. Their real life is hidden in Christ, and their visible, daily lives should be conformed to him and conducted in Christlike ways. Thus, Paul continues his practical instruction by stating in no uncertain terms what Christians must avoid and what they must do.

The Personal Behavior of Christians (3:5–17)

The theological connection between chapters 2 and 3 is provided by baptism and the image of dying and rising with Christ. The practical import of the theology of 2:8–19 is worked out in 3:5–17. The text's principle of organization is found in 3:2. The Colossian Christians are not to set their minds "on things that are on earth." These are the same things that are to be "put to death" in 3:5–11. Instead, they are to sets their minds "on things that are above," the things to be "put on" in 3:12–17. "Put off" (3:9) and "put on" (3:10,12,14) continues the imagery of 2:11–12 most closely, and employs a widely used metaphor in the ancient world for initiation and spiritual change, that of changing clothes.

Within the general structure of "put to death"/"put on" are two lists of five vices and one list of five virtues. Each is related to a central idea: 3:5 lists sexual sins; 3:8 sins of the tongue/attitude; and 3:12 Christlike qualities that bear on social relationships. Paul borrowed the use of vice and virtue lists from the teaching methods of the hellenistic world. The form was used extensively by the Stoics, hellenistic Jews, and early Christians.

Jewish vice lists are exemplified in Wis 14, especially 14:24-27. (Paul's, and the New Testament's longest list, Rom 1:29-31, follows Wis 13-14.) Jews tended to employ random lists of sins that were understood to be the result of a primal fault. (In Wis 14, for example, the sin is idolatry.) First century hellenistic Judaism developed a regular form for denouncing Gentiles in which idolatry was linked with immoral actions (see 3:5). The lists of vice in the New Testament tend to be conventional and to have tenuous connection to their contexts.

Interestingly, virtue lists have no set Jewish precedents and are fewer in number in the New Testament than vice lists. It was the Greeks who developed ethical terminology, and the Jews were apparently hesitant to use it. Christians, however, were not so reticent, and New Testament virtue lists are related to Stoic catalogues, which sometimes seem to be used without any changes.

In the Pauline lists, vices and virtues are frequently linked with eschatological hopes (see Gal 5:21, 1 Cor 6:9). In Colossians the lists are introduced by the promise of Christ's appearance in glory (3:4) and contain warnings about ultimate judgment (3:6). Interestingly, Pokorny points out that the closest parallels to Colossians' vice and virtue lists are to be found in the literature of Qumran, which also had strong eschatological expectations.

Paul understands that if Christian faith is to be credible, the daily life of Christians must conform to it and reflect it. He discusses the ethical or moral life of Christians in terms of a series of relationships with all people (3: 5-7), with the church (3:8-17; 4:2-4), with the family (3:18-21), which includes one's work or professional life (3:22-4:1), and with the larger society (4:5-6).

Paul's shift from theological explanation in the early sections of the letter to the imperative mode here is even more dramatic when we recall that the letter was to be read aloud in the churches (4:16). The theological context, dying and rising with Christ in baptism, would be fresh in the hearers' minds. Paul asserts that because they have died with Christ in baptism, Christians must put to death earthly vices.

The "earthly" vices of 3:5 (sexual sins of any sort, impurity in the sense of any immoral intent, passion, lust in the sense of all evil longing, and covetousness) are the characteristic sins of paganism. They represent not only gross self-seeking but recall the sexual activity that was part of the idolatrous worship of the gods. The list is summarized by "covetousness," which implies using things and persons for one's own benefit and self-interest and which expands the scope of the condemned vices to include materialism of all sorts. Even the Roman moralists condemned *amor sceleratus habendi,* "accursed love of getting." For Paul, covetousness is idolatry because it puts desire for gain or for things before God. For him, and for all Jews, idolatry "is the beginning and cause and end of every evil" (Wis 14:27, NRSV), and would naturally lead to the ultimate judgment introduced in 3:6. (Recall, in this context, that in Rom 1:18–32 part of God's wrath is to abandon people to their sinful ways.)

Paul in no way minimizes "earthly" vices, here understood as the insidious tendency to use ourselves and others for ignoble ends. In fact, he reminds the Colossians of the alienation of such sin from which they have been rescued by Jesus Christ. They once "walked" (the same metaphor for the lifestyle used in 2:6 and 4:5) or "lived" (implying the attitude from which action comes) in earthly ways. "But now" they must "put them all away" (3:8). The contrast between what was and what is constitutes the root of much of Paul's ethical exhortation, and that same comparison is at work here.

The Colossian Christians must also rid themselves of vices of the tongue (cf. Jas 3:6–12), which both disrupt Christian fellowship and represent sins of attitude toward other persons. The Greek root of "anger," (*orgēn*) is the same root as the word "orgy." "Wrath" implies the sort of anger that is manifested in outbursts or temper tantrums. "Malice" describes that vicious nature which delights in harming others. To belittle (*blasphēmian*) someone or cause her to fall into bad repute or reputation is to slander her. (The word is from the same root as "blaspheme.") "Foul talk" includes not only "dirty words," but abusive language in general. The vices Paul condemns here are particularly insidious because they not only make community life impossible, but they corrupt the inner life. Anger, wrath, and malice can be internalized and become habitual attitudes before slander and foul talk are even verbalized.

Lying is perhaps the cardinal sin of the tongue (and thus summarizes the list) because it destroys the trust without which relationship cannot grow. In 3:9–10 Paul returns to the baptismal imagery of chapter 2 as he reminds the Colossian Christians that they have put off completely and irrevocably the practices that were part of their unredeemed nature and have put on a new nature which is constantly being renewed. The present passive participle *anakainoumenon* ("to renew") suggests that renewal is continuous and has an outside source; the preposition at the beginning of the compound verb suggests not the restoration of some prior state but a contrast to what existed before. The Christians are being made new in knowledge (again, proving the vanity of the claims of the false teachers in 2:8–23) "after the image of its creator." "Image" (*eikona*) recalls 1:15, Christ "the image of the invisible God," the same Christ "in whom are hid all the treasures of wisdom and knowledge" (2:3). The idea is that Christians are in the process of being recast in the image or being of Christ.

"Here," that is, in the new humanity made after the image of its creator, old "earthly" divisions, castes, and labels no longer apply. Instead, there must be a unity of believers. In a verse reminiscent of Gal 3:28, Paul explains how Christlikeness destroys national divisions (Greek and Jew), religious divisions (circumcised and uncircumcised), and social/economic divisions (slave and free man, a possible introduction of the discussion in 3:22–4:1). Even barbarians (non-Greek speakers, including not only those lacking culture but Persians and other highly developed Asian cultures) and Scythians (understood as wild people from the trackless wastes, whom Josephus called "little better than wild beasts," *Contra Apionem* 2.269) are united through Christ, who "is all and in all" (3:11). Again, what matters is not the outward appearance but Christ within effecting the mysterious transformation of human personality that results in a unified Christian community (see 3:1–3).

As is characteristic of his style, Paul follows negative prohibitions with positive instructions. In some ways 3:12–17 is a continuation of the discussion of the baptized in chapter 2. The focal point of the section is the list of virtues in v. 12 that the Colossian Christians are to "put on" along with (and reflecting) their new and renewed nature.

Paul understands that the church is now the "chosen people" (cf. Rom 8:33; 16:13). Positive qualities that will advance human relationships are the garment its members are to put on. God's chosen are described as "holy and beloved," the same terms used in the Old Testament of Israel of the spirit. The virtues expected of the elect are the same used to describe God and Christ (see, for example, Rom 2:4; 12:1; 2 Cor 1:3; 10:1). They are social in nature and have the well-being of the community as their goal. Thus, they provide the corrective to the vices in 2:5 and 2:8 which destroy communal life.

"Compassion" might be translated "bowels of mercy" since *splagxna* are literally the internal organs, which were understood to be the seat of human emotion. (When the Gospels refer to the "compassion" of Jesus, they use the same root word.) "Kindness" implies generosity and courtesy expressed in attitude and deed. "Lowliness" or humility was a slave virtue and connoted a spirit of modesty and a disregard for status. "Meekness" describes the gentleness and restraint of the personality of the one who has brought herself into subjection to God's will or who has made himself submissive to God. "Patience" (*makrothymian*) is a compound word meaning literally "long tempered" (as opposed to the lustfulness of v. 5 or the anger of v. 8, both of which share the same root word). It speaks of the long suffering of one who has the right to retaliate but does not do so, of one who bears injustices without the desire for revenge. (The prime example, of course, is Jesus on the cross. See Luke 23:34.)

These relational virtues are to be exercised through the forbearance and forgiveness enjoined in 3:13 (which is an expansion of v. 12). Paul probably has no specific grievance in mind here but is lifting up general principles. Continual forbearance and forgiveness are how meekness and patience are exercised and are how members of close communities remain in continual fellowship with one another. Paul sets forth Christ himself as the model of forgiveness. In 2:13 he has shown how Christ is the mediator of God's forgiveness. Christians are to forgive each other because they have been forgiven. It is the same principle that is set forth in the Lord's Prayer (Matt 6:12; Luke 11:4).

While this catalogue of positive attitudes is important, Paul realizes that love is the fundamental Christian virtue (cf. 1 Cor 13, Gal 5:6, Rom 13:8). Love is "above" (cf. 3:2) all other virtues and is thus the motive and force behind Christian action and the principle of cohesion in the Christian community. Throughout the passage, Paul's focus transcends personal rectitude and is corporate in its concerns and intention. Love as the most important moral force in the Christian's life will result in "perfect harmony" (which here might be better translated "complete maturity"). Love is the binding agent, the "super glue," of Christian community life.

The repetition of "put on" in v. 14 signals a new variation on the theme of Christian virtue. Verses 15 and 16 are roughly parallel as the Colossians are told to "let the peace of Christ rule in your hearts" and "let the word of Christ dwell in you richly." "Rule" (*brabeuetō*) in Greek carries with it the idea of an umpire in athletics or an arbitrator of disputes. If peace adjudicates the conflicts and governs the activity of the heart, the center of the person and thus of life, both the individual and his/her community will be governed by peace. "Word of Christ" is an objective genitive, so literally should be translated "word about Christ," that is, the gospel (or the truth, see 1:5b–6). The Word takes residence in Christians and leads to the same pedagogical process described in 1:28. The wisdom with which they teach and admonish is from Christ, and their singing is an expression of gratitude to him. ("Psalms and hymns and spiritual songs" in v. 16 are to be understood as synonyms.) The primary characteristic of the Christian life is thankfulness in all circumstances (see 1:3, 12; 2:7). Thankfulness or gratitude, which is stressed three times in three verses, is rooted etymologically and actually in grace (*chariti*).

Whether forbearing, forgiving, loving, teaching, admonishing, or singing with thankfulness, the Christian is to do all in the name of Jesus, that is, with his sanction and under his ownership. (For a full exposition of the meaning of the name of Jesus in early Christianity see chapter 4 of my study *Spiritual Life in the Early Church* [Minneapolis: Fortress, 1993].) In 3:17 Paul places all of life under the lordship of Christ, through whom God the Father is approached. Here, as throughout the Colossian letter, Jesus Christ is focal.

Some scholars have noted that 3:16–17 and 4:2–4 are about Christian spiritual practice or worship. They suggest that 3:18–4:1 is an intrusion or an insertion in that discussion. The passage is clearly a *Haustafel* or household code which is introduced in the context of doing "everything in the name of the Lord Jesus" (3:17) to illustrate how life in Christ affects their most intimate and immediate personal relationships. The whole parenetic section moves from discussion of relationship with all people (3:5–7), narrows the focus to those within the church (3:8–17), and then, more narrowly, within the domestic sphere of the family, which, paradoxically, would include slaves and thus one's work or profession (3:18–4:1), and, finally, returns to the broader focus of relationship to the church (4:2–4) and the larger society, "outsiders" (4:5–6). If Paul's plan is to move from general to specific and back to more general arenas of Christian life, then the *Haustafel* is not a random insertion but integral to the movement of his passage.

The Domestic (and Professional) Relationships of Christians (3:18–4:1)

At the outset of the parenetic section of Colossians Paul pointed out how new life in Christ should affect the believer's personal life. He stressed the communal nature of Christian life and how it must be marked by love, peace, and thanksgiving. Now he turns to the arena of domestic life (which included what we would call "professional relationships). In effect the household code depicts the principle given in 3:17 being worked out in that sphere.

Colossians preserves the first example in early Christian literature of the household code (which Luther called a *Haustafel*), a listing of the duties of the members of a household. Other instances occur in Eph 5:22–6:9; 1 Tim 2:8–3:13; 6:1–2; Titus 2:1–10; 1 Pet 2:13–3:7; *Didache* 4:9–11; *Epistle of Barnabas* 19:5–7, and *1 Clement* 21:6–9. Not surprisingly, the form has received extensive scholarly attention.

Like the vice and virtue lists, the *Haustafel* form is borrowed from the hellenistic world. Its underlying idea can be traced to Aristotle's *Politics* (1.1254b), which argues that patriarchal domination of males over females enhances the proper functioning of the household and, ultimately, of the state. From this assertion, that a well-run household is the foundation of a well-run state, the *Haustafel* arose. The form is found extensively in Stoic sources (in Seneca, Epictetus, Diogenes Laertius) and in hellenistic Judaism (in Pseudo Phocylides, Philo, Josephus).

The number of *hapax legomena* in Col 3:18–4:1 suggests that the basis of the code existed before the writing of the letter, that Paul is again using traditional materials. Its form is characteristic of the genre in which each exhortation has an addressee (normally of one word) and a command, followed by the motive for obeying that command. As is usually the case in such codes, the first party addressed is subservient to the second. In Colossians Paul presents three sets of reciprocal exhortations (the reciprocal nature of the duties is believed to be the Christian addition to the codes) arranged from the closest to least close relationship. All household codes evince a special interest in wives and slaves, and this at least partially accounts for why Paul included one in the Colossian letter.

Certainly the general purpose of the Colossian *Haustafel* is the same as that of the vice and virtue lists, to delineate Christian behavior, here in the domestic sphere, from non-Christian. In their familial relationships, Christians must "do everything in the name of the Lord Jesus" (3:17) and must conduct themselves wisely, "making the most of the time" (4:5). More specifically, the *Haustafel* provides a check on the lax morality of paganism (cf. 3:5–7) and safeguards the social order and the Christian's place in it.

I have argued elsewhere that in its earliest form Christianity gave women much more freedom than they enjoyed in the wider cultural context (see *The Widows* [Minneapolis: Fortress, 1989]). In the hellenistic world the most telling criticisms of any group were those leveled against its women. As the expectation of an early parousia receded, Christians of the late first century were faced with the challenge of living in society for an extended period. The greater freedom of their women (and, relatively speaking, of their slaves) represented a threat to the existing society. Christian household codes were part of an attempt to limit that freedom, to see that Christian women were exempt from criticism by the larger society by teaching them to conform to the expectations of that society. (Crouch, too, notes the special stress on the subordinate members of the household and believes it to be a conservative reaction against too much freedom.)

Paul frames his household code with material on worship and devotional life (3:16–17; 4:2–4). His admonition to the Corinthians that all things be done decently and in order (1 Cor 14:40) comes immediately to mind. In 1 Corinthians, the limitations placed on women also occur in the context of Paul's teaching on worship (1 Cor 11–14). Here in Colossae, where false teachers encouraged pneumatic worship (2:18–19) and where Christians were under scrutiny from "outsiders," Paul reminds the faithful not only to place household relationships under the lordship of Christ but to conduct those relationships with appropriate decorum. Placing the household code in the context of worship stresses the need for order. And, since "liberated" women and slaves represent a potential source of threat and disorder, they, especially, are addressed with regard to the theological motivations for their subservience and humility.

Paul begins his instruction with wives and husbands because they form the basic unit in any household (3:18–19). As the subordinate party, wives are addressed first and are told to "be subject" to their husbands. The submission (*hypotassesthe*) enjoined here is based on recognition of the Christian order. It is "in the Lord." 1 Corinthians 7:3–6 suggests that Paul thought of submission as being mutual. The overarching principle is that Christ rules the new person formed by the two in marriage. The humility by which submission is manifested has been demanded of all Christians (3:12) and not placed as a burden on wives alone. "As is fitting," however, indicates that Paul accepts the subordination of women that was the norm in both the Greek and Jewish cultures of his day.

There is, however, a positive motivation for a wife's subjection to her husband; it is her husband's love for her. Love manifested in mutual affection was not necessarily part of the marital equation in antiquity, so the personal love depicted here is unusual. Furthermore, Paul has just stressed love as the supreme Christian virtue that "binds everything together in perfect harmony" (3:14). This is as true in marriage as in the larger Christian community and places the burden of marital stability on the husband (cf. Eph. 5:25-33). Husbands are enjoined to practice Christian love, which puts concern for the other before self interest. "Harshness" (*pikrainesthe*), implying authoritarian rule, is the opposite of Christian love (and the first vice of the list in Eph. 4:31).

Children and fathers (the *paterfamilias,* who represented "parents" and authority in the family) are also called to understand that their relationships to one another are based on mutual interaction and are under the lordship of Christ (3:20-21). Consideration for children as persons and individuals is novel in the hellenistic period because children were generally held in low esteem in Greco-Roman society. Christian children are to be obedient "in everything" (which is more than the subordination asked of wives), "for this pleases the Lord."

Note that the subordinate members of the household (wives, children, and slaves) are given theological motivations for their behavior. Improper behavior will displease not only husbands/fathers/masters but the Lord himself. In contrast, husbands/fathers are given practical, human reasons for their behavior. Only the master is reminded of his thralldom to Christ, perhaps because there were few legal or societal checks on his behavior toward his slaves. If husbands are harsh with their wives, the wives will become unruly and surly. If fathers provoke their children, the children will become discouraged. That the "ante is upped" for the subordinate household members is not to underplay what is asked of the dominant member. Paul revokes the paternal license to tyrannize children, perhaps fearing that such treatment would turn them from Christian faith. Constantly provoked and irritated children lose heart, become spiritless, and, finally, moody and sullen. Paul would spare Christian families such unhappiness. The remarkable modernity of his insights with regard to children (if not to wives and slaves) in his era should not be overlooked.

Finally, the longest injunction in the Colossian *Haustafel* is addressed to slaves and masters (3:22-4:1). This is not surprising since the slave Philemon and his master Onesimus are from Colossae (see 4:9 and the letter to Philemon). The Colossian church has already had to face in practice the changes that Christianity makes in the master–slave relationship.

(This section of the household code is best read in tandem with Philemon.)

As was the case with his focus on children, Paul's attention to slaves is remarkable, even though he accepts slavery (as he accepts the subjugation of women) as part of the social order with no sense that it is morally wrong. His teaching here is much like that in 1 Cor 7:21–24. (For a full treatment of slavery in the period, see S. Scott Bartchy, *First-Century Slavery and 1 Corinthians 7:21* [SBL Dissertation Series 11; Missoula, Mont.: Scholars Press, 1973].) In the *Politics* (1.2.4–5, 1253b) Aristotle suggests that slaves have no rights. But in the community made up of those who have put on "the new nature" (3:10) "there cannot be" slave and free man (3:11). In society a man may be slave to a master, but in the church both are brothers and this has consequences for their relationship in the larger society.

In Colossians, the bulk of the instruction is directed to slaves (3:22–25) both because there were more slaves than masters in the Christian community but also because their Christian "license" (see 3:11) was a potential source of conflict between Christians and the social order. Thus Paul, toeing the expected line, says that slaves, like children, are to obey their masters "in everything." His basic theological point, however, is that of "true motivation"; the labor of slaves must spring from their inner conviction as Christians rather than from fear of punishment or reward or any earthly motive. In v. 22 two compound words (which occur only here and in Eph 6:6) exemplify the idea. Slaves are not to engage in "eyeservice," literally "eyeslavery," (*ophthalmodoulia*) or to be "people-pleasers" (*anthrōporeskos*); that is, they are not to work conscientiously only when someone is looking, because, ultimately, their work will not be judged by an earthly master but by the Lord. Christian slaves work for Christ, not for earthly masters; in reality, the master is Christ (3:23).

The new attitude that Paul calls for among Christian slaves has a new center of reference (Christ). Because this is the case, they will "work heartily" (*psychēs ergazesthe*), literally, "from the soul" (3:23). Likewise, there is a new reward that also comes "from the Lord" (3:24). Paul calls this reward "the inheritance" (*klēronomias*), a striking choice of word since by Roman law slaves could not inherit earthly possessions. The Christian slave shares with his Christian master and with all Christians "the inheritance of the saints in light" (1:12).

Just as those who serve willingly will be rewarded, those who are "slackers" and who do wrong will be recompensed. The promise of reward in v. 24 is balanced by the warning of punishment in v. 25, which serves as a consolation to slaves and a warning to masters. Disinterestedly and without bias, God will avenge all wrong (see Deut 32:35a). God's impartiality is a standard feature of Christian teaching (cf. Acts 10:34; Rom 2:11; 1 Pet 1:17), and in this context not only warns slaves to work fairly but puts masters on notice that they, too, will appear before the judgment seat of God. As in the Christian community, so in the Kingdom, the slave/master distinction (or any social or economic distinction) is unimportant to God.

The principle of reciprocity is carried out in the injunction to masters in 4:1. Not only slaves but also masters have "a master in heaven." In a world in which slaves had no legal rights, Paul sets down two principles for their treatment by Christian masters: justice and fairness (both norms of Stoic morality in popular philosophy).

In the hellenistic world slaves were understood as part of the hierarchically ordered household of husbands/fathers, wives/mothers, children, and, finally, slaves. However, they also represent the world of business and economics, what we would call "professional relationships." What Paul says to Christian slaves and masters in the first century can be applied to Christian people in business and workers in the present century. Thus the *Haustafel* both shows how Christ should influence the most intimate of the Christian's relationships (within the nuclear family) and moves outward into the wider arena of work life (and, finally, toward "outsiders" in 4:5) to demonstrate Christ's effect on the Christian there.

The essential concern of the Colossian household code is the relationship of the subordinate to the dominant member of the pairs addressed. This cuts both ways. Because women, children, and slaves in the Christian community had more status there than in the larger society, they were a potential source of criticism of Christianity by that larger society. Therefore the household code instructs them to behave in ways that would not offend society or bring censure on Christianity. On the other hand, that same code places limits on the attitude and authority of the dominant members (husbands/fathers/masters) of the Christian (and hellenistic) community. They are under the lordship of Christ and must behave toward their subordinates in ways that reflect their own subordination to Christ. As Lohse pointed out, the content of the directives is from the cultural environment, but the motivation is tied to subordination to the Lord.

The household code probably presents the most difficult problems of interpretation and application for the general modern reader in the whole letter. It seems wrong to assume that Paul's understanding of the domestic hierarchy and societal ordering of the hellenistic world is the correct pattern for every age. (If it were, modern Christians would own slaves, which, of course, they would treat properly!) I do not think that the immortalizing of the first century social order is the crucial issue. For his own day, Paul wanted to prove that the "otherness" of Christians was not a threat to their society. What is valid in every age is the understanding that all of life is under the lordship of Christ, and that the Christian's submission to him is manifested in humility in all of life's relationships, with those who are both "higher" and "lower" in standing. Unfortunately, this point has often been lost in the fervor to point out who should be subject to whom. Whatever the century, the way the Christian behaves in her ordinary relationships and in his daily round is the best apologetic for the gospel in a non-Christian environment.

The Final Exhortations (4:2–6)

The final pericope of the parenetic section of Colossians exemplifies the third form of literature that Paul borrowed from hellenistic moral exhortation, *topoi*. Parenesis, exhortation to seek virtue and avoid vice, gives rules for proper thought and action in daily living in forms that allow for wide applicability. *Topoi* are self-contained, brief teachings, often with loose or arbitrary connection to their context, dealing with the same general subject. Several sentences dealing with the same subject are united by the existence of a recurring word, a *stichwort,* that binds the units together. The form probably developed as Stoic and Cynic teachers repeatedly confronted the same questions and developed a stock set of answers to those questions. (For a fuller exposition, see D. G. Bradley's article in the bibliography immediately following.)

These *topoi* in Colossians are related to the general topic of church life, as Paul in 4:2 picks up the discussion of personal piety of 3:16–17 and places it in the context of evangelism. The final exhortation, then, is made up of two units: 4:2–4, which deals with the Colossian support of Christian mission through prayer, and 4:5–6, which deals with support of Christian mission through their behavior. Each section begins with an imperative (v. 2, "continue"; v. 5, "conduct") and ends with an "ought" statement (v. 4 and v. 6). In 4:2–4 the focus is within the church, and in

4:5–6 the focus is on relations with "outsiders," but the concern through-out is with what we would call evangelism.

At the outset of the letter Paul has stated that he and his colleagues have been in constant prayer for the Colossians (1:9). Now he commands that they, too, continue (*proskartereite* suggests persistence and deter-mination; cf. Rom 12:12) in prayer. Paul tells the Colossians to "watch and pray," the same admonition Jesus gave the disciples in the Garden of Gethsemane (Mark 14:38). They are to be watchful in prayer "with thanksgiving," reintroducing the attitude that Paul teaches must be char-acteristic of Christians (see 1:2, 3, 12; 2:7; 3:15, 16, 17).

Although God directs evangelistic efforts and their results, the Colos-sians have a part in the Pauline mission. They are to pray for it. Paul asks not that they intercede for his release from prison (literally, from "being bound," *dedemai,* which is both literal—cf. 4:18—and a pun, since Paul thinks of himself as Christ's slave), but "that God may open to us a door for the word" (4:3), that is, provide an opportunity for preaching (evan-gelism). The "mystery of Christ" is the substance of his preaching (1:26; 2:2) and the reason he is imprisoned, and Paul wants to be able to con-tinue that activity with clarity. In contrast to the "tricky speech" of 2:8, it is Paul's desire to display or reveal or make known (*phanerōsō*) Christ. He needs the prayerful support of the Colossians to be able to do so.

In 4:5–6 Paul turns his attention to their relations with unbelievers, but his focus on those outside the church is still evangelistic. Verse 5 is filled with marvelous ambiguity. Again using "walk" (*peripateite*) as a metaphor for the conduct of life, Paul suggests both that there is no need to offend outsiders unnecessarily (see the discussion of 3:18–4:1 above) and that Christians must use every available opportunity with regard to them. Paul cleverly makes wisdom a matter not of esoteric knowledge (as do the rival teachers), but of manner of life, because Christian con-duct itself has a missionary function.

For the first century, as for our own, time is the most precious com-modity. "Time" (*kairon*) here is not, however, a point in time, but time as a space of possibility. Perhaps the phrase might better be translated, "making the most of the opportunity." "Making the most" (*exagora-zomenoi*) is a strong commercial word which means literally "buying at the marketplace"; the prefix *ex* indicates intense activity. Framed as the verse is by a discussion of evangelism, Paul is suggesting that they use every available opportunity to show forth the gospel by how they live. By observing how Christians live, outsiders will be drawn to (or repelled by) their Christ.

The wisdom of their lives will also be reflected in their speech, which is always to be gracious. The idea is that their gracious attitude to outsiders should reflect God's grace (which comes from the same root word) toward them. The focus of 4:6 is as much on the manner of the speech as on its content. "Seasoned with salt" raises a variety of images. Salt was used both to preserve and to make palatable. The suggestion is that the gospel, while unchanging in its truth (i.e., "preserved"), is not "insipid" but "tasty," not to be dull but interestingly presented (cf. Matt 5:13–16). Since salt was a rabbinic metaphor for instruction in wisdom, Paul has here again introduced a subtle reference to the whole wisdom tradition which was behind his presentation of Christ earlier in the letter (and which is the alternative to the false wisdom presented by the rival teachers).

People are different, and the questions they ask will be different. The latter part of v. 6 speaks to "passive evangelism," to responding to other's initiatives with regard to the gospel. A variety of approaches will be necessary, and the Christian will have to prepare herself to be able to answer "everyone." Evangelism or witness alone is not enough, Paul suggests; it must be appropriate and informed.

One of the arguments for placing Colossians among the late, deutero-Pauline epistles of the New Testament has been that it does not reflect the immediate expectation of the parousia that is found, for example, in the Thessalonian or Corinthian correspondence. But this final exhortatory section of the letter evinces eschatological language and expectation. Watchfulness and prayer are key notes of eschatological expectation in the New Testament (see Mark 13:32–37; Luke 21:34–36; 1 Thess 5:6, 17; 1 Cor 16:22). "Making the most of the time" in 4:5 suggests, at the very least, that time is not limitless. It is true that making the most of time was a general philosophical truism in the period (see, for example, Seneca, *Epistles* 1:1), but coupled with the explicit reference to the return of Christ in 3:4 it suggests more than that here. *Exagorazomenoi* in its more customary New Testament sense means "to rescue." On one level, then, the Colossians are being told to rescue the time from the evil into which it has fallen. Although subtle, Pauline eschatology is not absent from Colossians.

Having used *topoi* to conclude his practical exhortation to the Colossians, Paul follows the form of the hellenistic letter and draws his epistle to a close with greetings to and from friends and co-workers.

W. Barclay, *The Letters to the Philippians, Colossians, and Thessalonians* (Philadelphia: Westminster Press, 1975).

D. G. Bradley, "The *Topos* as a Form in the Pauline Paraenesis," *JBL* 72 (1953): 238–46.

G. E. Cannon, *The Use of Traditional Materials in Colossians* (Macon, Ga.: Mercer University Press, 1983).

G. T. Christopher, "A Discourse Analysis of Colossians 2:16–3:17," *GTJ* 11 (1990): 205–20.

J. E. Crouch, *The Origin and Intention of the Colossian Haustafel* (Göttingen: Vandenhoeck & Ruprecht, 1972).

B. S. Easton, "New Testament Ethical Lists," *JBL* 51 (1932): 1–12.

E. G. Hinson, "The Christian Household in Col 3:18–4:1," *RevExp* 70 (1973): 495–507.

J. R. Levison, "2 Apoc. Bar. 48:42–52:7 and the Apocalyptic Dimension of Colossians 3:1–6," *JBL* 108 (1989) 93–108.

W. Lillie, "The Pauline Housetables," *ExpT* 86 (1975): 179–83.

E. Lohse, *A Commentary on the Epistles to the Colossians and Philemon* (Philadelphia: Fortress Press, 1971).

A. J. Malherbe, *Moral Exhortation: A Greco-Roman Sourcebook* (Philadelphia: Westminster Press, 1986).

C. J. Martin, "The *Haustafel* in African-American Biblical Interpretation," in *Stony the Road We Trod: African American Biblical Interpretation,* ed. C. H. Felder (Minneapolis: Fortress Press, 1991).

R. P. Martin, *Colossians and Philemon* (Grand Rapids: Eerdmans, 1985).

C. F. D. Moule, "The 'New Life' in Colossians 3:1–17," *RevExp* 70 (1973): 481–93.

W. Munro, "Col. 3:18–4:1 and Eph. 5:21–6:9: Evidences of a Late Literary Stratum?" *NTS* 18 (1972): 434–47.

C. A. Newsom and S. H. Ringe (eds.), *The Women's Bible Commentary* (Louisville: Westminster/John Knox Press, 1992).

P. Pokorny, *Colossians: A Commentary* (Peabody, Mass.: Hendrickson, 1991).

E. Schweizer, *The Letter to the Colossians* (London: SPCK, 1982).

R. Yates, "The Christian Way of Life: Paraenetic Material in Colossians 3:1–4:6," *EQ* 63 (1991): 241–51.

THE GREETINGS AND CLOSING

Colossians 4:7-18

The Greetings (4:7-17)

Letters in the hellenistic world characteristically close with farewell greetings. The closing *errōso* (addressed to one recipient) or *errōsthe* (addressed to multiple recipients) (literally, "to make strong") was associated with wishing good health to the recipients of the letter and sending greetings to others. According to Jerome Murphy-O'Connor, this form is found only in the letters quoted in Acts (see Acts 15:29 and 23:30). Typical Pauline closings usually include hortatory remarks (like those in 4:5-6, 10b, 16), greetings (4:7-17), a wish of peace (absent in the closing of Colossians, but part of its standard opening), and a grace or benediction (4:18). In Paul's letters, greetings predominate before the final blessing. (The notable exception is Rom 16:21-23.)

The greeting section of the Colossian letter is unusually extensive. In a lecture at the Ecole Biblique in Jerusalem in 1993, Jerome Murphy-O'Connor pointed out that Paul mentions individual persons only in letters to churches he didn't found and in which he was not personally known. As is the case in Romans 16, Murphy-O'Connor feels it is not necessary to assume that Paul has met all these people. Murphy-O'Connor believes the point of these long greetings is to establish relationships with those he has not met.

The case is slightly different in Colossae. Here, the people Paul mentions are either known to him and the church in Colossae or are known to him and being introduced to them. The greeting falls into three sections. Paul commends the messengers bringing the letter (4:7-9), conveys greetings from his fellow prisoners and associates (4:10-14), and, finally, sends his own, personal, greetings and messages (4:15-17).

Since the theological and practical content of the letter is complete, it would be easy to pass over rapidly the greetings. However, the greetings often give "flesh and blood" to Pauline epistles. Paul had real people around him for whom he cared and who cared for him. The greetings in his letters give some insight into his friends and relationships within the church; they show Paul's personal and pastoral interests and thus justify attempts at historical reconstruction which use the Acts of the Apostles and deutero-Pauline epistles as source material. The discussion that follows, then, attempts to give something of Paul's "human geography" at the time he was writing Colossians. (Nevertheless, I admit both the speculative character of some of the following material and the caution with which I draw it from its sources.)

The greeting opens as Paul commends the carriers of the letter to Colossae (4:7–9). Tychicus and Onesimus are entrusted with three tasks. First, they are to deliver the letter. "I have sent him" (*epempsa*, v. 8) uses an "epistolary aorist," a way to attach a message in a letter that mentioned the carrier of the letter and suggested that he could fill out its contents with verbal reports. Second, they are to encourage the Colossians (v. 8). And, finally, they are to share news of Paul and his associates ("that you may know how we are," v. 8; and "They will tell you of everything that has taken place here," v. 9). The unit of text begins and ends with "will tell you" (vv. 7 and 9).

Tychicus was a common name in inscriptions in Asia Minor. This Tychicus Paul calls a "beloved brother" (meaning, a fellow Christian), "a faithful minister" (*diakonos* probably does not yet signify a clearly defined church office), and a "fellow slave" (in and of Christ). Acts 20:4 mentions a Tychicus from Asia who accompanied Paul through Macedonia. It was also a Tychicus whom Paul sent to Ephesus (2 Tim 4:12) and as a messenger to Crete (Titus 3:12). If these references are to the same man, he served extensively as Paul's emissary.

Onesimus was a common slave name which literally means "useful one." There is no proof that this is the same Onesimus who is the focus of Philemon, but that is the customary association, since he is referred to as "one of yourselves" (v.9). Behind the mention of Onesimus, then, is the whole issue of how slaves and masters were to be related to each other in the Christian community. The Colossians must have been well aware of the specifics of this particular relationship, since Philm 2 indicates that the letter discussing Onesimus and his master is to be read to the whole house church. Onesimus, too, is a "faithful and beloved brother." Unlike the rival teachers, Tychicus and Onesimus are "faithful," that is, committed to the apostolic message. They come carrying this teaching with its apostolic authority in the Lycus Valley.

The most extensive section of the greeting, vv. 10–14 conveys the greetings of Paul's fellow prisoners and associates to those in Colossae. Aristarchus, Mark, and Jesus (Justus) are, like Paul, Jews and are his fellow workers and a comfort to them (v. 11).

Paul calls Aristarchus a "fellow prisoner" (*synaichmalōtos*). The word literally means "a prisoner of war" and is to be understood as an honorific title (see 2 Cor 2:14 and 10:3–4). Acts introduces a person named Aristarchus who worked with Paul in Asia. He was among the crowd in the riot in Ephesus where he is introduced as a Macedonian and travel companion of Paul (Acts 19:29). He accompanied Paul through Macedonia (Acts 20:4), which was his home, and (as a fellow prisoner?) on the ship to Italy (Acts 27:2). The letter to Philemon names him as a fellow worker who sends greetings (Philm 24).

Mark is introduced parenthetically as a cousin of Barnabas, implying that he is not widely known. (Apparently the Colossians are acquainted with Barnabas, who provides Mark with legitimacy.) If this is the John Mark of Acts, the son of Mary whose home in Jerusalem was a meeting place for Christians (Acts 12:12), his history as a missionary is fascinating. He was brought to Jerusalem by Barnabas and Saul after their early mission (Acts 12:25). He began the Cypriot mission with Paul but left to return to Jerusalem (Acts 13:5, 13). Paul declined to take him with Barnabas and himself on a visit to established churches, probably because of his earlier desertion, and this led to the rupture between Barnabas and Paul (Acts 15:36–41).

In Colossians, it seems that Mark has been rehabilitated as a worker for the gospel and a companion of Paul. The Colossians have "received instructions" about him, suggesting there has been some discussion of his work, and are to receive him. Philemon 24 lists him as a fellow worker who sends greetings. And by the time of the writing of 2 Timothy he seems to have regained his reputation and is described by the author as "useful in my ministry" (2 Tim 4:11). It is possible to see in John Mark's story an example of how Christian workers can have a serious "falling out" and yet be reconciled and again come to work fruitfully together.

Little can be discerned of Jesus called Justus. "Jesus" was a very common name in the period. "Justus," of course, means "the just." Double names were common among Jews who took hellenistic names similar to their semitic ones. (Recall John Mark or Saul/Paul, for example.) Jesus Justus, like Aristarchus and Mark, is literally "of the circumcision" (v. 11). The phrase most obviously seems to mean they are Jews, but it has been interpreted to suggest Christians who were concerned with living a Jewish lifestyle and men of the circumcision party (like those in Galatians), although this latter interpretation has not won wide acceptance. *Parēgoria* means "comfort" in its most profound sense. The word has been found on gravestones and in a letter of condolence. Do these men offer Paul comfort in the face of death? If that is the suggestion, it certainly increases the intensity of the plea in this letter.

Epaphras, like Onesimus, is a Colossian whom Paul here describes as "a servant of Christ Jesus" (the only other of his associates so described is Timothy in Phil 1:1) and in Philm 24 as a "fellow prisoner." It is he who has brought the gospel (1:7, 2:5) and who still bears responsibility for the Colossian church through his prayers. Earnest prayer hardly conveys the sense of *agōnizomenos,* which is the same word used to describe Jesus' prayer in the Garden of Gethsemane (Luke 22:44), which Paul uses to describe his own strivings for the gospel (1:29), and which is related to the English cognate "agony." The substance of the prayer is similar to that in 1:3–12. Epaphras prays that they will be mature (*teleioi*) and fully assured (*peplērophorēmenoi*) in the will of God. The two words clearly allude to the claims of the rival teachers, so his prayer, like Paul's letter, is intended to oppose their "philosophy." Paul's confidence in Epaphras and his commendation of him are intended to raise his status among the Colossians and further to inspire their confidence in him.

It has been noted that Paul's expressions of confidence in those he addresses appear most frequently in the closings of letters and are intended to help secure a favorable hearing for his positions. In praising Epaphras, Paul, the consummate psychologist, is praising the Colossians (Epaphras is "one of yourselves" v. 12), and thus encouraging their faithfulness to his gospel.

Essentially, Luke and Demas are mentioned in passing. Colossians is the origin of the tradition of Luke the "beloved physician." A person named Luke is also mentioned in Philm 24 as a fellow worker who sends greetings and in 2 Tim 4:10–11 as the only one who has stayed with Paul. Here, and in Philm 24, Demas seems to be one of Paul's fellow workers and associates. In 2 Tim 4:10, however, a Demas "in love with this present world has deserted me and gone to Thessalonica." If Mark can represent the happy fact of reconciliation of the estranged, Demas can represent the sad fact of rifts in fellowship in the Christian community even in its earliest days.

That Onesimus, Epaphras, Mark, Aristarchus, Demas, Luke, and Archippus also appear in Philemon serves further to link the two letters. Those who argue for the pseudonymity of Colossians suggest these names are introduced to root the letter in the life of Paul. But it can equally be the case that they were, indeed, Paul's associates, as are Tychicus and Nympha who are not mentioned in Philemon and who cannot otherwise be accounted for.

Having passed along the greetings of those attending him, Paul now sends his own greetings in 4:15-17. As is characteristic of the uncontested letters, he uses a form of *aspasomai* to convey greeting. First, he greets "the brethren at Laodicea." (*Adelphous,* "brethren," can equally accurately be translated "brothers and sisters.") The verse raises a problem. Why would Paul send greetings to Laodicea via Colossae if, as v. 16 asserts, he sent Laodicea a letter? The mention of a Laodicean letter has led to much speculation. Among the suggestions are that the letter to Laodicea is the Ephesian letter, that it was a letter written by Epaphras, and that it was written by Paul but later suppressed or lost, perhaps in the earthquake of 60/61 C.E. in the Lycus Valley. The historical puzzle remains, and the letter in question has not yet been accounted for.

However, 4:15-16 does give information about life in the early Pauline churches. First, it provides a tantalizing, but incomplete, suggestion of how the letters were collected. Second, it was apparent from 1:24-2:5 that Paul intended his letters to be read aloud in the churches, and 4:16 makes this explicit (cf. 1 Thess 5:27; Philm 2). Third, it makes clear that Christians met together in homes in smaller groups and that these groups had fellowship with each other. There is ample New Testament evidence for house churches (see Acts 16:15, 40; Rom 16:5, 23, for example).

Nympha, like Lydia (Acts 16:11-15, 40), seems to have been a householder who provided one of the churches in the area with a place to meet. There is textual uncertainty about whether "Nympha" is a male or a female name. The change to the masculine interpretation seems to have happened in the course of the transmission of the text. As Bernadette Brooten has demonstrated, this same "sex change" happened to Junia in Romans 16:7 (see "Junia . . . Outstanding among the Apostles," in *Women Priests,* ed. L. Swidler and L. Swidler [Mahwah, NJ: Paulist Press, 1977]). Nympha is another example of the prominence of women in the early church generally, and in the Pauline churches in particular. Like Lydia, she was head of her own household, which may have included children, relatives, and slaves (cf. 3:18-4:1), and, as such, was a businesswoman of sorts. (For an alternative reading of the textual evidence, see Ralph Martin, *Colossians and Philemon* [Grand Rapids: Eerdmans, 1985], 136-37.)

Finally, Paul reminds Archippus to be faithful to the ministry he received in the Lord. Again, the verse tantalizes but does not reveal. Is he to be faithful to his ministry generally, or to some specific task to which Paul has called him? Is the verse a warning or a positive reminder? Is "received in the Lord" (*parelabas en kyriō*) technical language, so that v. 17 reflects (as v. 7 does not) the beginning of a diaconate? Like the recipient of the letter to Philemon, Archippus will be given his instruction from Paul in the public meeting of the church. Whatever it is he is to do will be known and expected by the community. Paul has placed not so subtle pressure on Archippus and the accomplishment of his ministry!

An Archippus is mentioned in Philm 2 as a member of Philemon's household and a "fellow soldier" of Paul. John Knox has argued that it was Archippus who was the owner of Onesimus. The verse in Colossians, he asserts, is to remind him of what he had been instructed in the letter to Philemon. Whether or not this is the case is a matter of discussion.

Who were Tychicus, Onesimus, Aristarchus, Mark, Jesus, Epaphras, Luke, Demas, Nympha, Archippus? We know little about them. Most of what we can construct is speculative. But there is no doubt that these names represent the living examples of Paul's genius for friendship. Thankfully, they lead us away from a modern stereotype of Paul as a thorny and unlikeable pious dictator. They introduce us to Paul the pastor and Paul the man, the Paul who had as his primary concern the eternal destiny of those about whom he cared and to whom he brought the "word of truth."

The Closing (4:18)

The closing of the letter begins with an autograph. In antiquity when one used an amanuensis to write a letter, one added his or her own signature or mark at the end to guarantee the authenticity of the contents of that letter. (We do the same today with letters written by secretaries.) The standard phrase used was *hoc manu mea,* "in my own hand."

As was the custom, Paul used secretaries to write his letters (Rom 16:22 names its scribe as Tertius). In three uncontested letters, Paul mentions writing or signing in his own hand (1 Cor 16:21; Gal 6:11; and Philm 19). It is especially important that the letter to the Colossian church be authentic. First, it will circulate in the Lycus Valley and have a wide hearing. Second, and more important, it represents apostolic authority in the face of the rival teachers. In 2 Thess 2:2 the author mentions letters sent in his name that are not his. This letter, the signature asserts, is Paul's. His own hand is a mark of his sincerity, of his affection for the Colossians, and of his personal interest in them.

The hand that Paul raises to sign the letter is bound by a chain. If Colossians is "heavy handed" it is because the hand that signs it is chained. (If Paul were literally chained in prison, he would be chained by his right hand to the soldier's left hand so that the soldier's right hand was free to use his sword. This fact hardly diminishes the symbolism.) "Remember" recalls 1:24 and all the apostolic suffering of Paul, which is part of his authority. The church is to recall (*mnēmoneuete*) his bonds (*desmōn*), what ties him to Christ and to them. The command brings the letter to a close on a note of solemn authority.

Colossians opened, "grace to you ... from God our Father" (1:2), and it closes, "grace be with you." In the uncontested letters the blessing of grace is a genitive of origin with "the Lord Jesus Christ." It is made explicit that Jesus is the mediator of grace. We do not know why reference to Jesus Christ is omitted here. Perhaps since the whole letter focuses on Christ, Paul felt no need to reintroduce his name here. The ending of Colossians is the briefest of any of the letters. The most developed closings occur in Paul's severest letters, as if he felt he must compensate in closing for his tone in the body. Again, since Colossians is not a severe letter, perhaps Paul feels an abbreviated ending is in order.

In any case, the apostolic greeting that opened the letter also brings it to a close. In a real sense, grace has been the subject of the Colossian letter, for Paul has explained what God has done in Jesus Christ and the all embracing sufficiency of that action. To bless the Colossian Christians with "grace" is, quite literally, to protect them from the rival teachers and ground them in the source of that grace, Jesus Christ, the firstborn, the creator, the head of the church, the firstborn from the dead, the fullness of God, the reconciler who makes "peace by the blood of his cross" (1:20).

C. P. Anderson, "Who Wrote the Epistle from Laodicea?" *JBL* 85 (1966): 436-40.

E. E. Ellis, "'Those of the Circumcision' and the Early Christian Mission," *StudEvan* 4 (1968): 390-99.

M. D. Goulder, "The Visionaries of Laodicea," *JSNT* 43 (1991): 15-39.

P. N. Harrison, "Onesimus and Philemon," *ATR* 32 (1950): 268-94.

J. Knox, *Philemon among the Letters of Paul* (New York: Abingdon, 1959).

G. E. Ladd, "Paul's Friends in Colossians 4:7-16," *RevExp* 70 (1973): 507-14.

S. Olson, "Pauline Expresions of Confidence in His Addressees," *CBQ* 47 (1985) 282-95.

N. T. Wright, *Colossians and Philemon* (Grand Rapids: Eerdmans, 1991).

DEUTERO-PAULINE
CHRISTIANITY

DEUTERO-PAULINE CHRISTIANITY

Toward the end of the first century, the church's self-understanding began to change; that change is evident in its literature. By about 70 C.E. the original twelve apostles called by Jesus and St. Paul himself were probably dead. The parousia (or "second coming"), which the first generation of Christians had expected as imminent, was apparently delayed, and so, also, the expectation of the immediate end of time. From preparing for the end, the work of the church became how to live in the Empire and adapt to a longer "stay."

The ethnic composition of Christianity also was changing. Second- and third-generation Christians were more likely to be of Greek or pagan heritage than of Hebrew or Jewish. Within the church, these Christians had to deal with challenges to the teachings of the apostles (see, for example, Col 2:8-23), and from without, their theology was increasingly influenced by Hellenism, especially Gnosticism in the second century. It soon became clear that "the saints" (a Christian self-designation probably drawn from esoteric Judaism) could sin! Restoration of erring Christians, authority, and church order became of crucial importance. And the suffering and anxiety caused by persecutions like those which led to the writing of the book of Revelation could not be ignored.

Disciples and followers of Paul had to face these challenges, and they took up the task, and that of preserving Paul's teaching with modifications for their own day and their own difficulties. The process was not unlike that of the evangelists who preserved the teachings of Jesus with modifications for their communities. Disciples of Paul began to produce literature in his name.

Pseudonymity (writings "under a false name") was not uncommon in biblical writings. Jewish apocalyptic works of the second and first centuries B.C.E. claimed the authorship of heroes like Daniel, Baruch, and Enoch. To King Solomon was attributed Proverbs, Ecclesiastes, Wisdom of Solomon, and Psalms of Solomon. Pseudonymity was also common in the hellenistic world. Plato's use of Socrates' name is probably the most widely known example of it.

Early Christians would not have considered pseudonymity dishonest or plagiarism. Our modern notion of the ownership of "intellectual property" was not part of the thinking of the ancients. Thus, pseudonymity is not a moral, but a historical issue. It was considered a tribute to a master when his disciple attempted to write as he had written. Furthermore, letters circulated under the name of a teacher were believed to carry his authority, thus, names were chosen for letters to give authority to their contents. The issue was not that of "making things up," but of preserving the teachings of a master while modifying those teachings for current situations, making them "relevant" by applying them to new situations.

This is exactly what the followers of St. Paul did. In an attempt to preserve his teaching, enhance his reputation, and speak to the church's struggles, they produced letters in his name. Most scholars currently hold that the deutero-Pauline canon (or "secondary" Pauline canon) includes Ephesians, 2 Thessalonians, and the Pastoral Epistles (1 and 2 Timothy and Titus). (Although I argued earlier in this volume that Colossians was written by Paul, some scholars do deem it deutero-Pauline.)

Deutero-Pauline works have noticeably different literary characteristics than the earlier and authentic Pauline writings. The sentences are longer. Meditations on a single subject are interrupted by other things. Hymn fragments and liturgical materials are inserted, and other hellenistic religious, philosophic, and literary forms and materials are used extensively. The vocabulary is often different from Paul's, and even Pauline words and phrases can be used with new or altered meanings.

Theological differences also occur in these later writings of the church. Emphasis shifts to the whole cosmos. The "mystery of Christ" is spoken of in terms of the reconciliation of the whole universe through his death and resurrection. Christ has broken down divisions in the cosmos, as well as the walls that divided people. The image of the church as the body of Christ is extended as Christ is described as the head of his body the church, whose members grow in grace toward him in heaven (rather than awaiting his return to earth). The emphasis on Christ as head reflects the church's concern for authority.

In deutero-Pauline writings the practical issues of unity, holiness, and authority are focal. The Holy Spirit is no longer the standard by which unity is determined. Therefore, the church needs the symbolic unity that is manifested in uniformity of belief and practice. Writings that address false teachings and teachers exhibit this concern.

Christians, members of Christ's body, could, and did, sin. In order to deal with this reality, the church began to develop ethical codes, codes of Christian conduct. These are found in the long parenetic sections of the letters, which incorporate hellenistic ethical forms like vice and virtue lists and household codes. The restoration or exclusion of erring sisters and brothers is addressed.

But perhaps the most important practical issue is authority. What happens after the original apostles die? Who has authority, and how is it to be exercised? Hellenistic mystery teachers, for example, said they had special revelations of knowledge and teaching. Did they? Deutero-Pauline letters were written to preserve the apostolic traditions as they were taught in the Pauline gospel.

Historically, deutero-Pauline Christianity struggled to come to terms with the delay of the parousia, the increasing possibility of (and, in some instances, the reality of) persecution, and the destruction of Jerusalem and the Temple in 70 C.E. Incipient forms of Gnosticism, hellenistic religions, and other philosophic-religious systems increasingly threatened to invade and influence Christian teaching. How far could syncretism be allowed to go? Ironically, at the same time the church was struggling against these "pagan" ideas, it made increasing use of hellenistic religious traditions and philosophical literature and its forms. Thematically and theologically the pseudonymous letters emphasize Christ as reconciler as well as head of the church and emphasize the unity of Jew and Gentile in Christ's body.

In the remainder of this volume, two pseudonymous or deutero-Pauline letters will be examined, Ephesians and 2 Thessalonians. Although Paul may not be the author of these letters, they carry his authority. And, more significantly, because they are included in the canon of the New Testament, the church has made clear that they represent apostolic tradition that is binding on Christians, no matter who wrote the works. In short, "pseudonymous" does not mean "false."

EPHESIANS

INTRODUCTION

The City of Ephesus

Ephesus was a major city of antiquity, the leading city in western Asia Minor. Greek legend suggests that Ephesus, a port at the mouth of the Cayster River, was founded by the Amazons. First colonized by Ionian Greeks, it was the city of Croesus of Lydia who took it in 560 B.C.E., dedicated it to Artemis, and moved it from the mountains to the southern plain. (Actually, the location of the city moved five times due to silting of the harbor.) Croesus was defeated by Cyrus of Persia in 547 B.C.E., and the city came into Alexander's empire in 334 B.C.E. After being ruled by the Seleucids, Ephesus was added to the Roman Empire in 133 B.C.E.

The city was at the height of its prosperity and power in the first and second centuries C.E. Strabo's *Geography* (14.1.24) described it as "the largest emporium in Asia this side of the Taurus." It was the fourth largest city in the Roman Empire, the capital of the Roman province of Asia, and residence of the proconsul, and boasted a quarter of a million inhabitants. Its prosperity was due to its natural harbor, and when this silted up, the city declined in importance.

From antiquity, Ephesus was a religious center. It had a shrine to the Anatolian Mother Goddess whom the Greeks called Artemis and the Romans worshiped as Diana. Her cult included both magic and astrology. According to Strabo, the first temple of Artemis was built by the architect Chersiphron. In Paul's time it was one of the seven wonders of the world and supported a large votive and pilgrim/tourist industry. Emperor worship was also practiced in Ephesus, and it seems to have been one of the first centers of Gnostic thought. Acts reveals that Ephesus had a synagogue and "Jewish exorcists," indicating that the tradition was not unaffected by its environment.

At the time Paul was in Ephesus, the city was laid out on a hellenistic plan and had a theater with perfect acoustics, a stadium that seated twenty-four thousand, and no fewer than six public baths. Its colonnaded main street was half a mile long. The bank at the Artemesian was the largest in Asia Minor. (The library of Celsus, which dominates the present ruins, was built in 135 C.E., and attests to the city's continuing importance.)

Ephesus has been extensively excavated by Austrian archaeologists, and a huge model of the ancient city has been reconstructed and is on display in Vienna.

J. Finegan, "Ephesus," *IDB,* 2:114–18.

C. Miller, "Ephesus," *HBD,* 270–72.

B. Thurston, *Spiritual Life in the Early Church* (Minneapolis: Fortress Press, 1993), chap. 7.

The Church in Ephesus

Ephesus is mentioned no fewer than twenty times in the New Testament. Paul did not found the church there. Priscilla and Aquila preceded him (1 Cor 16:19; Rom 16:5), and the church may have existed when they arrived. Apollos is associated with Ephesus (Acts 18:24), as are disciples of John the Baptist (Acts 19:1, 7; 20:16).

The Acts of the Apostles gives an extensive account of Paul's ministry in Ephesus (see Acts 18:24–20:1; 20:16–21:1). By Lukan reckoning, Paul was in Ephesus for two and a half to three years (about 54–57 C.E.). Paul taught for the first three months in the synagogue and then for two years in the lecture hall of Tyrannus. Apparently his primary opponents were Jewish exorcists (who lost status because of the spread of Christianity) and Demetrius the silversmith who represented the votive industry of Artemis (which, because of Christian inroads in Ephesus, was experiencing a decline in business).

Helmut Koester thinks the only useful historical information in the account in Acts is the statement of Paul's length of stay (two years, three months, Acts 19:8,10) and the location of his teaching. (Koester also puts Paul's stay in Ephesus around 52 C.E.) It is true that Luke does not mention Paul's correspondence from Ephesus, which includes the majority of his extant letters (1 Corinthians, part of 2 Corinthians,

Philippians, Philemon, and perhaps Romans and Colossians). Nor does Luke allude to Paul's imprisonment (traditionally in a cave; cf. 1 Cor 15:32; 2 Cor 1:8-9).

Paul's work in Ephesus probably involved its organization as a missionary center and headquarters for other work in Asia. The Ephesian church continued to be prominent after Paul's time. It was governed by Timothy and John and associated with John the Evangelist and the Virgin Mary, who is said to have lived out her life there. Ephesus is one of the seven churches in the book of Revelation and in 431 C.E. was the site of one of the major councils.

H. Koester, *Introduction to the New Testament* (Philadelphia: Fortress, 1982), vol. 2.

B. Robinson, "An Ephesian Imprisonment of Paul," *JBL* 29 (1910): 181-89.

D. Rowlingson, "Paul's Ephesian Imprisonment," *ATR* 32 (1950): 1-7.

The Relationship of Colossians and Ephesians

Even a cursory comparison of Colossians and Ephesians reveals remarkable similarities between the two letters. (For example, compare Col 3:12-13 and Eph 4:1-2; Col 3:16-17 and Eph 5:19-20; Col 4:7-8 and Eph 6:21-22.) Statistically, about a third of the words in Colossians are found in Ephesians; 73 of the 155 verses in Ephesians have parallels in Colossians. In addition to verbal parallels, the two letters are stylistically similar and follow the same general structure.

A variety of theories have been put forth to account for the similarities. In 1838 Mayerhoff argued that non-Pauline Colossians was dependent on Ephesians, and his argument has been revived by both F. C. Synge (1941) and J. Coutts (1958). In 1872 Holtzmann suggested that the short epistle of Paul to the Colossians was used as a basis for Ephesians and was added to by the writer to make our present book of Ephesians. Dibelius (1947), noting that both letters contain a great deal of traditional parenetic material, decided that Colossians and Ephesians were independently determined by a common tradition of which, in some cases, Ephesians exhibits the more primitive form. (Ernst Percy also puts forth a theory of common origin.)

T. W. Manson, following Marcion, said that Ephesians is the letter to the Laodiceans, who are mentioned in Col 4:16, or, perhaps, he speculates, a circular letter like those in Rev 1-3. C. Masson (1950 and 1953) rejected the circular letter theory as a phenomenon unknown in the ancient world. He argues that Colossians as it appears in the New Testament is not the original form of the letter. Paul, he contends, wrote a brief letter which a disciple developed into Ephesians as we have it, but which was originally addressed to the Laodiceans.

Perhaps the most widely known theory is that of Goodspeed (1933), who believes that Ephesians was written by a Pauline disciple as the first work in a collection of Paul's writings. This author used Colossians as source material for his thought. C. L Mitton (1951) adopted and expanded Goodspeed's work. He thinks the author of Ephesians knew the whole Pauline corpus well, and Colossians almost by heart, and had it at hand as he wrote. The writer's purpose, Mitton suggests, was to present to Gentiles a summary of Paul's teaching apart from specific problems of local churches but stressing elements of Paul's thought that were applicable to his own day.

Although some traditionalists maintain that Colossians and Ephesians were both written by Paul at about the same time, this volume accepts the Goodspeed–Mitton hypothesis. Acceptance of this theory requires assuming the non-Pauline authorship of Ephesians.

For a full discussion of the issue with bibliography, see M. Barth, *Ephesians* (Garden City, N.Y.: Doubleday, 1974), 1: 36–41.

C. Anderson, "Who Wrote the Epistle from Laodicea?" *JBL* 85 (1966): 436–40.

J. Coutts, "The Relationship of Ephesians and Colossians," *NTS* 4 (1957/58): 201–7.

M. Holtzmann, *Kritik der Epheser- und Kolosserbriefe* (Leipzig, 1872).

E. Mayerhoff, *Der Brief an der Kolosser* (Berlin, 1838).

C. L. Mitton, *The Epistle to the Ephesians: Its Authorship, Origin and Purpose* (Oxford, 1951).

J. Polhill, "The Relationship Between Ephesians and Colossians," *RevExp* 70 (1973): 439–50.

The Question of Authenticity

From earliest times Ephesians was placed in the Pauline canon, and its claim to Pauline authorship was assumed. Questions arose in the eighteenth century, and by the end of the nineteenth most German scholars denied Pauline authorship. What caused this shift?

According to the text of the letter, Paul is under arrest and sends Tychicus to supplement the letter with oral information (3:1–2; 6:20–22). The letter makes it clear that the writer and readers are unknown to each other (1:15; 3:3). That, however, seems unlikely if Paul spent nearly three years in Ephesus. Furthermore, the phrase "in Ephesus" in 1:1 does not appear in the best manuscripts. Irenaeus about 180 C.E. mentions Ephesus, but Marcion about 140 C.E. indicates the letter was "to the Laodiceans." A popular, though much later, suggestion made by Archbishop Usher in 1654 was that Ephesians is an encyclical to Gentile Christians (2:11; 3:1), and a blank was left for the bearer (Tychicus) to insert the name of the recipients as required. (Conjecture about the circumstances of the writing has continued and will be discussed below.)

There are linguistic, stylistic, historical, and theological arguments against the Pauline authorship of Ephesians. Linguistic arguments against the letter's authenticity include the fact that there are about ninety words in Ephesians not used elsewhere in the Pauline corpus, and Pauline vocabulary is used in ways foreign to the apostle. Most Pauline letters use more nouns than verbs; Ephesians uses more verbs. Käsemann and several more recent scholarly works have commented on the similarities between the terminology of Ephesians and that of the documents from Qumran.

Stylistically, Ephesians contains sentences that are long and slow moving, with many relative clauses and particles. Paul's style in the uncontested letters is much crisper. The Ephesian writer is inclined to combine nouns and to connect them by means of prepositions and to pile up synonyms. These techniques have led to notoriously difficult problems of translation.

In addition to the great interdependence between Colossians and Ephesians mentioned above, Ephesians exhibits significant dependence on the seven unquestioned Pauline epistles. It has even been suggested that Ephesians is made up of phrases from those letters. Since the best manuscripts of Ephesians lack an address, since the letter contains no personal greetings, and since the work addresses no specific problem, it has been argued that Ephesians is not really an example of an hellenistic epistle.

Historically, the conditions of church life reflected in the letter are not those of Paul's time. For example, the Jew/Gentile tension that appears in Galatians and Romans (and in Acts 15) seems to be completely settled. And the church herself is viewed in much more universal terms than in the genuine Pauline epistles. This introduces the issue of the theology of Ephesians.

The ecclesiology of the letter is different from that in the uncontested letters. In Ephesians the church (Gk., *ekklēsia*) is always universal, never the local congregation. The reference to the apostles and prophets as foundational in the church (2:20) is striking, because Paul always asserted that the church's foundation is Christ.

Since I take Colossians to be written by Paul, it seems significant that in Eph 2:16 Christ is the subject of the verb "to reconcile"; in Col 1:20 the subject is "God." Likewise, in Eph 4:11 Christ calls apostles and prophets; in 1 Cor 12:28, God does so. The Christology of Ephesians seems different from that of earlier letters. But so does the attention to practical matters. For example, the expectation of the parousia is all but absent from Ephesians. Marriage, instead of a concession to the flesh as in 1 Corinthians, is here treated with the highest honor.

Nevertheless, there are strong counterarguments that speak in favor of Pauline authorship. First, earliest reference to it assumes Paul is the writer. Second, the text itself claims Pauline authorship (3:1). Third, many genuinely Pauline letters contain examples of words that appear infrequently, so vocabulary alone is not decisive. Romans and the Corinthian correspondence contain over one hundred such words, and the proportion of *hapax legomena* in Philippians is larger than in Ephesians. Fourth, the differences in style could have resulted because Paul was older, more reflective, and had more time to think out his writings since he was imprisoned and not in the midst of his work and journeys. Fifth, literary relationships with other letters can be seen to support authenticity, because the several works can arguably be from the same hand. Sixth, Paul's excellent and agile mind could well change; his theology could be adapted to new circumstances. And, in any case, it is argued, the thought of Ephesians agrees substantially with that of the earlier letters. Finally, proponents of Pauline authorship ask the important question, Why would someone other than Paul produce a letter and ascribe it to him?

The fullest defense of Pauline authorship is found in Ernst Percy's *Die Probleme der Kolosser- und Epheserbriefe* (Lund: Gleerup, 1946). He thinks that the following three features argue decisively for Pauline authorship: first, the numerous similarities between Ephesians and genuine epistles; second, the personal authentication of the letter in 3:1–13; and third, the difficulty of discovering a satisfactory aim for the letter in the post-Pauline situation.

As was the case with Colossians, it is finally impossible to establish with certainty the authorship of Ephesians (or even its original recipients). I am inclined to accept the arguments against Pauline authorship as telling. Those who support pseudonymity must create a plausible *Sitz im Leben* for the work, so several well-known speculations (and they are just that) follow. Regardless of who wrote Ephesians, it represents the apex of Pauline thought and is treated as such in this commentary.

M. Barth, *Ephesians 1–3* (ABC; New York: Doubleday, 1974).

R. Batey, "The Destination of Ephesians," *JBL* 82 (1963): 101.

H. Cadbury, "The Dilemma of Ephesians," *NTS* 5 (1958/59): 91–102.

F. Howard, "An Introduction to Ephesians," *SWJT* 22 (1979): 7–20.

E. Käsemann, "Epheserbrief," in *RGG.* 3d ed. II (1958).

C. Mitton, "The Authorship of the Epistle to the Ephesians," *ExpT* 67 (1955/56): 195–98.

The Circumstances of the Writing

While there have been many theories about the origin of Ephesians, they tend to follow one of three lines of thought. Ephesians is understood as a summary or circular letter, or as a homily or liturgical document, or as written for a historical purpose, to address specific problems in Asia Minor. (These various purposes can, of course, overlap.) Such theories tend to hold that although Ephesians does exhibit several epistolary characteristics, it is not an occasional letter like the works in the Pauline canon. (These shall be highlighted in the commentary that follows.)

Goodspeed is probably the best known proponent of a summary/circular letter position. Briefly, he believes that someone, probably Onesimus, was stimulated by the writing of Acts about 85 C.E. to search for and collect the letters of Paul. His purpose was to awaken the churches from lethargy and formalism, to unite them against sects, and to acquaint them with the great religious values in Paul's letters. To commend his collection, he wrote a general work in the epistolary style, Ephesians, as a "preface."

Both John Knox and F. W. Beare in the IBC adopt Goodspeed's point of view. Beare sees the author of Ephesians as both commending Paul and as being a great theologian in his own right. Also in agreement is C. L. Mitton, who in his NCBC volume notes that Ephesians is written to "present Pauline teaching in its universal and eternal aspects." Mitton also emphasizes the liturgical interest of Ephesians.

Käsemann is the champion of the liturgical origins of the letter. He thinks the work was built of liturgical materials already available in the church, and he stresses the connections between Ephesians and baptism. Dahl, examining the baptismal language in 1:13–14; 4:5; 5:8, 26, suggests Ephesians was written to new congregations to teach them, with Paul's authority, more of what they had received through baptism. Schille, Coutts, Porkorny and Kirby all see Ephesians as a discourse on baptism directed to Gentiles.

Recent speculation about the origins of Ephesians tends to argue for a historical purpose, to address issues that arose in the church in Asia Minor. Chadwick thinks the work originated from a pastoral purpose, to remind the Gentile church of its Jewish origins and thereby to emphasize the unity of the church. Weizsäcker thought both Colossians and Ephesians were written to counter the thinking introduced into the church in Asia Minor by the Johannine literature, which was being produced about the same time.

Several scholars have connected Ephesians with a Gnostic threat to Christianity. Koester is the strongest proponent of the view (although it also figures in Martin's thinking). He argues that the author of Ephesians drew from Gnosticism the theological categories that made his universalism possible. The writer used the intellectual equipment of Gnosticism to oppose it.

After establishing Asia Minor as the origin of the Ephesian letter and establishing that area, and Ephesus in particular, as a center for magical practices, Arnold argues that Ephesians was written to affirm the supremacy of Christ over "the powers." (Thus, its purpose is not unlike that of Colossians.) People in Asia Minor, he argues, felt oppressed by the demonic realm. The writer of Ephesians assures them that identification with Christ provides all the necessary resources to resist such hostile powers.

Goulder thinks that Ephesians was the letter to Laodicea, written to counter Jewish-Christian visionaries. Apocalyptic Judaism, of which Christianity was a form, insisted on revelation through visions. Those who had such visions also had spiritual authority. According to Goulder, the writer of Ephesians opposes this view.

Although Barth believes Paul wrote Ephesians from Rome at the end of his life as a summary of his thought, he makes an important point for those who accept the pseudonymity of the work. Barth points out the advantage of recognizing that Ephesians has many purposes. Those who are willing to grant this fact will be more receptive to the actual contents of the letter. Submitting all the details to a single theory can be a danger in interpreting such a rich document. Barth is correct in stating that Ephesians has many dimensions and should not to be examined under one aspect only.

To summarize, what are the probabilities surrounding the circumstances of the writing of Ephesians? The ethos of the document suggests that it was written for a church in Asia Minor. "Ephesus" is the earliest guess about the location. (If addressed to the churches in Asia Minor, the work would certainly have been read in Ephesus.) It was written for a Christian community that was predominantly Gentile.

The author cannot be identified with certainty (although, in addition to Paul, Onesimus and Tychicus have been suggested). This writer knew Colossians well (indeed, there appears to be literary connection between the two works), knew the Pauline corpus, and viewed Paul as the greatest Christian missionary. The author wrote in a declaratory, liturgical style appropriate to the worship in which the work would be heard. His primary concern, the unity of the church, was best addressed in this context.

The letter is probably later than 70 C.E., but its latest date of composition is uncertain, although Ephesians was known to the author of *1 Clement* (95–115 C.E.). Most scholars favor a date of about 90 C.E. (or the period of the Johannine writings, which probably also were being produced in Asia Minor).

In the final analysis the traditional pronouncement of the *IBD* accurately describes Ephesians. It is an original, brilliant composition in the Pauline manner.

C. Arnold, *Ephesians, Power and Magic* (Cambridge: Cambridge University Press, 1989).

E. Goodspeed, *The Meaning of Ephesians* (Chicago: University of Chicago Press, 1933).

M. Goulder, "The Visionaries of Laodicea," *JSNT* 43 (1991): 15–39.

J. Kirby, *Ephesians: Baptism and Pentecost* (Montreal: McGill University Press, 1968). (Pp. 3–55 survey the literature on circumstances of writing and give full bibliography.)

C. Mitton, *Ephesians* (NCBC; Grand Rapids: Eerdmans, 1981). (Pp. 25–32 also provide an excellent summary and full bibliography.)

The Structure of the Letter

Ephesians sets forth the divine plan of God, accomplished through the death and resurrection of Jesus, to reconcile Jews and Gentiles to God. God's final purpose is unity and harmony in the universe, and the church (which is not Jew or Gentile, but Christian) with Christ as its head is the instrument for accomplishing that purpose.

The unity of all things is found only in Christ. As did Colossians, Ephesians asserts the cosmic dimension of Christ's power and of the church's destiny. Because the letter speaks in cosmic terms, it exhibits a certain speculative tone. Stylistically, it is prayerful, liturgical, "doxological." It resembles panegyric (festal address praising someone, in this case, God).

Structurally, Ephesians follows the pattern of a Pauline letter. It begins with an address (1:1-2) and closes with a blessing (6:23-24). Chapters 1-3 are doctrinal or dogmatic, and chapters 4-6 are parenetic or didactic. Characteristically, praxis follows theory; ethics follows theology.

Barth's monumental two volume commentary modifies this pattern slightly. He believes that 1:3-14 is prologue to the whole letter; 1:15-2:22 describes God's perfect work; 3:1-4:24 praises the ongoing work of God's revelation to people; 4:25-6:20 encourages people to "let their light shine."

The following outline provides the large divisions for the commentary which follows:

1:1-23   The Salutation, Blessing, and Prayer of Thanksgiving
2:1-22   The Church in Christ Jesus
3:1-21   The Mystery of God's Plan
4:1-6:20 The Parenesis
6:21-24 The Closing

Note that the work is both framed and divided by prayer (1:1-23; 3:14-21; 6:23-24).

B. Metzger, "Paul's Vision of the Church: A Study of the Ephesian Letter," *TheoT* 6 (1949): 49-63.
B. Viviano, "The Letter to the Ephesians," *BibT* 102 (1979): 2019-26.

THE SALUTATION, BLESSING, AND PRAYER OF THANKSGIVING

Ephesians 1:1-23

A central theme of the Ephesian letter is the divine plan of salvation. Temporal terms form an inclusion marking off the first half of the letter, which sets forth that plan. God's design began "before the foundation of the world" (1:4) and extends "to all generations, for ever and ever" (3:21). God's plan for the creation began in the past (1:4; 3:9) and extends into the future (1:10; 3:21). The theological or doctrinal half of the letter is framed in cosmic terms by time immemorial extending both into the past and the future.

This section of the letter is also delineated in literary terms. It begins and ends with doxologies. It opens with the traditional form "blessed" (*eulogētos,* 1:3) and closes with the type of doxology that ascribes glory to God (3:20-21). These doxologies reinforce the inclusion which marks off a distinct unit of the letter.

This first section of the letter is basically a sustained prayer. It is as if the writer is addressing God and is only overheard by the hearers or readers. The prayer begins with an initial benediction (1:3-14), which is followed by thanksgiving (1:15-23) and intercession. The intercession begins at 3:1, is interrupted by a meditation on the mystery of God's plan (3:2-13), but resumes at 3:14-19 and ends with doxology (3:20-21; cf. 1 Thessalonians, which is also dominated by prayer). Within this prayerful exposition, liturgical language predominates, and 1:3-14; 1:20-23; 2:4-10; and 2:14-18 have been designated by various scholars as hymns.

The question has been raised whether Ephesians is an epistle in the sense that the uncontested writings of Paul are epistles. Certainly the writer of this work uses the standard conventions of a hellenistic letter to present his thought. The work opens as do most epistles of the period with a salutation, a thanksgiving, and a prayer. However, between the salutation (1:1–2) and the prayer of thanksgiving (1:15–23) there is a long, explanatory blessing (1:3–14), which sets forth the themes of the whole letter.

The Salutation 1:1–2

Following hellenistic conventions, the letter opens with the name of the writer, the address, and a greeting. This standard opening contains three features that are especially worthy of note.

First, the writer is anxious to set forth the authority behind the letter. Paul is listed as the writer, and no coauthor is named. This material purports to come from the apostle and from no other. Of the genuine Pauline epistles, only Romans cites no coauthorship. In all the uncontested letters except Philippians (where there has been no challenge to Paul and, therefore, no need to establish his authority) and Philemon (where Paul is making a request and, therefore, finds it politic not to assert his authority), Paul designates himself an "apostle." As if to underline apostolic authority (and echoing 1 and 2 Corinthians, Colossians, and the extended explanation in Gal 1:1–2), the writer reminds us that Paul's apostleship is "by the will of God." Paul is an apostle not by human, but by divine, agency. Therefore, whatever he says should carry special weight in the Christian community the letter addresses.

Second, v. 1b is of particular interest because of what it does not tell us about the recipients. The difficulties of translation due to the awkwardness of syntax in the Greek are legion. It is the absence of a geographical destination for the letter that has caused both the translation problems associated with 1:1b and the historical problems associated with the letter as a whole. The oldest manuscripts, and those known by Marcion, Tertullian, Basil, and Origin, do not contain the phrase "in Ephesus." Scholarly attempts to provide an answer to this absence of detail have been summarized in the introduction to the letter above.

Furthermore, in all the genuine Pauline letters but Galatians and 1 Thessalonians (where the assembly is addressed), the recipients are called "saints." The term literally means "holy people," but undoubtedly designated members of the church. Here it is the saints "who are also faithful" to whom the writer speaks. Unlike the Colossian letter where Paul is, indeed, setting the faithful apart from those who have fallen away, here the writer speaks to believers who are united "in Christ." (In fact "faithful" is sometimes translated "believers.") Those addressed are a group of individuals who have placed their faith in Christ Jesus.

Third, and finally, there is interest in the standard greeting in 1:2. The greeting is exactly the same as in Romans, 1 and 2 Corinthians, Galatians (which adds extended material), Philippians, Philemon, and 2 Thessalonians. "Grace and peace" appear in all the greetings of the Pauline writings. The secular, Greek greeting of the time was *chairein;* Paul uses the similar form *charis,* "grace." *Shalôm,* the traditional Jewish greeting, was also understood as God's gift to humans. Both grace and peace are understood to be bestowed by God and to be concepts that were social in application. Thus, while the greeting is the normal one for a Pauline letter, it serves the Ephesian writer's purposes especially well. Just as the letter will argue that God has brought Greek and Hebrew together in the church, a Greek and a Hebrew term brought together in the letter's greeting foreshadows that unity. The gifts of grace and peace come from God and from "the Lord Jesus Christ." The writer introduces a form of the earliest Christian confession ("Jesus Christ is Lord"), thereby reminding those addressed of the agency of the unity he defends. This is the great mystery that the first half of the letter reveals; Greek and Jew are brought together under Christ's lordship.

The Blessing (1:3–14)

Before the thanksgiving and prayer for the recipients of the letter, the author of Ephesians issues a long blessing or benediction, which begins with an early christological formulation, "Blessed be the God and Father of our Lord Jesus Christ." "Blessed be the God who . . ." is a common expression of Jewish piety. It is called *berakah* or benediction, and it usually praises the grace, action, and revelation of God. The form was taken over by the early Christians (it is found, for example, in 2 Cor 1:3 and 1 Pet 1:3), and its use here has suggested not only the language of worship, but, to some, the introduction of an early Christian liturgy.

On the basis of this departure from the hellenistic letter form and of the liturgical language in vv. 3–14, some scholars argue that the whole passage is an insertion. I think the writer is setting forth fundamental theological assumptions at the outset, and rather than concentrating on the liturgical character of the passage (which has been widely discussed), the focus in this commentary is on its trinitarian structure. Throughout, God is the chief actor, and the agent of God's action is Jesus

Christ. "In him" and "in Christ" appears more than eight times here (with "in the Lord," thirty-six times in the whole letter). "The God and Father of our Lord Jesus Christ, who" functions effectively as the acting subject of vv. 3–10. Verses 3–6 describe what God does. With "in him" at the beginning of v. 7 and continuing through v. 12, Jesus comes to center stage as the agent. Verses 9–12 set forth the central purpose of God's work in Christ, and vv. 13–14 introduce the contribution of the Holy Spirit, "the pledge of our inheritance," to that purpose. So the passage describes the work of God, Christ, and the Holy Spirit. In English after v. 3, each subsequent sentence is logically dependent on the preceding one, a reflection of the one, long statement in the Greek. Therefore, the strophic arrangements of the text that have been suggested by those who view the passage liturgically are not entirely satisfactory.

In vv. 3–9, which focus on the action of God accomplished in Jesus Christ, the Greek text contains a series of six aorist verbs followed in all but the last case by an accusative plural pronoun. (That break in the pattern at v. 9 to a dative plural pronoun is one indication of a shift in focus.) God is the one who "blessed us" (v. 3), "chose us" (v. 4), "destined us" (v. 5), "bestowed upon us" (v. 6), "lavished upon us" (v. 8), and "made known to us" (v. 9). In each case what God did was done in or through Christ (vv. 3, 5, 9), "in him" (v. 4), "in the Beloved" (v. 6), or through the grace made available by redemption "through his blood" (vv. 7–8). Two important facts are established by this pattern. What God does is done through Christ. And God is deeply involved in the life of the believer (indicated by the fact that "us," those who believe in Christ, is the object of the verbs).

First, then, God "blessed us in Christ with every spiritual blessing in the heavenly places" (v. 3). The blessing or praise offered to God is the response to the blessing God has granted to believers. "Every" (*pasē*) might also be translated "all," "every kind," or "whole." The blessings bestowed by God are of a piece, entire, complete. That they are spiritual means not only that they are the result and evidence of the Holy Spirit, but that they are inner, part of the hidden, unseen, and eternal life of the believer, which is manifested publicly in action. "In the heavenly places" is peculiar to Ephesians (see 1:20; 2:6; 3:10; 6:12). In the writer's mind, the heavens are part of the created universe, not geographically understood, but understood as the realm of unseen forces that exert their influence on human beings. God's blessing on believers "in the heavenly places" asserts God's presence, power, and, indeed, supremacy in that realm. (For a fuller discussion of the idea, see the commentary on Col

2:8–23.) Every blessing of every sort in every realm of existence has its origin in God, the Father of the Christian's Lord, Jesus the Christ.

Second, God chose believers "before the foundation of the world" to be "holy and blameless before him" (v. 4). The writer of Ephesians continually stresses that the initiative in this choosing is God's. Therefore, human holiness and blemishlessness (*amōmous* is also used to describe sacrificial animals that are without defect) comes not by human accomplishment but because of God's selection. This choice was not random or last minute, but part of a strategy in force since the creation, the foundation, literally the "throwing down" (*katabolēs*), of the world. The goal of God's plan was the coming of Christ. "In him" (and through "us"!) a whole cosmic process is being accomplished.

Related is the fact that God "destined us" to be offspring or heirs (appropriate translations of *huiothesian* in v. 5). "Destined" (*proorisas,* literally, "to mark out a boundary beforehand," "appoint") is to be understood in connection with "chose" (*exelexato*) in v. 4. God's "predestination" (a much misunderstood theological term) does not imply coercion by God. The God and Father of the Lord Jesus Christ does not, like the Fates, spin an unalterable thread that determines human destiny, but gives human beings the choice of whether to accept election or reject it. The strict meaning of "chose" in v. 4 and "destined" in v. 5 implies repeated action. The act of election is repeated every time God's call is heard and obeyed. The faithful are chosen "in him" and destined "through Jesus Christ." Acceptance of Christ activates God's election. In the author's mind, faith and obedience are linked to "destiny."

"In love" can be either the final phrase of v. 4 (as in the NRSV, NIV, NAB, JB) or modify "destined" in v. 5 (as in the RSV). Thus it is interpreted either as the essential quality of the holy and blameless life to which Christians are called (v. 4) or as God's chief motivation in the plan of election (v. 5). Certainly love characterizes both God's benevolent design and those who choose to cooperate with it. The whole scheme is according to God's "good pleasure," a stronger translation of *eudokian,* which suggests the delight that God takes in these plans, emphasizes what has been implied by "destined," and exemplifies the writer's propensity to multiply qualifying phrases.

Note that throughout the passage the author emphasizes how all that has been done and is being done is part of a plan or purpose devised by God. *Oikonomian* (literally, "purpose" or "plan"), a term from household management, appears in vv. 5, 9, 10, 11. The root word "destined" appears in vv. 5 and 11, and God's will is stressed in vv. 5, 9, 11. Contrary to the hellenistic notion of the Fates, or the determinism of popular Greek and Roman religion manifested at the time by an avid interest in astrology, human history is not unalterably determined, random, or without significance. Even before creation (v. 4), God has been enacting a plan. History was, is, and will be in God's hands, not controlled by any other "power" or force in this world or in the spiritual realm. To the author's pagan readers this was good news, indeed!

As part of the plan, God has "freely bestowed on us" grace (v. 6). The verb *echaritōsen* has as its root *charis,* "grace." To describe how believers are "graced with grace," the writer has fixed on the word Paul characteristically uses to sum up God's attitude to humanity. This grace is freely given "in the Beloved," a messianic formulation found also in Col 1:13, and in similar forms in the synoptic accounts of the baptism and transfiguration of Jesus. (Those who argue for a liturgical, baptismal origin of this passage find support for their view in this allusion.) The messianic reference introduces the focus in vv. 7–12 on what the Son has accomplished.

First, redemption (*apolytrōsin,* literally, "purchasing with a price") is effected through Christ's blood, both a reference to a specific event (Jesus' death on the cross) and a metaphor for sacrifice. The word would resonate in both audiences addressed. Slaves bought by ransom were "redeemed," the same word used in the LXX for Israel's release from Egypt and from Babylon. Second, Jesus' sacrificial death forgives trespasses (literally, "wandering away" or "falling aside," v. 7). This release (*aphesin*) from or removal of transgression is evidence of God's grace that was "lavished upon us" (v. 8). "Lavished" (*eperisseusen*) literally means "overflowing," and is consistent with the exuberant and superlative terminology used by the writer to describe God's gracious action. What has been suggested all along is now made explicit: Christ is the agent by whom God has blessed, chosen, destined, bestowed, and lavished. Through him, as the immediately following verses attest, the mystery, purpose, and plan of God is revealed.

Verses 9 and 10 are central to the passage and to the whole epistle. Christ makes known God's purpose, which is to unite all things in him. God "has made known to us in all wisdom and insight the mystery of his will" (v. 9). Use of the term *sophia,* "wisdom," is another example of a vocabulary that would have resonances in both the Jewish and Gentile Christian communities. For Jews wisdom was religious and practical; for Greeks it was metaphysical and speculative, but it, like insight (*phrōnesei,* literally, "manifestation of wisdom in practical action"), was highly prized by both. All intellectual knowledge and its practical application are made known by God in Christ. Verse 9 summarizes the whole argument of Colossians 1–3; Christ is all sufficient to manifest and bring to fulfillment the purposes of God.

"Mystery" (*mystērion,* which occurs six times in Ephesians) was also a term of special interest to hellenistic Christians. It implies the secret plans that, for example, a king would share only with trusted advisors. God's mystery, which in Greek religions would be entrusted only to a select few, is now made available to all. Summarily, it is God's plan to unite all things in Jesus Christ. The phrase "fullness of time" implies a progression of events that is now coming to completion reinforcing the "purpose/plan" theme of the passage (cf. Mark 1:15; Gal 4:4). This *kairon,* this moment of great significance, is described as "gathering under one head" (*anakephalaiōsasthai,* literally, "the arithmetic total of a sum"), bringing separate items into one whole. (Paul uses the same word in Rom 13:9 to describe love as the summing up of the law.) The scale of this unity is cosmic, affecting "all things" in heaven and on earth. All the powers of the universe, unseen spiritual powers, political and economic power, social and religious power (what Colossians referred to as "the principalities and powers") are to be united in Christ. In the beginning, creation was "thrown down" (v. 4) and now it is "gathered up" (v. 10).

Although vv. 11–13 still focus on Christ as the one who accomplishes God's purpose of unification, the writer makes a subtle distinction between "we who first hoped in Christ" (v. 12) and "you also who have heard the word of truth" (v. 13). "We" may mean the first generation of Christians and "you" the second, or "we" may refer to Christians like Paul, of Jewish origin, and "you" to those of Gentile origin (the majority of the Ephesians?). If the latter is the case, the writer's thinking seems to be that whereas the Jewish people had a specially "destined and appointed" role to play in God's plan, now they, too, exist to praise Christ's glory. In both communities, faith results from hearing the word (see Rom 10:14, 17). Both Jews and Gentiles who responded to the gospel ("the world of truth, the gospel of your salvation"; cf. Col 1:5) have been sealed with "the promised Holy Spirit."

That the Holy Spirit was promised, known, expected, and anticipated (cf. Acts 2:17, quoting Joel; Luke 24:49; Gal 3:14) reinforces the writer's argument that history is proceeding according to a plan. What was formerly promised is now delivered, and its arrival is the promise of something else yet to come of which the Holy Spirit serves as a seal. Seals were used in the hellenistic world both to indicate ownership of the thing sealed (slaves, for example, were branded with their owner's seal) and to guarantee the contents of a package or a letter (see 2 Cor 1:22). To be sealed by the Holy Spirit is to be marked as belonging to God and thus guaranteed the inheritance of God's children (cf. 1:5). Recall that an inheritance comes not for good behavior but because one is a member of a certain family (cf. 1:4). (There is lively discussion about whether "sealed" in v. 13 directly refers to Christian baptism.) The "guarantee" or "pledge" (*arrabōn,* literally "down payment"; cf. 2 Cor 1:22; 5:5) is a deposit ensuring that the full amount will be paid. There is no hint in the text that full possession will not be delivered. Note that the inheritance (*klēronomias*) is "ours"; in Christ "we" and "you" become "us." Ephesians accurately represents Paul's understanding of Christian life; the Christian hears, believes, and receives the Holy Spirit (v. 13). Reception of the inheritance of the children of God will show forth God's glory and result in God's praise.

The importance of Eph 1:3–14 cannot be overstated. With its focus on God's plan, Christ's agency, and the Holy Spirit's guarantee, it summarizes the whole epistle. The keynote of the passage is vv. 9–10, which state God's purpose to unite all things in Christ. Most startling of all, God's plan is to be achieved through redeemed humanity, those who believe and are unified in Christ. It is for that faithful community that the writer prays in the following verses.

The Prayer of Thanksgiving (1:15–23)

After a formulaic opening (1:15–16), the writer requests two things for the recipients of the letter: a spirit of wisdom and revelation (1:17) and enlightenment of their hearts to know the hope, inheritance, and power that is theirs in Christ (1:18–19). The mention of Christ leads from intercession to an exposition of what God has accomplished in Christ (1:20–23). It was suggested above that the benediction section (1:3–14) was trinitarian in structure. It has also been argued that the first half of the letter is trinitarian. Having discussed God's will in 1:3–14, 1:15–2:10 reveals the work of the son, and 2:11–3:21 discusses life in the spirit. Certainly 1:15–23 focuses on how God has used Jesus Christ to effect divine purposes.

This unit of the writer's thought is clearly marked off by the phrase "for this reason" (1:15). (In the first half of the letter, each of the three times the writer begins a prayer, some form of *touto* appears; cf. 1:15; 3:1; and 3:14.) The letter opened with a benediction form with origins in Judaism. This served the author's purpose well as it reminded his predominantly Gentile audience of their roots. Now the standard Pauline thanksgiving is employed. Here, as in 1 and 2 Thessalonians, 1 and 2 Corinthians, Philippians, Romans, and Colossians the essential elements of the thanksgiving are an expression of gratitude and the reasons for that gratitude. The opening chapter of Ephesians exhibits both continuity of form and novelty.

The Christians addressed have heard the gospel and believed it (1:13). This is the "reason" (*dia touto*) that elicits the intercession. Furthermore, the author does not cease to give thanks because he has heard of their "faith in the Lord Jesus" and "love toward all the saints." They have exhibited the two cardinal Christian virtues, faith and love. Faith characterizes their relationship to Christ; and love, their relationship to each other. They have not only heard the gospel and believed it, they are living out its ideals in their daily lives; their "relational parameters" are entirely Christian. (Paul taught that faith "works through love"; Gal 5:6.) The writer commends this behavior; thus, one function of a thanksgiving, to secure the good will of a letter's recipients, is emphasized. The Pauline formula in v. 16 not only expresses thanksgiving, it introduces what the writer will ask God to do on the recipients' behalf.

The writer prays that they will have a spirit of wisdom and revelation and have the eyes of their hearts enlightened (1:17–18). As in 1:3 the focus of the reference to God is christological. God is the God of "our Lord Jesus Christ," emphasizing the Christian's identification with the Lord, and "the Father of glory," emphasizing Jesus' relationship to God as Father. And as in 1:3–10 God is the principle actor. God "gives" wisdom (*sophias,* which was identified with Christ in 1:9) and "revelation (*apokalypseōs*) in the knowledge of him." The composite noun "knowledge" (*epignōsei*) suggests deep and profound knowledge, not superficial awareness (cf. 1 Cor 13:12). In the New Testament, revelation is always the activity of God. Here both wisdom (insight) and knowledge (perceptivity or discernment) are associated with Jesus and gained through acquaintance with him.

Second, in a wonderfully vivid and penetrating metaphor, the writer prays that they may have "the eyes of their hearts" enlightened. The heart was understood to be the organ of understanding, intuition, and will more than of emotion. In both Greek and Jewish literature of the period, light is associated with understanding. So the prayer continues to be for spiritual illumination. The parallel construction, marked off in Greek by clauses introduced by the pronoun *tis* ("what"), makes the substance of this spiritual understanding clear. They are to know (*eidenai* from *oida,* meaning "to know by experience") what is the hope to which he has called you (v. 18); what are the riches of his glorious inheritance in the saints (v. 18); and what is the immeasurable greatness of his power in us who believe (v. 19). They are to know and experience hope, inheritance, and power.

"Hope" (v. 18) finishes the triad of faith and love (v.15). Hope was an inheritance previously reserved for Israel. Now the Gentiles, too, are "called" (*klēseōs,* a Pauline word for vocation, indicating a deliberate choice or election by God) to share not only hope but a "glorious inheritance." This inheritance was introduced at 1:14. The idea of an inheritance figured prominently in early Christianity (see Gal 3–4; Col 1:12; Heb 9:15; 1 Pet 1:3–5). Perhaps because so many of the first generation of Christians were poor and powerless the notion of an inheritance appealed. More importantly, a promised inheritance gave (and gives) hope for the future. Hope for an inheritance in (or "among") the saints assures a confident future because, as Barth noted, hope is equated with the thing hoped for.

Finally, the writer prays that they will know the "immeasurable greatness" of God's power. It is not a potential reserve that exists in the abstract, but is "in us" and "working," that is, effectual in those who believe. It is important to note both that the power comes from God and that human faith enables it to work. (This is consistent with the teaching of Jesus in Mark 9:23; Matt 9:29; cf. Mark 6:5–6.) The spiritual power of God working in the life of the believer is the characteristic element of the Christian life as depicted by Ephesians. The multiple synonyms used in v. 19 are characteristic of the writer's style. "Immeasurable greatness," "power," and "great might" emphasize the strength of God, the "Father of glory."

God's might is most clearly evident in what God accomplished in Christ (v. 20). Reflecting on the power of God leads the writer to think of its clearest manifestation, so he moves from prayer and intercession in 1:15–19 to exposition in 1:20–23. These verses affirm the absolute power and dominion of Christ. Again, God acts. Here two aorist active participles (*egeiras* and *kathisas*) and two aorist active indicative verbs (*hypetaxen* and *edōken*) indicate what God did.

The resurrection of Jesus is the fundamental conviction of the Christian faith. Thus the primary and greatest evidence of God's "great might"

(v. 19) is that he raised Jesus from the dead (v. 20). Throughout the New Testament, resurrection is an act of God, not self-generated by Jesus. Early Christians understood the risen Christ to be both alive and in their midst and with God in heavenly glory. That God made Christ sit "at his right hand" indicates both the sovereign power of God and the privileged position of Jesus, because the right hand was the position of honor given by eastern potentates. The verse may allude to Ps 110:1, which is used with messianic implications at several points in the New Testament (see Mark 12:36; Acts 2:34; Heb 1:13) and in reference to Jesus in Mark 16:19; Rom 8:34; Col 3:1; Heb 10:12; and 1 Pet 3:22.

The phrase "in the heavenly places" (v. 20) would have had powerful resonances for the epistle's recipients since they believed in spiritual powers other than "the God and Father of our Lord Jesus Christ" and probably in degrees of angelic beings and a hierarchy of powers. Thus v. 21 qualifies "heavenly places." "How high?" or "how extensive are they (and thus is Christ's rule)?" might be the questions in the minds of the hearers. "Far above all rule and authority and power and dominion and above every name that is named, not only in this age but also in that which is to come" is the writer's answer. As in 1:9-10 the supremacy of Christ over all spiritual forces–in heaven and on earth, in the present and in the future–is stressed. Christ is more powerful than "every name," a reference to the fact that names of deities were thought to have divine power, and so names themselves were evoked and venerated. (Recall how often works are done "in the name of Jesus" in Acts.) This same emphasis on the sufficiency and power of Christ is seen in Col 1:15-20.

The supremacy of Christ continues to be focal as the writer explains that God put "all things under his feet" and made him head over "all things" (v. 22). Again Ps 110:1 ("till I make your enemies your footstool") seems to lie behind the first metaphor (see also Ps 8:6). Victorious heroes put their feet on the necks of those they conquered. The second phrase, "made him head over all things for the church," again carries the idea of God's "giving," since *edōken* followed by the double accusative might more literally be translated, "he gave him as head," that is, God "appointed" or "installed" him. The emphasis is on Christ's authority as given by God.

In the New Testament *ekklēsia* ("church") means a gathering of people, the Christian congregation, in a house or a particular area. Much has been made of the etymological meaning "called out," and the related term *eklektoi,* "elect." In Paul's genuine epistles, *ekklēsia* usually refers to a specific, local group of Christians. Only in Ephesians does it have a universal connotation, "all churches" or "all Christians." The writer's decision to modify "church" in v. 23 has led to serious interpretive complications.

The phrase "for the church, which is his body" (vv. 22-23) may well echo Colossians in which the church is also called the "body of Christ" (Col 1:18, 24) and where in Col 1:18-19 *plērōma* ("fullness") also appears. The theological problem raised is whether the church can be the fulfillment of Christ without violating what has just been said about Christ's supremacy (much less the Christology of the rest of the New Testament). The interpretations offered rest on three grammatical and linguistic problems: whether the meaning of *plērōma* is active or passive (that which fills or that which is filled); whether the voice of *plēroumenou* is passive, middle, or middle with active significance; and whether the sense of the phrase *ta panta en pasin* is adjectival or adverbial.

Translations and interpretations that view *plērōma* as active in meaning and in apposition to *sōma, plēroumenou* as a passive participle, and the phrase as adverbial seem to offer the best solution to the problem. This requires that Christ be understood in v. 23 as an inclusive personality into which Christians are incorporated. The focus of vv. 20-23 is the power of God at work in the resurrection and exaltation of Christ. We know from 1:3-14 that the goal of salvation history is Christ's reconciliation of humanity. As Christ has represented the many in his work of salvation, the many come to represent Christ through his body, the church.

Essentially, the intercession in 1:15-23 is for the recipients' awareness of the power available to them. The writer has heard of their attitude of faith and their activity of love and, therefore, praises God and asks God to give them wisdom, knowledge, and illumination to know the hope, inheritance, and power that is theirs. That power is best attested by God in Christ whom God raised and exalted above all things to rule for the sake of his body, the church. Ephesians 1:15-23 promises believers four things: spirit and revelation; the hope of a calling; the riches of a glorious inheritance; and the power of faith.

M. Barth, *Ephesians* (ABC; New York: Doubleday, 1974) 1:170-210.

A. Borland, "God's Eternal Purpose," *EQ* 34 (1962): 29-35.

J. Bowman, "The Epistle to the Ephesians," *Interp.* 8 (1954): 188-205.

B. Corley, "The Theology of Ephesians," *SWJT* 22 (1979): 24-38.

M. Goulder, "The Visionaries of Laodicea," *JSNT* 43 (1991): 15-39.

A. King, "Ephesians in the Light of Form Criticism," *ExpT* 63 (1952): 273-276.

J. Sanders, "Hymnic Elements in Eph 1-3," *ZNTW* 56 (1965): 214-232.

R. Yates, "A Re-examination of Ephesians 1:23," *ExpT* 83 (1972): 146-151.

THE CHURCH IN JESUS CHRIST

Ephesians 2:1–22

H aving described what God has done in Christ, the writer of Ephesians turns in chapter 2 to "you" (*hymas*), the recipients of the letter, who formerly were unbelievers with all that state implied. The Pauline gospel ("by grace you have been saved") is set forth in 2:1–10 and 2:11–22 outlines the unity effected by Christ.

The two units of chapter 2, 2:1–10 and 2:11–22, are similarly organized. At the outset of each (2:1–3 and 2:11–12) the writer draws a vivid picture of the condition of persons without God. The particle *de* is used as a conjunction at 2:4 and 2:13 to link what follows with what went before. The particle is usually translated "but," the English conjunction that rhetorically cancels out whatever precedes it. What God did in Christ and the life and unity made possible in him is then discussed in 2:4–10 and 2:13–18. Finally, since the "household of God" is described in 2:20–22, both chapters 1 and 2 end with a characterization of the church.

As a whole, chapter 2 continues the exploration of what God has done, namely, redeemed from sin and united what was estranged. In 2:1–10 the focus is the individual in Christ and the salvation Christ brings to her or him. In 2:11–22 the writer moves to the wider arena of the reconciliation of communities and the new community that is constituted in Christ.

Saved by Grace through Faith (2:1–10)

The passage is a summary of Paul's teaching on what it means in one's personal life to be a Christian. The writer presents Pauline soteriology in a nutshell, so it is not surprising to find a great many phrases borrowed from Paul's earlier letters. As noted above, the text's structure is "before and after"; life before Christ is described in vv. 1–3 and vv. 4–10 depict what Christ achieved.

Two theological issues are of particular importance in this passage. First, the passion of Christ is foundational to the writer's thinking. What happens to individual believers is precisely what God has done in the life of Jesus Christ. As the RSV puts it, "you he made alive when you were dead" (v. 1). The parallel is so important that the writer inverts and repeats it in v. 5: "when we were dead . . . [God] made us alive." The passion event of Jesus becomes the model or symbol for the life of the believer; each was dead and brought to life as in the crucifixion and resurrection of Jesus.

Second, Paul's great theme of justification by faith, which is spelled out in detail in Galatians and Romans, is emphasized, parenthetically in v. 5 and then straightforwardly in v. 8. Just as Jesus was raised from the dead (resurrection was not his own doing), so believers are saved by grace. Salvation is not of their own doing. Throughout Ephesians, God is the great doer, and Christ is the agent of that doing. Through him Christians can participate in the great plan of God. (But that is getting a bit ahead of the argument of the text.)

"You" in v. 1 certainly refers to the recipients of the letter (perhaps it can be inferred from v. 11 that those addressed are Gentiles), but the condition described is universal: life without Christ is death. "Trespasses" (*paraptōmasin*), the same word used in 1:7 and meaning "deliberate breaking of a known law," and "sins" (*hamartiais*), meaning "missing the mark," cover what the Anglican confession calls "things done and left undone." Both produce in persons an internal and spiritual callousness that is life-denying and thus leads to death (which here must be understood both metaphorically and literally).

"Walk" (*periepatēsate*) indicates a way of life; it is a Hebraism for a habitual mode of conduct, a "lifestyle" (a thoroughgoing Pauline word; it occurs most frequently in Ephesians). In vv. 2 and 3 the writer discusses both external and internal pressures that lead to a life of sin. As noted, people in the hellenistic world believed in powerful spiritual forces that exerted influence on the material world and life in it. The "course of this world" probably means "this age" with its negative connotations especially since "course," literally *aiōna*, can also be translated "age" or "period," thereby alluding to the term's Greek philosophical and Hebrew religious history. The "prince of the power of the air" is associated with Satan and also with the powers alluded to in 1:21. (They will reappear at 6:11–12. In John's Gospel, Satan is the ruler of this world [see John 12:31; 14:30; and 16:11].) "Air" (*aeros*) in ancient cosmology is the area between earth and heaven; it can mean the climate of opinion, the *Zeitgeist*, and is the arena of the "children (*huiois*) of disobedience," a Semitism suggesting not only amoral pagans, but God's rebel subjects. The point is that both this world and the powers of evil exert on human beings pressure toward sin. The picture drawn is of an evil environment in the grip of evil powers.

The believers whom the writer addresses were once associated with this environment and its inhabitants (v. 3). They, too, once lived "in the passions of our flesh, following the desires of body and mind." "Flesh" (*sarkos*) means not only the physical body but unredeemed human nature, a selfish rather than a divine life orientation. More is implied than physical appetites, as the writer clarifies when he speaks of desires of the body and of the mind. Both physical desires and intellectual or spiritual dispositions are included in these internal pressures toward sin.

Identifying with those to whom he writes, the author notes that "we were by nature children of wrath." This is another Hebraism indicating that, left to do what naturally "feels good," the human tendency is toward evil. "By nature" humans trespass and sin. No one is "naturally" reconciled to God. Reconciliation requires initiative on God's part and response (conversion) on the part of human beings.

The whole tenor of the text changes at v. 4. From describing the plight of those without Christ, the author moves to the change Christ has made in Christians. (It has been suggested that vv. 4–7 and 10 are fragments of a pre-Pauline hymn of initiation into which vv. 8–9 are inserted as interpretation.) The initiative is God's whose motive flows from the divine nature which is mercy (*eleei*, "compassion" or, more strongly, "pity") and love (*agapēn*) (cf. Exod 34:6 or Deut 7:6–9). God acted out of love for people, not in a "just" response to what their nature and actions deserved. Even while humans were "dead through ... trespasses," God made them alive "together with Christ" (v. 5). Note again the identification made with the passion of Jesus, since to "make alive together with" (*synezōopoiēsen*) in the majority of New Testament usages means "to raise." "Saved" is a perfect passive participle indicating that what has happened continues to be true. What happened to believers is participation in Christ's once-and-for-all resurrection, which continues in the life of each one who believes.

As God raised Jesus to heavenly position and authority (1:20–23), so

God raises believers to sit with him "in the heavenly places" (v. 6). "Made us sit" or "caused to sit down together with" (*synēgeiren*) can describe what has already happened or can have a future referent (cf. v. 7). "Sit" in the Greek implies sharing a common meal rather than occupying a throne. (Apparently, the seats at the kingdom's banquet are assigned!) The idea that rescue from spiritual death is understood in terms of elevation into the company of the inhabitants of heaven also appears in 1QH 11:10–12 and 1QH 3:19–22, leading some scholars to argue that the tradition behind Eph 2:6 is not Gnostic, as is frequently suggested, but that of the theology of the Qumran community. The force of the verse is to emphasize the Christian's close identification and relationship with Christ, as a comparison of 1:20 and 2:6 reinforces.

The phrase "immeasurable riches of his grace" (v. 7; cf. 1:18–19) prepares for the classic Pauline expression of the concept in vv. 8–10. The key phrase from v. 5 is repeated here for emphasis. Grace is God's initiative. And faith, the writer now explains, must be the human response. "Grace" expresses the very essence of the gospel: God's great, even reckless, generosity and love expressed in Jesus Christ. The referent of "this" (*touto*, v. 8) can be "grace," or the verb "saved," or "faith," that utter openness to God which allows God to operate in the life of the believer. Faith, itself, is a gift of God. The idea is reinforced in v. 9, as the writer makes explicit that neither salvation nor faith comes from "works," from what a person does. "Boast" in v. 9 is hardly a strong enough word to translate *kauchēsētai*, which means something like "glory in" and describes a prideful and self-congratulatory attitude (cf. 1 Cor 1:29).

Although "works" do not save, they are not without importance. Verse 10 explains that the new person created in Christ Jesus, God's workmanship or God's "artifact," is made for good works. "Works" is a Pauline term; "good works" appears in post-Pauline writings like the Pastorals, Hebrews (cf. 10:24), and Matthew (cf. 5:16). It was these "good works" that illustrated faith for the writer of the book of James (Jas 1:18). Salvation is demonstrated by quality of life. As T. W. Manson noted (quoted in C. L. Mitton, *Ephesians* [NCBC; Grand Rapids: Eerdmans, 1983], 98), works are a requisite of faith, not a prerequisite. But even the good that believers do is a direct result of God's initiative, the fruit of God's action in the believer's life.

The writer of Ephesians makes clear that, in persons pressured from without and within to live outside the divine will, God has taken the initiative to save. God's grace requires the individual believer to exhibit the receptiveness of faith and the active life of obedience and "good works."

Having outlined the process on the individual level, the writer turns his eye to the communal or societal aspects of God's reconciliation.

Reconciled in Christ (2:11-22)

At 2:11 the writer's focus shifts from what Christ has done in the individual's life to what Christ has done to reconcile communities. His main point is that the estrangement of the Gentiles is now overcome, and thus Gentile Christians and Jewish Christians are being built into God's house. While this reconciliation is treated as an accomplished fact, it would have been unnecessary to emphasize what was not problematic. Was there some theological or social uneasiness in Ephesus? Were the Gentile Christians, who were in the majority, unaware of or questioning the Hebrew roots of their faith? Were the Jewish Christians insisting on prominence because of that heritage? It is impossible to know. Clearly the writer is reminding his readers of their pre-Christian past in terms of their status as Gentiles in comparison to Israel to show the greatness of what has been done by Christ on their behalf. Recent scholarship is demonstrating the affinity of this section of Ephesians with documents from Qumran. There is more than a little irony in the fact that the passage that affirms the full acceptance of the Gentiles by God relies on Hebrew traditions.

The section is made up of three parts: vv. 11-12 describe the condition of the Gentiles "without God"; vv. 13-18 describe Christ's work of reconciliation; and vv. 19-22 describe the community created by Christ. The whole passage relies on a "before and after" format and on a series of comparisons between without Christ and in Christ (vv. 12, 13); far and near (vv. 13, 17); peace and hostility (vv. 15,16,17); broken down and built up (vv. 14, 20-22); aliens and citizens (vv. 12, 19); and strangers without God and members of God's household (vv. 12, 19). The primary purpose of this contrast schema is to demonstrate the enormity of what Christ has done for both Gentiles and Jews.

Whereas the parenetic section of the letter is replete with imperatives, only one occurs in chapters 1-3, "remember" (*mnēmoneuete*) at 2:11. The writer commands Gentile Christians to recollect what they were before their conversion. (That this is treated as a past event takes the theology of Ephesians beyond that of Romans.) In Greek "Gentiles" occurs with the definite article (*ta ethnē*), indicating that a class of people is being considered. To be called "uncircumcised" by a Jew was to be subjected to an epithet of utter contempt. But circumcision as a Jewish rite was "made in the flesh by hands"; that is, it was human and material as opposed to spiritual. "Flesh" in rabbinic literature was a euphemism for sexual organs, so the writer is emphasizing the physical nature of the acts, and "made . . . by hands" (*cheiropoiētou*) is the word the LXX uses for the making of idols. Clearly, the writer intends that Jewish Christians, also, must attend to what he is saying.

It is not only separation from Israel but from Christ that the writer finds problematic for the uncircumcised (2:12). There are four "strikes" against the uncircumcised Gentile. He was alienated from the "commonwealth of Israel," and, therefore, a stranger to the "covenants of promise." All that God had promised the obedient was unknown to the Gentiles. No wonder they were both without hope (cf. 1 Thess 4:13) and without God, *atheoi,* the word from which "atheist" is derived.

But God's action in Christ has changed all that as the writer explains in vv. 13–18. These verses have generated a great deal of commentary. If difference in language and style from surrounding material is the criteria for quotation, Eph 2:14–18 may be treated as a hymnic fragment inserted here to illustrate the author's point. Certainly vv. 13–18 exhibit a rabbinic cast of mind and seem to be framed by references to Isaiah 57:19, "Peace, peace, to the far and the near, says the Lord" (NRSV). If, as I think may be the case, the writer of Ephesians used Colossians to frame his epistle, then 2:13–18 may be the exposition of Col 1:20, "and through him [Christ] to reconcile to himself all things . . . making peace by the blood of his cross."

Whatever its composition history, the text as we have it is clearly delineated. It begins and ends with references to far and near (vv. 13 and 17) and within those verses the terms "peace" (*eirēnē*) and "hostility" (*echthran*) alternate as follows:

v. 13	far/near	a
v. 14	peace	b
	hostility	c
v. 15	peace	b
v. 16	hostility	c
v. 17	peace	b
	far/near	a

Evidence for the use of chiasm (and related patterns) in ancient rhetoric is obscure, even if modern scholarly preoccupation with it is not. Perhaps it would be most accurate to say that the writer uses comparison to emphasize how Christ overcomes the hostility and distance that previously characterized relations between Gentiles and Jews.

Two fundamental assertions are made at the outset: you who were once far off have been brought near in the blood of Christ, and he is our peace (vv. 13, 14). The shed blood of Christ functions as a symbol of the surrendered will. The assertion is that he, and he alone, is peace. (Recall that the peace offered by Isaiah is not an abstraction, but a person. See 9:6; 52:7.)

This same Christ has "broken down the dividing wall of hostility" (v. 14). The verb translated "broken down" (*lysas*) is used in the New Testament both to describe the destruction of the temple (Matt 24:2; 26:61, for example) and the setting aside of the law (Matt 5:17; John 5:18, for example). "Dividing wall" (*mesotoixon*) is simply a variant term for the wall between two houses or a partition within a house and is roughly synonymous with *phragmou,* a fence for protection. Although some commentators have suggested it is a reference to the Temple curtain that was torn at the crucifixion of Jesus, it is generally assumed that the wall the writer had in mind was that separating the Court of the Gentiles from the inner portions of the Temple that were open only to Jews. This is supported by the famous inscription found in 1871 ("No foreigner to pass the parapet and barrier round the precinct. Anyone caught will have himself to thank for his ensuing death"), which was posted, in Latin and Greek, on the inner side of the Court of the Gentiles in the Temple. Interestingly, *phragmos* is the word the LXX (Isa 5:2) and Mark (12:1) used for the protective hedge that God planted around the vineyard, Israel. The "wall," then, is a metaphor for the separation between the nations and Israel which was maintained by means of the law and was experienced as enmity between Gentiles and Jews and between human beings and God.

Verse 15 makes explicit that the hostility between Jew and Gentile was embodied by the law, which to Gentiles seemed petty and meaningless. Whether "in his flesh" refers to occasions in Jesus' ministry when he defied the law, or to his body which was crucified, the point is not that moral standards no longer apply, but that what divides has been removed. (In this regard, Mitton's suggestion that "in his flesh" be translated "by what he said and did" is helpful.) Two natures and two peoples have been brought together in the one Christ.

This reconciliation occurs only by means of the cross (cf. Rom 5:6–11; Col 1:21–22). Christ brings Gentile and Jew into one body, one community, by the cross. That "both" are reconciled implies that each party needed reconciliation, Jews no less than Gentiles. Behind the human alienation from other humans stands human alienation from God. Through the cross both enmities are abolished.

The Christ who died on the cross to reconcile "preached peace" (v. 17). "Preached" (*euēggelisato*) refers to a primary activity of Jesus and suggests a royal proclamation that hostilities are ended. (Perhaps in contrast to the name calling in 2:11?) Behind vv. 17 and 18 are not only Isa 52:7 but images of life in a royal court with its proclamations and audiences. (Compare with the "enthronement" verses, 1:20–23 and 2:6.) "Access" (*prosagōgēn*) in v. 18 refers to the right of free approach to a king's presence. By means of the cross of Christ (and by no other means), both Jew and Gentile are free to approach the throne of grace. Those who without Christ were aliens from the commonwealth and strangers to the covenants (v. 12) are now, with Christ, fellow citizens with the saints and members of the household of God (v. 19). Those without legal rights have gained them; the transients have become permanent residents. Through the cross, Christ has broken down the walls that separated and abolished the law, making two groups of people one, creating in himself one new humanity and reconciling both to God.

At v. 19 the metaphor shifts from royal courts to construction. No fewer than ten words that refer to building occur in vv. 19–22, which describe the "household of God." A community viewing itself as a "holy temple" was not original to Christianity. The Qumran community believed that the Hasmonean priests had defiled the temple in Jerusalem. Since a temple could not be built outside Jerusalem, the concept of "temple" was transferred to the people of Qumran. The building language in Eph 2:19–22 is also found in 1QS 5:5ff.; 8:4ff.; 9:3ff.; 11:7–8; and 4QFlor. Throughout Eph 2:11–22 the assertion of the reconciliation of Gentiles and Jews is firmly rooted in Hebrew tradition.

The "foundation" (*themeliō*) of God's household is the apostles and prophets (associated again at 4:11), the primary recipients of revelation. The apostles provided clear link to Jesus and thus authority and stability in the early church. "Prophets" were those who spoke the mind of Christ in their own day and thus provided on-going guidance and revelation. Christ is the "cornerstone" or "keystone" (*akrogōniaiou,* a term about which there has been much debate), that which completes the building and holds it together. The allusion is to Isa 28:16 or Ps 118:21–23.

But the structure is not complete; it is still "growing" (*synoikodo-meisthe,* present tense; v. 21). The mixed metaphor of building and growing, which is alluded to again at 3:17 and 4:16, is Pauline (cf. 1 Cor

3:5–17). For the Jews, the Temple was the place where God was uniquely present. Now, for Christians, be they Jews or Gentiles, God is uniquely present in the church, which owes its sanctity to Christ (the point at which all else is joined). Each believer is "built into" (v. 22) this temple; *synoikodomeō* literally means "built together with the others" and occurs only here in the New Testament. The implication is that, without other Christians, we cannot be "built." It is in the church and in Christians that God is understood to dwell.

In 2:19–22 the image of the household of God is that of a building which is dependent upon Christ. But the building is not static; new stones are constantly being fitted in. "Upbuilding" is the point, and the individual parts exist for this purpose, as 4:1–16 will make clear.

The writer of Ephesians believed that both Gentile and Jew were disadvantaged, estranged from each other and from God. ("Far" and "near" subtly emphasize this fact.) Salvation did not occur in a vacuum, but in the context of God's dealings with Israel, as the many Hebrew traditions evident in the passage attest. Now a new and startling union has been effected between Jew and Gentile. The established peace is horizontal, but its binding link is vertical. Jews and Gentiles are reconciled to each other, and both are reconciled to God via Christ's death on the cross. In Christ both groups were linked with each other by being linked to God. This equal partnership of Gentiles and Jews is perhaps the fundamental theological claim of Ephesians, and the "mystery" of which the writer speaks in the following passage.

M. Barth, *Ephesians 1–3*, 1:228–32; 261–62; 283–87.

A. Lincoln, "The Church and Israel in Ephesians 2," *CBQ* 49 (1987): 605–24.

T. Matson, "Theology and Ethics in Ephesians," *SWJT* 6 (1963): 60–70.

B. Metzger, "Paul's Vision of the Church: A Study of the Ephesian Letter," *TheoT* 6 (1949): 49–63.

C. L. Mitton, *Ephesians* (NCBC; Grand Rapids: Eerdmans, 1983).

M. Moore, "Ephesians 2:14–16: A History of Recent Interpretation," *EQ* 54 (1982): 163–68.

J. Murphy-O'Connor and J. Charlesworth (eds.), *Paul and the Dead Sea Scrolls* (New York: Crossroad, 1990).

J. T. Sanders, "Hymnic Elements in Ephs. 1–3," *ZNTW* 56 (1965): 214–32.

D. Smith, "Cultic Language in Eph 2:19–22," *RQ* 31 (1989): 207–17.

THE MYSTERY OF GOD'S PLAN

Ephesians 3:1-21

Several commentators view Ephesians 3 as a long intercession (vv. 1-19) followed by a doxology (vv. 20-21). However, the repetition of "For this reason," (*toutou charin*) at v. 1 and v. 14 effectively divides the chapter into two sections—a "digression" on Paul's ministry which contains the heart of the message to the Ephesians and which is the most personal and "letterlike" passage in the work (vv. 1-13), and the prayer proper (vv. 14-21). Apparently, the writer began the prayer at 1:15, but recognized the need to authenticate his message as Pauline. As he understood it, the mystery revealed to Paul was that the grace of God had been extended beyond the confines of Israel to include all people (cf. Acts 26:15-18). For the writer, the partnership of Gentile and Jew in the church sets forth God's "manifold wisdom" and is at the heart of Paul's gospel.

The Mystery of God's Plan (3:1-13)

"For this reason" (v. 1, a phrase not found in the genuine Pauline epistles) refers to what immediately precedes it. In 2:19-22 the writer has set forth the nature of the Gentiles' salvation in the church. Reference to the ministry of Paul serves as a framework on which to hang his "insight into the mystery of Christ" (v. 4) and "the plan of the mystery" (v. 9). The passage is notoriously difficult to divide into units in English, and in the Westcott-Hort Greek text, vv. 1-12 comprise a single sentence. The following division, while helpful, is admittedly inadequate: vv. 1-3 ministry; vv. 4-6 mystery; vv. 7-8a ministry; vv. 8b-12 mystery; v. 13

ministry. The ensuing discussion is arranged thematically under the headings "Paul's ministry," "the mystery," and "the plan."

First, however, is the issue of the apparently biographical material and the pseudonymity of the letter. Those who hold that Ephesians is Pauline take 3:1–13 to be what it appears to be, autobiography. However, these verses never assert Paul authored them; they simply describe Paul's ministry. It was common practice in hellenistic writing for an author to ascribe his own work to the person he sought to represent. This both honored the subject and gave authority to the contents of the work.

If the writer is not Paul, the thought is certainly Pauline. This passage, and indeed the whole letter, reflects a deep understanding of the teachings of the apostle. Furthermore, these Pauline ideas are couched in the same style and vocabulary as the rest of the epistle. This argues against the assertion that the biographical material was an editorial insertion into a liturgical document. The similarities noted between Eph 3:1–13 and Col 1:23–27 suggest that the author of Ephesians is dependent on the biographical material he found in Colossians. What is most significant is the author's understanding of the Pauline ministry (and this is true whether or not the author is Paul himself).

The intensive use of "I, Paul" (v. 1; cf. Gal 5:2; 2 Cor 10:1; Col 1:23) stresses Paul's authority. "He" speaks because of all God has done for people ("for this reason"), and he speaks as a prisoner. The Greek text literally reads "a prisoner of Jesus Christ," meaning in his grip and power. The writer understands that Paul was imprisoned both by Christ and for Christ "on behalf of you Gentiles." He was persecuted by Jews because he insisted that Gentiles were "fellow citizens" and "heirs of the promise." The prisoner is conscious of his mission to the whole world.

Verse 2 is interesting because it hints that the readers may not have heard of Paul's ministry. This would be odd if Paul were the writer, especially since he spent significant time in Asia Minor and was probably imprisoned in Ephesus. Perhaps the writer has introduced this material to acquaint the recipients with Paul. A steward (*oikonomian*) is one entrusted with managing a household. It is understood that Paul "managed" or "administered" God's grace (here in v. 2, a special favor granted to Paul) for the benefit of the church. God's grace was given to Paul for others. (A similar idea appears at 4:12.)

The "mystery" that the writer reveals was granted Paul by revelation (cf. 1:9–10). This is exactly what Paul says of his message and his apostleship (see 1 and 2 Corinthians; Gal 1:1; and Col 1:1, for example). The revelation he received on the Damascus road had not come from study or human teaching. It was unexpected, unpredicted, and of compelling authority (see. Gal 1:12, 16). "As I have written briefly" (v. 3) probably alludes to chapters 1 and 2 of this letter, but might refer to other Pauline correspondence (even the lost letter to Laodicea?). As Barth notes, *prographō* can mean "to write above," "to write earlier," or "to write up publically."

The author understands the origin of Paul's ministry to be divine. This awareness is reinforced in vv. 7 and 8. Verse 7 echoes the thought of v. 2. Everything Paul has, even his servanthood (*diakonos*), results from God's grace. The expression of humility reminds the reader both that his circumstances mitigated against Paul's apostleship and that he was a persecutor of the church (cf. 1 Cor 15:9–19 and Gal 1:13). Paul understood his ministry in terms of preaching to the Gentiles (cf. 1 Cor 1:17; Gal 1:16). The substance of that preaching is the "unsearchable" (*anexichniaston*, literally, "bottomless" or "untraceable") "riches of Christ." What Christ offers to the Gentiles is not subject to rational explanation (cf. Rom 11:33).

The writer understands that Paul is called not only to preach, but to "make all men see . . . the plan of the mystery" (v. 9). "See" (*phōtisai*) has the same root as the word used in 1:18, where the writer prayed that the recipients might have the eyes of their hearts enlightened; it describes an illuminating power (literally, the act of making something shine) which Paul intends to be universal. The language of v. 9 includes several other terms found in Gnostic thought, notably "plan" (*oikonomia*, cf. 1:10; 3:2) and "mystery." Unlike the hidden knowledge of the Gnostics, God's plan for redemption is being made evident to all. (God's plan for history is very much in the mind of the writer throughout Ephesians.)

Finally, the writer understands Paul's ministry in terms of the suffering it involves. Paul's sufferings (*thlipsesin*, literally, "tribulations"; see 1 Thess 3:3) in prison are also for "your glory" (v. 13). The life of Paul provides a concrete example of the union of believers, which the writer set forth in chapter 2 (cf. Col 1:24). To be obedient to the plan of God, Jesus himself chose to suffer on behalf of those he came to save. Likewise, those who follow Jesus cannot expect to avoid suffering, but that suffering is given meaning in the context of the community of believers in which it occurs.

It is the mystery of what God has done in Christ that is the focal insight of the ministry of Paul as the writer of Ephesians understands it. Paul's role is to reveal a mystery. The term *mystērion* had many resonances in

Paul's world. Originally, it was a Greek military term from the days of the Ptolemies in Egypt. The battle plans drawn up by the royal family and kept secret even from the generals before battle were "mysteries." In Greco-Roman religions the word had an almost technical meaning connected with religious rites. In these rites the initiated received secret information that led to immortality. Finally, the term is used in the Qumran scrolls in connection with God's wise providence and the mystery of salvation heretofore hidden in God but revealed to the teacher and, through him, to the community (see 1QS 4:18–19; lQS 11:56; lQpHab 7:13; and 1QH 1:21). The recipients of the letter would have understood the term in vv. 3, 4, 5, and 9 against this background.

The point here is that the mystery, formerly unknown to "the children of men" (v. 5, a Hebraism for "humankind") is now (*nyn*, indicating the immediate present) made known by revelation to the apostle Paul (v. 3) and to Christ's "holy apostles and prophets by the spirit," that is, by direct inspiration (v. 5). Part of the emphasis in Ephesians is on revelation to the leadership of the church; such revelation guarantees their authority. (See the discussion of deutero-Pauline Christianity presented earlier.)

Verse 6 sets forth the substance of the mystery: the Gentiles are fellow heirs, members of the same body (a term for naturalization in a state), and partakers of the promise (cf. 1:12–13; 2:12, 19) with the Jews "in Christ Jesus through the gospel." The three benefits the Gentiles now enjoy with the Jews are expressed with words using the preposition *syn* ("with") to emphasize a new unity, the accomplishment of which is highlighted by the instrumental use of "in" and "through." The gospel proclamation is that all the privileges of God's family are made available to all people in Christ. All believers are members of one body, a universal community of Christians (cf. 3:13). Here in 3:6 the message of 2:11–22 is summarized.

This now manifest mystery is part of a great plan of God that was made known to Paul (3:3), to apostles and prophets (3:5), and now to all (3:9). Verses 10–12 explain straightforwardly God's plan and are at the heart of the letter. It is God's *oikonomia* (v. 9) that through the church, the manifold wisdom of God be known. "Manifold" (*polypoikilos*) is a *hapax legomenon* in the New Testament that can also be translated "diversified" or "comprehensive." It originally signified an intricately embroidered pattern (cf. Wis 1:3–14). This is the crucial task of the church, to make God in God's variety and completeness known both on earth and "to the principalities and powers in the heavenly places." Once again, the writer alludes to the spiritual forces that were so potent to his readers. These powers were real in his world, and only the comprehensive nature of Paul's God was capable of disarming them.

It is God's plan that the church speak for the divine reality in heaven and on earth. The church is to be the visible manifestation of God. This is possible because in the church the dividing walls are down (see 2:14ff.). In the world of Ephesians these walls were real. Jews scorned Gentiles as outside the workings of God's providence. Gentiles scorned barbarians like the Jews as without culture and reason. The unity effected in the church is the proof of God's ability to repair human society. (Paul had already established that God had defeated "the powers." See Rom 8:37–39; 1 Cor 2:6–8; 15:24–28; Col 2:15.) God's plan means not only a broken barrier but peace between hostile peoples and forces.

The role of the church is part of an "eternal purpose" that was realized in Christ (v. 11). Through Christ believers have not only access to God, but boldness (*parrēsian*, the freedom of speech of those who have nothing to conceal) and confidence of access (*prosagōgēn en pepoithēsei*, entrance through having been persuaded). The approach to God is through faith in Christ, and that faith is the source of confidence that God is benevolently disposed toward humans (v. 12).

The closing phrase *pisteōs autou* is translated by the RSV "faith in him." However, when *pistis* is followed by the personal genitive, the genitive is nearly always subjective. Therefore the phrase also means "through the faith of him," that is, the faith Jesus himself had. The faith of Christ was seen most clearly in his obedience to the will of God, his working out of the divine faithfulness to the promise to Abraham that all the nations of the earth would be blessed through him. Even the smallest details of the Ephesian writer's thinking reinforce his understanding of the unity accomplished by God through Jesus and now made manifest in and through the task of the church.

Behind Eph 3:1–13 is the unification of Jews and Gentiles. Three theme words pervade the passage: mystery, grace, and plan. The mystery of grace is that God conceived this plan of unification. Perhaps the most astonishing aspect of this mystery is the central role of the church in the redemptive work of God. Bruce Metzger writes in "Paul's Vision of the Church," "God's ultimate purpose is to achieve unity and harmony in the universe, and to accomplish this the church is his instrument." The author's confidence in this fact has its origin in God's eternal and enabling will as the doxology which closes the chapter makes clear (3:20–21).

The Summary Prayer (3:14–21)

The prayer in 3:14–21 follows as logically from 2:22 as from 3:13. "For this reason" (v. 14) picks up the interrupted prayer (v. 1) and is an example of the free access to God which is promised in 3:11–12. The writer adores God for the generosity of the divine plan of salvation and asks that the Ephesians be strengthened to understand the plan and be filled with God's fullness.

Scholars who view Ephesians as a liturgical document about baptism view this text as a prayer for the newly baptized. However, form-critical research has not discovered hymns or traditional material behind the prayer, although immediately preceding their doxologies, Jewish prayers often end with the request that God's gifts be rightly received (see, for example, Ps 106). So, the author of Ephesians apparently wrote this prayer following a customary form.

Although vv. 14–19 are one sentence in Greek, the structure of the prayer is simple; vv. 14–15 are an invocation of adoration, vv. 16–19 are petition; and vv. 20–21 are doxology. However, two subtle thematic patterns are also noteworthy. First, there is an implicit trinitarian pattern in the reference to the Father (vv. 14–15, 20–21), the Spirit (v. 16), and the Son (vv. 17–19, 21). And second, the prayer comes full circle from God as the source of life in v. 15 to God as the goal of humanity in vv. 19 and 22, so that the overarching pattern of chapters 1 to 3 is repeated in the closing prayer of the section (see 1:4 and 3:21). Structurally, the prayer serves to mark the end of one section of the letter and the beginning of another.

Three aspects of the invocation are noteworthy. The first is the writer's attitude: "I bow my knees." The Jewish attitude of prayer was to stand looking heavenward with hands outstretched. In Hebrew scripture bowing, or kneeling, was associated with Baal worship. However, bowing (literally, prostration) was more common among the Gentiles the writer addressed. When coming before a king, Gentiles were required to "bend the knee." Perhaps the writer has in mind the bended knee that will signal the cosmic submission to God (Isa 45:23) and to Christ (Phil 2:10–11).

Second, in Greek there is a play on the words "father" (*patera*) and "family" (*patria*). A family is a group descended from the same ancestor. The idea is that every human and divine family has its identity in reference to God. (Thus, the unity of Jew and Gentile which is at the heart of chapter 2 appears again here.) God is the prototype of all fatherhood, and God gives names to families belonging to God (see Gen 17:5; 32:28).

Third, then, the aspect of naming is important. Behind v. 15 is the idea that a name stands for the identity or character of the one named. In Semitic tradition, the father names, and thus legitimizes a birth (see Gen 16:15; Matt 1:25; Luke 1:57–63). To receive a name from God is to be included in God's power and presence. God not only "owns" all the families of earth and heaven, but God has included them all in the circle of divine concern.

The petitionary part of the prayer (vv. 16–19) consists of three intercessions formed in Greek by *hina* clauses, the first two of which are followed by parallel infinitives. The author prays

I. that
    a. they may be strengthened . . . through God's spirit
    b. Christ may dwell in their hearts through faith
II. that
    a. they may comprehend the love of Christ
    b. they may know the love of Christ
III. that
    they may be filled with the fullness of God

The prayer in chapter 1 sought an increased knowledge of the vastness of the divine power working on the Ephesians' behalf. The prayer of Eph 3 asks that they experience the inner, divine strengthening of that power.

The writer's first petition is that "according to the riches of his glory" God "may grant you to be strengthened with might through his Spirit in the inner human" (*anthrōpon*). God's riches of grace in Christ have been a theme of the letter (1:7; 2:7; 3:8). God's generosity matches God's abundance and makes spiritual empowerment possible. The Holy Spirit is the means by which God deals with the real or spiritual nature of human beings. The Spirit strengthens (*krataiōthēnai*), fortifies, and invigorates interior life, which, for Greeks, would include the reason, the conscience, and the will.

"Heart" (v. 17) is another way to refer to this interior life. God's action by the spirit meets the human response of faith (which is instrumental) so that Christ may dwell (*katoikēsai*), that is, have permanent habitation, there. (Compare Gal 2:20 and John 1:14. Henry Lyte's hymn "Abide With Me" asks that God "Come, not to sojourn, but abide with me.") The mixed metaphor of "rooted and grounded" is a Pauline favorite (cf. 1 Cor 3:6–12 and Col 2:7). It recalls the image the writer has used of the church "built on the foundation of the apostles and prophets" which "is joined together and grows into a holy temple" "for a dwelling place of God" (2:20–22). The metaphors are used here, as they were at the end of chapter 2, to reinforce the hearer's understanding of their relationship to the Trinity, which appears with this constellation of images in both passages. Love is the substance in which they are rooted and grounded, and thus is the source of life, growth, and stability.

Verse 18 is an attempt to express the all-embracing quality of the love of Christ. Scholars have found similar formulas in the mystery cults and in the *Corpus Hermeticum.* The writer of Ephesians is struggling to communicate the full scope of Christ's love and power, and Severianus (4/5th century C.E.) was the first, but not the only commentator to see in his phrase an allusion to Christ's cross. St. Jerome wrote that Christ's love reaches up to heaven and down to hell and embraces those striving toward heaven and wandering away from Christ.

The writer prays that his hearers will be strong enough or able (*exischysēte*) to grasp intellectually (*katalabesthai*) this love. But note that it must be understood "with all the saints." No individual Christian comprehends it alone. The implication is that all are needed for full understanding of a concept which "surpasses knowledge" (v. 19). Recall that the love of Christ and the inadequacy of human knowledge was also an important theme in the Corinthian correspondence. Understanding of the love shown on the cross goes beyond the human faculties of knowing (see 1 Cor 8:1, 13). Such love is only experienced in the community that God has drawn together in Christ across almost impossible boundaries.

Astonishingly, it is not just understanding the love of Christ that the writer desires for the Ephesians. He prays that they "may be filled with all the fullness of God" (*to plērōma tou theou*). The phrase was undoubtedly chosen with the religious environment of Ephesus in mind since it carries associations with the hierarchy of heavenly "powers" in the mysteries and with Gnostic thought (cf. Jer 23:24 for possible Hebrew resonances). In Christ, believers are filled with all that is God, are part of the supreme power in the universe. Little wonder the writer breaks into doxology!

Verse 20 follows logically from v. 19 as the writer gives glory to God, whose power works in believers and is able to do vastly more than even they can imagine. The language reflects the highest form of comparison imaginable because what has been done for believers now is done in them. And so God the doer is given glory in the church (stressing again, as does chapter 2, its importance) and in Christ Jesus "to all generations, forever and ever." Verses 14 and 15 speak of existing families; v. 21 includes all families existing and yet to be in God's glorious plan. The "Amen," so be it, indicates the end of this section of the epistle. The prayer opened with adoration of God, and it closes with an exuberant glorification of God.

The primary purpose of Eph 3:14-21 is to intercede for the saints in Ephesus, for their inner fortification, their understanding of the dimensions of God's love, and their perfection with God's perfection. But it also serves to summarize the major ideas of chapters 1-3 by repeating or paraphrasing key terms and ideas (cf., for example, 3:15 and 2:19; 3:14-15 and 2:19; 3:15 and 1:10). "Riches of his glory" echoes earlier uses of "riches," as the reader is reminded of God's rich grace (1:7; 2:7) and of the "unsearchable riches of Christ" (3:8; cf. also 1:18). The "dimensions" of the love of Christ (v. 17) expands the extent of God's power depicted at 1:21 and sheds light on the destruction of the "dividing wall" (2:13-18). The "fullness of him who fills all in all" closes the prayer of 1:15-23 and is the goal for which the author prays in 3:19. The term reinforces the claim of Christ's authority over the cosmos (1:10) by relying on the hellenistic associations of *plērōma*.

The prayer also serves as an introduction to the parenetic material that follows in 4:1-6:20. The concept that links the two sections is love (an important word in Ephesians; various forms of *agapē* appear nineteen times in the letter). The writer prays for the indwelling of Christ by faith and firm establishment of the Ephesians' lives in love so that they may progress to a deep understanding of God and come to act as God acts. In the Greek world the spiritual danger was of a faith built on intellectual knowledge alone (cf. 1 Cor 1:22; Col 2:18, 23), which is why the heart of the prayer contrasts love and knowledge.

If there is no love, the spirit of Christ is not present and understanding cannot progress. The author prays not just that they comprehend (*katalabesthai*, v. 18), which implies grasping something mentally, but that they know (*gnōseōs*, v. 19), which implies practical apprehension through personal experience. To "know" in this sense is to make personal application. The content of the "knowledge" to be applied is God's love, the "love of Christ which surpasses knowledge." To know is to love, to be an "imitator of God" (5:1), to "walk in love, as Christ loved us and gave himself up for us" (5:2). This way of loving requires a community, "all the saints" of v. 18. Full knowledge, that is, full application of love, is attained in the church. It is not an individual but a communal achievement. The parenetic section of Ephesians contains a series of instructions to love (4:2, 15, 25ff.; 5:2, 25, 28, 33; 6:24). It is from the "love of Christ" (which the prayer of 3:14-19 asks that they understand fully) that the "new life" described in practical terms in chapters 4-6 proceeds. Chapters 1-3 demonstrate the meaning of God's love, and chapters 4-6 provide practical instruction on how to live it out.

M. Barth, *Ephesians* 1:370-84.

J. Blevins, "The Church's Great Ministry: Ephesians 3," *RevExp* 76 (1979): 507-16.

G. Howard, "The 'Faith of Christ,'" *ExpT* 75 (1974): 212-15.

B. Metzger, "Paul's Vision of the Church," *TheoT* 6 (1949): 49-63.

C. Story, "Peace: A Bible Study on Ephesians 2:11-3:21," *ERT* 9 (1985): 8-17.

B. Thurston, *Spiritual Life in the Early Church* (Minneapolis: Fortress, 1993), chap. 8.

THE PARENESIS

Ephesians 4:1–6:20

The prayer and doxology at the end of chapter 3 signals the end of the theoretical section of the Ephesian letter. Chapters 4–6 turn to practical matters. In chapters 1–3 the author has described God's work in Christ of unifying Jew and Gentile, heaven and earth. The assumption behind chapters 4–6 is that the lives of persons living that reality will reflect it. Like Paul's, the writer's understanding of morality is theological. The parenetic material, like Christian unity itself, grows from life "in Christ."

The instructions preceding the household code (5:21–6:9) are difficult to divide into units. The long section 4:1–5:20 is a sustained exhortation contrasting the life in Christ with the old life of "futility" (4:17). Throughout, Christ is the "measure," (4:13), the example and standard of conduct (see 4:13, 15, 20, 21; 5:2, 8, 17, 20). C. H. Dodd suggests the following division on thematic grounds: 4:1–16, promoting the church's unity; 4:17–5:20, breaking with pagan ways; 5:21–6:9, building Christian homes; 6:10–20, putting on the armor of God. The commentary that follows employs Dodd's divisions and further refines the progression of thought within those units.

A Life Worthy of Christ's Calling (4:1–16)

The parenetic section of Ephesians begins as does the hortatory section of 1 Thessalonians (4:1) and Romans (12:1) with "therefore I beseech," and with a listing of the qualities of life that enhance the unity and fellowship of the church (vv. 1-3). The character of Christian life is expected to reflect the theological unity that the author envisions in its confession (vv. 4–6). That unity is maintained because of gifts bestowed by Christ. The mention of Christ's gifts (v. 7) leads to a brief digression on Christ (vv. 8–10), and the gifts themselves are enumerated in vv. 11–12. That the gifts are "for building up the body of Christ" (v. 12) leads to the reflection on maturity with which the section closes. The point throughout is the promotion of Christian unity through growth in Christ-likeness.

The calling to which the Ephesians have been called is to be built into the household of God "for a dwelling place of God in the Spirit" (2:19–22). Christians have entered this life and fellowship as a result of God's initiative; God chose, destined, and appointed them for it (1:4, 5, 12). Now in terms that are both warm and urgent, the Ephesian writer begs (*parakalō*) them to "walk," (*peripatēsai*, cf. 2:2, 10), to live their lives and to conduct themselves worthily with regard to their calling. The adverb "worthily" (*axiōs*) literally means "balancing the scales." The Ephesian Christians are to live in ways that will maintain a balanced community.

Four attributes in the lives of individual Christians lead to this equilibrium (cf. Col 3:12). The first is lowliness or humility (*tapeinophrosynēs*), unassuming modesty that does not seek prominence for the self or insist on special rights or considerations but allows others to take leading roles and receive credit. Its root word, *tapein,* had the derogatory connotation of servitude in the Roman world. In fact, the author is commending a "slave virtue." However, it is also the main characteristic of Jesus, and one of only two he claimed for himself (see Matt 11:29; cf. Phil 2:3).

The second and third characteristics the writer encourages were both approved by Roman moralists. The second is meekness or gentleness (*prautētos*), and it describes persistent courtesy which is manifested by a person caught up in seeking a goal for the common good. The noun *praotēs* is used by Aristotle to describe a perfect balance between being too angry and never being angry at all. The word is also used of trained and controlled animals. Meekness, then, does not signify weakness, but the opposite of the "touchiness" that leads to taking offense, being malicious, and seeking revenge.

The third virtue is patience (*makrothymias*), which literally means "long heated," or "long tempered," and implies being able to deal with people who are difficult. Chrysostom said it was the spirit that has the power to take revenge but does not do so. "Forbearing one another in

love" amplifies "patience" and stresses its importance in community
life. It also introduces "love," the ultimate Christian virtue and the one
toward which this whole passage is moving (cf. vv. 15–16). Each quality
implies a form of self-restraint. The "unity of the Spirit in the bond of
peace" (v. 3) provides the motive for such self-discipline. The Ephesians
are called upon to be eager (*spoudazontes*), to take pains or make every
effort, to maintain their unity of Spirit in the peace that binds them
together (*syndesmō*).

The writer assumes that unity exists but must be maintained. Thus, he
sketches the nature of the unity in vv. 4–6. Because of the similarity of
these verses to 1 Cor 8:6 and 12:4–6 some have suggested they represent
an early confession of faith, a sort of Christian *Shema*. R. Williams points
out that the order here is almost the exact opposite of the logical order
of presentation—Father, Son, Holy Spirit, church—that appears in the
Nicean and other classical creeds. Ephesians' order is existential, beginning with the Spirit as experienced in the church and moving from it,
through Christ who bestows it, to its origin, God.

The "one body" was extensively discussed in the early chapters of the
letter. It is maintained by the one Spirit, which has drawn the Ephesian
Christians together and given them life and a common hope or goal. The
"one Lord" of the earliest creedal confessions (cf. Phil 2:11) unifies Jew
and Gentile, who share "one faith," one body of teaching, one confession, which was attested in baptism.

In the writer's understanding, the most potent ground of unity is the
universal fatherhood of God (v. 6). The Stoics understood divinity as per-
vading all existence; thus, once again we have the "dimensions" of God's
parental care (cf. 3:18). God is "above all," in control, supreme and tran-
scendent (a Jewish notion), "through all," actively at work in creation
(God's immanence is a tenant of Hellenism), and "in all" reinforcing the
idea that human lives become the dwelling place of God.

In Greek vv. 7–16 form one long sentence. At v. 7 the focus of the passage moves to the gifts of Christ. In the light of his understanding of
Christian unity, the writer must account for the differences among Christians. Unity, he explains, is not sameness; each Christian has received
grace through the generosity of Christ the giver (cf. 2:5, 8), and each has
a measure of Christ's gifts, a share, but a unique share. The church is still
unified, although its members are different by virtue of having been
granted different gifts for ministry.

At vv. 8–10, Ps 68:18 is introduced by the rabbinic formula *dio legei*
(which Paul also used in 2 Cor 6:2 and Rom 15:10) and is deliberately

altered to fit the Ephesian situation. The image in v. 8 is that of the triumphal procession of captives from war and the bestowal of gifts on the victorious conquerors (cf. 6:10ff.). Verses 9 and 10 express the completeness of Christ's experience. No condition is so low or so high that Christ cannot come to it, and this is true whether Christ's descent refers to the incarnation, the harrowing of hell, Pentecost, or the parousia, and whether his ascent is a reference to resurrection or ascension (the event in the life of Christ that made him available to all people everywhere). The point is "that he might fill all things," precisely the writer's understanding of Christ's nature as manifested in the church (1:20–23) and his prayerful hope for the Ephesian Christians (3:19).

Returning, then, to the gifts Christ offered, the writer lists the various gifts for ministry and their purpose in vv. 11–16. The gifts are to be understood as endowments of special abilities that equip believers for Christ's service; they are given to all (cf. 4:7), not to a small, ruling elite. The apostles were the original founders of the church; they represent rule and authority. Prophets "spoke for God," and reflect an early (and to us shadowy) function in the church associated with the ongoing revelation and communication of God's will (cf. 2:20; 3:5). Evangelists were those who spread the gospel, those with a special gift to speak to persons outside the church, according to Barth, missionaries who took the gospel into new areas. Pastors and teachers, whose functions are related, work with those already in the household of faith. Teachers are to give instruction in the faith, and pastors to give care. Among the lists of gifts for service in the early church (cf. 1 Cor 12:28 and Rom 12:4–8) these two are unique to Ephesians. They "equip" the saints for ministry. *Katartismon* literally means "to set bones," as in medicine, "to reconcile." The idea is that pastors and teachers put believers into their proper condition, readiness for practical service (*diakonias*).

Verse 12 makes manifestly clear the purpose of these gifts. First, they are to equip other Christians for service, and, second, they are to build up the body of Christ, to add to its numbers, to integrate its members into a harmonious community, and to promote cooperation among them. These tasks are not to be understood as "official positions." That they are gifts of Christ makes ministry a matter of divine commissioning, not appointment to an office. Ministry is Christ's program of service to the world and to the church, because it is entrusted to all Christians. Service is the goal and purpose of gifts until the fullness of Christ is attained.

The gifts of ministry are to bring the church to maturity and to protect her from dangers during that process. The first image the writer uses contrasts childhood and maturity (vv. 13–16). Childhood is impression-able, easily swayed by a variety of teachings. The chief danger is that of false teachers with unscrupulous ("crafty" and "deceitful") ways. The writer deems it a sign of immaturity to be unduly impressed, even gullible, in the face of new teaching. To "fall for" every new idea is to be like a boat tossed about on a rough sea (cf. Ps 107:23–27 and Isa 57:20–21 for similar uses of sea-storm metaphors).

In contrast to immaturity is growth, which implies a slow, natural process (v. 15). Its goals are the truth (loyalty to principles) and love (concern for people) that were perfectly balanced in Jesus Christ, the head. "Head" (*kephalē*) is the LXX translation for the Hebrew *rosh,* which can mean the anatomical head, the top, the ruling person, the first of a series, and the source.

God's plan for the church is that it be a harmoniously working whole, like a healthy, growing human body. Although terrifically difficult to translate, the emphasis in 4:16 (as it was at 2:21 which uses the same metaphor) is clearly on the community. Each person is understood to have a share in the building up, the maturation, of the whole. The fact that "love" is used twice in vv. 15–16 suggests that, for the sake of the church's life, it must be the chief characteristic of individual believers. The church originated in the love of God, and its already existing unity is maintained as its members strive to become more like the One who is love. Here, as in vv. 11–12, a personal quality functions for the sake of the whole community. All gifts, and especially love, are for the body.

Ephesians 4:1–16 makes a crucial point since it insists that the endow-ments of the individual are for the good of the community. No gift granted a Christian by Christ is for her own aggrandizement. A church built on this understanding can avoid the earthly distinctions about "greatness" which fritter away precious time and energy. The personal and corporate life of the church must show forth the Christ who took up a basin and washed feet. The abuses that have disfigured Christianity, dis-honored the reputation of Christ, and blinded the world to his truth have arisen largely because of an unholy interest in personal prestige and power rather than in the holy practices of humility and service. The life worthy of Christ's calling is the life of ministry, of building up the body, and of attaining and maintaining the unity of the faith.

M. Barth, *Ephesians* 2: 462–72.

C. H. Dodd, *Ephesians* (Abingdon, 1929).

R. Williams, "Logic Versus Experience in the Order of Creedal Formulae," *NTS* 1 (1954–55): 42–44.

Old Ways and New Expectations (4:17–5:20)

At 4:17 the author turns more pointedly to ethical matters and makes his appeal on the basis of the contrast between the old life and the new. (This pattern is sometimes referred to in the moralists as the "doctrine of the two ways.") When genuine letters of Paul address matters of conduct, they frequently have specific cases in view (see, for example, 1 Cor 5, 6, 8). Here, no specific crisis seems to be at hand; these are general teachings for Gentile Christians. Christians who were formerly Jews built their new lives in Christ on the strong moral foundation of the Torah. Gentiles had no such foundation, and their behavior, especially in sexual matters, was, even by modern standards, casual. The underlying danger that the writer perceives is the same one Paul highlights in Rom 1. Moral judgment can become so blunted that the ability to discriminate between good and evil is lost.

While this long passage cannot be neatly divided into subsections, some patterns are clear. The author opens his teaching with a picture of the darkness of the Gentile way (4:17-19), and he brings the section to a close with a warning against "unfruitful works of darkness" (5:11). What transfers believers from the world of darkness to that of light is Christ, who is lifted up as the agent of change and the example of the new way of life at 4:20-21 and 4:32-5:2. (The section also closes with a reference to Christ, which introduces the household code immediately following.) The metaphor of putting on and putting off or putting away dominates the comparison of the old way and the new in 4:22-32. A traditional Stoic vice list (5:3-5) precedes a general exhortation to virtue which is dominated by a light/dark metaphor, and in 5:18b-20 an alternative to the vice list of 5:3-5 is presented. (The listing of prohibitions and commands is a standard New Testament teaching form, probably borrowed from Stoic vice and virtue lists, but called by modern scholars "catalogical parenesis." For a discussion of the form see the commentary on Col 3:5-17.)

The passage begins with a description of the Gentile way of life (4:17-19); at its heart is the alternative of the godly life (5:1-2), with which the passage also closes (5:18b-20). Within this framework the writer alternates descriptions of what is and what is not to be done. Each negative injunction is balanced by a positive prescription. He never issues a prohibition without setting forth a positive alternative. This approach is clearest in 4:22-32, but it also appears as passages balance each other (for example, 5:3-5 and 5:18b-20).

Karl G. Kuhn has argued that the origin of the parenetic tradition of Eph 4:1–5:21 is to be found in the Qumran texts. In addition to the obvious comparison of the sons of darkness and sons of light which appears in the scrolls, he suggests that the prohibitions against fornication, impurity, greed, and idolatry come from the Essene tradition of priestly purity. His suggestions are worthy of consideration.

This commentary treats the passage in two sections, 4:17–32 and 5:1–20. However, it is to be understood that the two are closely related, that the division is arbitrary, and is done for the sake of convenience and not because of grammatical, linguistic, or thematic reasons intrinsic to the text.

4:17–32

"Affirm and testify" (*lego kai martyromai*), which opens the passage, reflects legal language and emphasizes the writer's authority. The fact that the writer speaks "in the Lord," indicates that the ideas presented are not just his own; they are the Lord's. His point is simple; Christians must not live as the pagans who surround them (cf. Rom 1:18–32). Pagan life is vividly described as "futile," "dark," "alienated," and "ignorant."

The manner of the Gentiles' life results from "the futility of their minds." "Futility" (*mataioteti*), a term that appears in Jewish polemic against Gentiles, implies vanity and emptiness. The comparable, and very accurate, modern slang term would be "air headed!" The idea is that the mind-set of Gentiles, their total attitude, was incorrect, and thus their lives were empty of meaning and value. Verses 18 and 19 vividly depict the results of this incorrect attitude.

The first result of an "empty" mind is darkened understanding. Use of a light/dark metaphor in a moral context is certainly Pauline (Rom 13:12; 1 Thess 5:4–5), but, in general, Jews referred to themselves as sighted and to others as blind (cf. Isa 42:6–7; 1QSb 4:27; Wis 18:4). Earlier in the letter, the writer prayed for the enlightening of their hearts (1:18) and described the darkness of life apart from Christ (2:3, 11–12; cf. Ps 36:9). The primary characteristic of this way is alienation from God (2:12). Their ignorance has led to nonresponsiveness, and it, in turn, to "hardness of heart." "Hardness" (*porosis,* literally, "petrification") described a stone harder than marble, but the term was also used in a medical sense to indicate the formation of a callus. The moral point is that, having done wrong repeatedly, the Gentiles no longer think of their actions as wrong.

The conscience has become calloused, petrified. Living immorally hardens the heart and makes it insensitive to spiritual truth (cf. Mark 3:5 and 6:52). Deliberate refusal of moral light inevitably leads to debauchery. That they have "given themselves up" to it indicates conscious choice. Now, they are past feeling, insensible (*apēlgēkotes*). The two vices highlighted here, licentiousness (*aselgeia*, literally "lack of restraint") and uncleanness (*akatharsias*, literally, "filthiness" or "impurity"), both have sexual connotations and will reappear at 5:3.

One can sense the horror with which the writer pens, "You did not so learn Christ!" (v. 20). Christians "learn Christ" as Jews "learn Torah." To learn Christ is to understand the will of God embodied in him. Christ himself is the substance of the lesson. The writer does, indeed, assume that the Ephesian Christians "heard about him" and "were taught" (v. 21). The verbs suggest the *kerygma*, the proclamation of the Christian message to gain converts, and the *didache*, the teaching of believers to build up the community (cf. 4:11–12).

Verses 22–24 introduce the metaphor that dominates the rest of this section of the text, the metaphor of changing clothes (cf. Col 3:8–10). The Ephesian Christians are to put off the old, Gentile manner of life, the way old clothes are put off. Perhaps they are to put it away as they put off their old clothes before baptism and are reclothed with new garments afterward (cf. Gal 3:27; Rom 13:12, 14). The contrast between the old self and the new person is made in absolute terms, and the infinitives "put off" (*apothesthai*), "be renewed" (*ananeousthai*), and "put on" (*endysasthai*) certainly have the force of imperatives.

The old nature belonging to the former manner of life was corrupted by "deceitful lusts" (v. 22). Lust deceives because it incites desire for the impermanent, and, ultimately, it robs one of the faculty of discernment (cf. vv. 18–19). The call to renewal is continuing, as the present tense of the verb indicates, and is understood to be an internal process. In the Greek world the mind (*noos*) was the organ of moral thinking and knowing, so moral regeneration rightly would begin, and continue, there (v. 23).

Jesus taught that it is not enough simply to put off the old; something new must take its place (Matt 12:43–45). Accordingly, one who puts off the old nature must put on the new. In contrast to alienation from the life of God (v. 18), this new life is created in God's likeness (cf. Gen 1:27). Where does one see God's likeness more clearly than in the face of Jesus Christ? Here the writer reinforces the point he made in vv. 20–21. This new nature is created in "righteousness" (*dikaiosynē*), to the Greeks a moral quality, but to Jews the essence of relationship with God, and "holiness" (*hosiotēti*), a word indicating devotion or piety. (The two qualities also occur together in Luke 1:75.)

In addition to introducing the controlling metaphor, vv. 22–24 set up a pattern of presentation that will be followed in the rest of the passage. The writer balances each negative behavior with a positive one. In vv. 25–32 five categories of sin are condemned (falsehood, anger, stealing, evil talk, grieving the Holy Spirit or sins of attitude) and five corresponding virtues are commended. The basic point is that evil behavior which harms others is to be avoided. But for Christians that is not enough; Christians must go on to practice the positive goods that will actively help others. While a general collection of catechetical material may lie behind the text, consonant with the first three chapters of the letter, the writer is paying particular attention to behaviors that would disrupt the unity of the church in Ephesus.

In v. 25 the "putting away," (*apothemenoi*), which in the aorist tense implies a once-and-for-all action or a decisive step, is understood to apply to all five categories of sin that follow. "Falsehood" (*pseudos*) is to be understood not just as "lying" but as any false attitude to life, any distortion of truth (cf. 4:17–18!). Falsehood is a social sin since it corrupts the root of relationship and is particularly devastating in the church because Christians are members of one body (see 1:10, 22–23; 2:14, 19–22; 3:6; 4:4). Instead of falsehood, Christians must continually speak truth (*alētheian*), a virtue also much praised by Roman moralists.

A series of scriptural admonitions lies behind vv. 26–27 (see, for example, Zech. 8:16–17; Ps. 4:4; the teaching of Jesus in Matt 5:21–22; and Jas 1:19, 20). The point is that falsehood generally leads to anger, and while anger is not, in itself, a sin, it usually leads to sin because it is seldom disinterested or true "righteous indignation." Instead of disturbing a night's sleep and allowing anger to smolder into bitterness or evil intentions, the Christian must be reconciled with the object or the cause of anger. (Plutarch reports the same teaching among disciples of Pythagoras.) Anger gives Satan a foothold, literally a place (*topon*), and that is to be avoided at all costs. (Interestingly, *diabolos* ["demon" or "devil"] is also the Greek word for "slanderer," "one given to malicious gossip.")

The need to enjoin the Ephesian Christians not to steal (v. 28) is to modern readers a potent reminder of the level of society from which many of the early Christians came. Jesus came for the sick, not the healthy, to save sinners, since the righteous had no need to be saved! Doing honest work with the hands would not only rule out sinful occupations (a prohibition which is worthy of our own consideration), but also the attempt to live off others, which is also a kind of stealing (cf. 1 Cor 4:12 and 2 Thess 3:6–13). It has been rightly noted that mastery of a long-standing bad habit requires a powerful incentive, one that reaches into the future. Thus former thieves are told to work not just for themselves, but for the benefit of those less fortunate (cf. Luke's account of Paul's last words to the Ephesian elders in Acts 20:33–35).

"Evil talk" (v. 29) does not really carry the force of the adjective *sapros,* which means "that which is rank, foul, rotten, putrid, thoroughly disgusting." This is the second sin of the tongue that the writer addresses. Foul conversation lowers the moral tone of the community and introduces corruption into discourse. Instead of being agents of corruption, literally breaking down, Christians are to be agents of edification, literally "upbuilding" (the same root word for building is used at 2:20 and 22). The Christian's conversation should not only be appropriate to the situation, which is really nothing more than a social nicety; it should "impart grace to those who hear." The injunction should not be passed over. God's grace is the centerpiece of the writer's thinking in chapters 1–3. A Christian's words are to introduce this same grace into her or his ordinary, routine contacts. It is a tall order.

The mention of grace no doubt triggers thought of the "Holy Spirit of God," who is "grieved" when believers use the gift of language in unholy ways (v. 30). Anyone who has experienced grief has vivid, experiential understanding of what dishonest or foul talk does to the Spirit who sealed believers (or marked them as belonging to God, cf. 1:13) for redemption.

To summarize this section of teaching, the writer returns in v. 31 to the "put away" metaphor of vv. 22 and 25, although here the root verb is not *apotithēmi* ("to remove" as clothes) but *airō,* "to remove," "sweep away," "take over," or "conquer." The vice list in v. 31 presents sins of attitude that are swept away or conquered by the virtuous attitudes listed in v. 32.

"Bitterness" (*pikria*) is actually a figurative word characterizing one who refuses reconciliation, cherishes resentment, and lives in a perpetual state of animosity. "Wrath" (*thymos*) denotes temper, or outbursts of anger or passion (cf. with forbearance, *makrothymias* in 4:2). "Anger" (*orgē,* from whence the English word "orgy") implies a permanent state of irritation which refuses to forget wrongs actual or perceived. "Clamor" (*kraugē*) connotes the noisy denunciation of loud, quarreling voices. "Slander" (*blasphēmia,* the English "blasphemy") involves not only speaking ill of others but the internal anger that leads to what the African-American church so vividly calls "scandalizing the name" of others, speaking ill of someone with the intent to destroy them. "Malice" (*kakia*) is used to summarize all kinds of bad feelings from which the vices that precede it originate. As Barth notes, the arrangement of vices in v. 31 is climactic.

The balancing virtue list of positive attitudes and actions once again sets forth Christ as model and agent of forgiveness. The word kind (*chrēstoi*) is, in Greek, an auditory pun on "Christ" (*Christos*). The word implies not just attitude, but goodness shown in helpful action. W. Barclay notes that the Greeks defined the quality as the disposition to think as much of the neighbor's well-being as of one's own (cf. Phil 2:3–4). It expresses the nature of God, constantly good and benevolent. "Tenderhearted" (*eusplagchnoi*) literally means to have "healthy bowels." The word is a vivid attempt to describe the deepest feelings of the inner self. Its root word, *splagchna,* occurs in the Greek word translated "compassionate," and it is used in reference to Christ (see, for example, Matt 9:36; 14:14; 15:32; Mark 6:34; 8:2; Luke 7:13).

"Forgiveness" (*charizomenoi*) crowns the virtues of attitude. Derived from the root word *charis* ("grace"), it means freely forgiving (cf. Matt 18:21–35). Whether or not the petition of the Lord's prayer is in the writer's mind, he certainly encourages the Ephesian Christians to treat others as God had treated them. In light of their pagan background and the wonderful mystery he has set forth earlier in the letter, God's generosity in Christ must have seemed almost unbelievable. Being forgiving as God is forgiving (cf. Luke 6:36) leads to the wider application in 5:1–2, which states the principle of which 4:32 is a specific example.

W. Barclay, *The Letters to the Galatians and Ephesians* (Philadelphia: Westminster, 1976).

K. Kuhn, "The Epistle to the Ephesians in the light of the Qumran Texts," in *Paul and the Dead Sea Scrolls,* ed. Jerome Murphy-O'Connor and James M. Charlesworth (New York: Crossroad, 1990).

5:1–20

There is no logical break in the thought from 4:32 to 5:1. On the contrary, the writer encourages the Ephesian Christians to "be imitators of God" (5:1) because "God in Christ forgave you" (4:32).

After stating the principle in 5:1–2 (a pattern which is repeated for the *Haustafel*, which begins at 5:21), the author presents what is essentially a vice list in 5:3–7. This is followed by a more general exhortation built around the metaphor of darkness and light (5:8–15). The writer continues his pattern set in 4:17–32 of presenting a positive alternative to forbidden actions; the vice list of 5:3–5 is balanced by a discussion of alternative behaviors (5:18–20), and the pagan way of life is contrasted to the Christian. N. Baker has looked at the passage from the point of view of its positive injunctions and suggests the writer is asking the Ephesians to be imitators of God in love (vv. 1–2), in purity (vv. 3–7), and in light (vv. 8–14). Heretofore, unity in love was modeled on Christ, and now purity of desire is rooted in Christ, the giver of light.

The first verse of chapter 5 gives wider application to the idea at the end of chapter 4. Christians are to be imitators (*mimētai*) of God. The exact phrase is found only here, although the idea is common in both the Old Testament and New Testament. As "beloved children," they bear a family resemblance to God. But what does this mean? What is the nature of God that should be imitated? It is love (v. 2). To reinforce the idea that love is not an emotion but the willingness to renounce self for the good of another, the writer lifts up the example of Christ, who "loved us and gave himself up for us." "Gave himself up" (*paredōken* from *para-didōmi*) is the same word used in connection with the death of Jesus. The point is that God's love is generous and self-giving, and these attitudes must be the hallmarks of Christian life. (This background makes the same phrase in 5:25 even more potent.)

To "walk in love" (again, *peripateite* is used to indicate the pattern of life or lifestyle) is to "sacrifice to God." As J. Murray wrote, "it is the service which we offer in the temple which we are." The "fragrant offering" is probably a reference to sweet-savor offerings of thanksgiving in the Jerusalem Temple, but it would have similar connotations for the writer's pagan audience (cf. Phil 4:18).

In direct contrast to Christ's self-giving way of love is the way of the pagan world, which is the focus of vv. 3–5. Once again, the writer hones in on sexual morality because of the laxity of the Gentile environment, and on speech because of its ability to make or break the unity of the church.

It may be that Christianity introduced chastity as a virtue into the Greco-Roman world. Cicero, for example, felt that forbidding the love of courtesans to young men was severe (see *Pro Caelio*). And in Athens, the proceeds of brothels were used to build a temple to Aphrodite. This is the sexual milieu from which the Ephesian converts had come.

Ironically, although fornication, impurity, and covetousness "must not be named among you" (v. 3), the writer does name them. There would have been no need to warn against sins that people were not committing! However, the point is that talk can lead to action. The word translated "fornication" by the RSV (*porneia*) really means any illicit sexual activity. Impurity (*akatharsia*) and covetousness or greed (*pleonexia,* literally, "insatiability") were also linked at 4:19. Both proceed from selfish desire and so are in direct contradiction to self-giving love since they exhibit a flagrant disregard for others.

The relationship between conversation and action comes into sharper focus in v. 4. Three vices of speech follow three vices of action. "Filthiness" (*aischrotēs;* literally, "obscene speech"), "silly talk" (*mōrologia,* a compound word meaning literally "foolish words"), and "levity" (*eutrapelia,* which really means "coarse jokes," but was used to refer to deceptive speech) are not proper for Christians. The writer, a good psychologist, has grasped the connection between the power of mental suggestion and behavior and knows it is especially strong in the sexual realm. Not only does bad talk lead to bad action, it cheapens life, harms others, and breaks down the community. To avoid improper speech, the Christian is to fill her mouth with praise. The subject of Christian conversation should be that of God's blessings. "Thanksgiving," (*eucharistia*) too, is a composite word form of *eu* ("good") and *charis* ("grace").

Beginning with an emphatic phrase that might be translated "know for sure," v. 5 picks up the vocabulary (and vices!) of v. 3. In the numerous vice lists of the New Testament, immorality, covetousness, and idolatry top the list of frequently repeated vices. The connection of covetousness and idolatry would be more apparent in the pagan environment of Ephesus than it is today, but the underlying understanding still holds. Covetousness is idolatry because it makes a god of what the heart is set on.

Ephesus was known for its facetious orators. Were false Christian teachers suggesting that the conduct of moral life was outside the purview of Christianity (cf. 1 Corinthians)? Or was the problem simply that Christian demands reversed the popular standards? We cannot know with certainty (and, in any case, false teachers are not the focal issue in Ephesians that they are in, for example, Colossians). But the problem of false teaching is not the only thing at issue in v. 6. The phrase "wrath of God" makes it clear that a principle of retribution is built into the structure of an orderly universe. As Rom 1:24–32 and Gal 6:7–8 also make clear, God allows people to reap the results of their own disobedience.

Christians are not even to associate with the disobedient (v. 7). Not only does bad company exert a powerful negative influence on Christian behavior, but it jeopardizes the reputation of the Christian community. What conclusions will outsiders draw about Christianity if Christians are constantly seen in the company of evildoers?

The extended reflection in 5:8–17 is based on a potent metaphor, that of light and darkness. Both Greek and Jewish thought perceived a cleavage in the universe. Greeks spoke in terms of the powers of light and darkness (and this became a fundamental dichotomy in Gnostic thought). Jews used the same metaphor to set forth two ways of life. The way of light was the way of obedience to God with its resulting blessings, and the way of darkness was the way of disobedience resulting inevitably in God's judgment and punishment. In both systems, light was the sphere in which God dwelt.

Again here, as in 2:11–22 and 4:17–24, the "past" life of the Gentile Christians is contrasted with their present life. Before their conversion, Gentile Christians not only were in darkness (cf. 4:18), they were darkness. Now, they are "light in the Lord," and they must "walk as," that is, live like, "children of light" (cf. 5:1). The proof of their "lightness" will be seen in their actions. Using the "fruit" metaphor of Jesus (see, for example, Matt 12:33; or Gal 5:22, where Paul presents all Christian virtues as "fruits of the spirit"), in v. 9 the writer introduces a trio of virtues to balance the vices of vv. 3 and 5. "Goodness" (*agathōsynē*) literally means "kind in action" or "actively benevolent." "Righteousness" (*dikaiosynē*) (with all its Jewish associations) implies justice with regard to the claims of others. According to W. Barclay, the Greeks defined it as "giving to men and to God that which is their due." "Truth" (*alētheia*) was one of the cardinal virtues of the Greek moralists and implied sincerity in word and deed, the absence of pretense or deceit (cf. 5:6). The principle is stated in v. 10: "try to learn what is pleasing to the Lord." This is a guideline for conduct, not a precise rule, and so it avoids legalism. Likewise "to learn" (*dokimazontes,* literally, "to find out by experience") does not mean to memorize instructions, but to discern in each situation what pleases God.

At v. 11 the writer brings together the metaphors of light/darkness and fruitbearing. In matters of practical morality, neutrality is not enough. Avoidance of evil actions is not enough. The Christian must actively oppose evil. It is the duty of Christians to root out evil from the community (see 1 Cor 5). Verse 12 continues the irony of v. 3 proclaiming it shameful to speak of what the author has just discussed! The point has already been made; speech can lead to action. Christians must not dwell on the evils to which they inevitably will be exposed. By implication, what is done "in secret" is done "in darkness" (cf. Matt 10:26–27). This assumption lies behind v. 13, which, even in the Greek, is obscure. It seems to relate to the judgment theme of v. 6 and to the idea that conviction of sin results from the presence of light. If Christians expose the works of darkness, the secret things, they, in fact, bring them to the light (to Christ). A redemptive pattern is at work here as the following quotation attests.

The same phrase that introduced the scriptural quotation at 4:8 appears at 5:14, giving the quotation the same weight as a canonical Psalm. The quotation is apparently from an early Christian hymn which may well have been part of a baptismal rite. Undoubtedly "light" is what brought the quotation to mind. "Awake" (*egeire*) literally means "rise," and is a word used for resurrection. One who sleeps, is one in darkness (i.e., in a state of absence from God), but Christ can give that one light. ("Sleep" is also a common metaphor for death from which Christ also calls believers.) Christ delivers people from the dominion of darkness to that of light (cf. 1 Pet 2:9), and Christ will give light for the resulting new life.

Verses 15–20 return to a more general exhortation and rely on the contrast between wise/foolish and drunk/filled with the spirit. By means of the repeated use of "walk" for "live" (cf. 5:2, 8) Ephesian Christians are reminded to be careful about their lifestyles. In the writer's understanding, to be wise is to discern the will of God (see v. 10; cf. Ps. 111:10; Prov 1:7; and Matt 10:16). And in moral terms, wisdom also includes the ability to anticipate the consequences of an act before it is done. The present tense of the verb indicates continual action; constant vigilance is required. A note of urgency appears for the first time in v. 16. The implications is that a limited time is available (cf. Col 4:5; 1 Cor 7:29; Matt 6:13), and so Christians must make the most of every opportunity not only to avoid the evil of their times, but to practice Christian love. The participle *exagorazomenoi* literally means "buy up at the market place," implying both "seizing an opportunity" and "buying back." Again, the point is "to understand what the will of the Lord is" (v. 17; 5:10).

The question of drunkenness undoubtedly arises in the Gentile environment because a variety of sects used alcohol to induce ecstatic states. But the same confusion appeared at Pentecost (Acts 2:12; and see Prov 23:29–34). Drunkenness was forbidden not only because of its pagan religious connections (the Bacchus festivals in the worship of Dionysus, for example), but because it leads to other shameful acts and is, in any case, a poor substitute for the joy that is available to the Christian in the Holy Spirit. (For interesting contemporary treatments of drunkenness see Philo's treatise "On Drunkenness.")

Instead of exhibiting "debauchery" (*asōtia*, which means "excess" and implies one who is profligate or dissolute), Christians are to live in ways that exhibit their life in the Holy Spirit. Verse 19 suggests not only that joy should characterize the life of the Christian community, but that the attitude of joy in our hearts is like a song to God. "Speak to one another" implies gathering in a meeting small enough for common participation, one that would be spontaneous and flexible, in short, under the control of the Holy Spirit. If pagans gather to drink, Christians gather for praise. "Psalms" were songs of praise; the verb form of the word suggested the plucking strings, so it was used to mean sacred songs accompanied by instruments. "Hymns" referred to sacred poetical compositions for praise. "*Ōdais*" meant any kind of song, so the writer qualifies it with "spiritual" (*pneumatikais*).

Finally, the Christian's duty and joy is "to give thanks in the name of our Lord Jesus Christ to God the Father" "always" and "for everything" (v. 20; cf. 1 Thess 5:18). "Always" suggests that thanksgiving must be habitual for Christians. And "everything" makes the difficult point that thanks must be rendered for more than the apparent "goods" of life. The Christian's heart must be grateful in all circumstances since it recognizes that God can bring good out of all situations (cf. Col 3:15, 17).

The long parenetic section 4:17–5:20 works primarily on the basis of comparing the old, pagan life with the new, Christian life. E. Best has noted that converts usually see their preconversion lives in the most negative of terms. As a Jew, the author of Ephesians probably would not have thought of his past as particularly negative. His readers, however, were Gentiles who saw their past lives as full of sin. The absolute presentation of contrast in the text is geared to their perception.

Furthermore, small sects, as Christianity was in the empire at this time, have a tendency to see those outside their own group in negative terms. Once within the security of the Christian community, former pagans did, indeed, judge outsiders harshly. As Best notes, "generally speaking, the moral exhortations of the second half of the letter relate to activity within and affecting the community and not to the relation of the community to those outside it." If overcoming estrangement was the great theological theme of the first half of the letter, maintaining the unity of the new community is the concern of the second half.

N. Baker, "Living the Dream: Ethics in Ephesians," *SWJT* 22 (1979): 39–55.

W. Barclay, *The Letters to the Galatians and Ephesians* (Philadelphia: Westminster Press, 1975).

M. Barth, *Ephesians* 2: 598–603.

E. Best, "Ephesians: Two Types of Existence," *Interp* 48 (1993) 39–51.

J. Murray, *The Epistle of Paul to the Ephesians* (Cambridge: Cambridge University Press, 1933).

C. Rogers, "The Dionysian Background of Ephesians 5:18," *BibSac* 136 (1979): 259–57.

L. Thompson, "Hymns in Early Christian Worship," *ATR* 55 (1973): 458–72.

R. Williams, "Logic Versus Experience in the Order of Creedal Formulae," *NTS* 1 (1954/55): 42–44.

The Household Code (5:21–6:9)

Form-critical analysis has noted that in many New Testament works it appears to have been the practice to introduce the themes of obedience and subordination after that of worship (see Rom 12; Col 3; Heb 13; Jas 1; 1 Pet 2). That pattern is at work in Ephesians. This being the case, arguments that would make 5:21–6:9 an interpolation must be discounted.

The household code (or *Haustafel*) as a form of moral teaching was discussed in the commentary on Col 3:18–4:1. The reader is referred to the commentary on the passage in Colossians for general remarks. The Ephesian writer, while maintaining the order of presentation in Colossians, greatly expands the material, especially with regard to wives and husbands. Before beginning the commentary on this text, let us consider a somewhat different approach to the household codes.

Generally speaking, household codes are applied by modern interpreters to the nuclear family. Charles H. Talbert raises the question whether it might be more appropriate to apply the codes to the modern family business. His proposal has significant merit (and, incidentally, it does not denigrate what the code tells us about Christian domestic relations).

The Greco-Roman household included not only what we would think of as members of the nuclear family (parents and children), but extended family members (sometimes distant relatives), slaves, freedmen, and business acquaintances. The household was as much a business unit as a family unit (cf., for example, Acts 16:11–15, 40 and the discussion of Lydia's household).

This assertion is borne out by the actual, architectural structure of the house itself. The residences in which Christian evangelism was done in places like Thessalonica, Corinth, Colossae, and Ephesus were probably not the *domus,* owned by only the very wealthy, but the *insula,* a type of apartment building that housed most people in the cities of the empire. The typical *insula* contained a row of shops on the ground floor that faced the street. Behind the shop, or above it, was living space for the owners, their families, guests, and retainers, including employees, servants, and slaves. The same complex would have manufacturing space for the goods sold. Such a household bears little resemblance to the modern nuclear family or its homes (at least in the Western world).

The shrill polemics that have surrounded interpretation of the New Testament household codes in recent years might be abated somewhat if we could view the household not so much as a family unit as a business unit. As Talbert suggests, the *Haustafel* may be a flowchart for a family business, basically the same flowchart used by pagans and Jews, and thus a common cultural convention. The fact that all members of Christian households shared the same Lord and worshiped together would not have negated the need for divisions of labor and responsibility in the business.

This line of thought does not contradict the overarching theme of unity in Ephesians. The process of unifying the church still begins in the home. And the basic principle found in 5:21, which introduces the code, still holds: all Christians, whether Greek or Jew, slave or free, male or female, must still voluntarily surrender their freedom to each other for the sake of Christ. The general rule in the church is mutual subordination, each person showing more concern for the rights and needs of others than for his or her own (cf. Phil 2:3–4). When this is the case, subordination becomes identification.

Following the verse expressing the principle (5:21), the text falls into three units: 5:22–33, which deals with wives and husbands; 6:1–4, which deals with children and fathers; and 6:5–9, which deals with slaves and masters. All household codes begin with the relationship between wives and husbands, but marriage is also related to one of the central points of this epistle, the lordship of Christ and his great love for those who dwell in union with him. One wonders if the writer expands the usual, brief instructions to wives and husbands because of the pattern of *hieros gamos* (or sacred marriage) that was ritually enacted between human beings and gods in a variety of the pagan religions represented in Ephesus. Perhaps he is stressing the vitality and blessing of the real union in contradistinction to that presented in the pagan ceremonies. In any case, in a culture in which the *paterfamilias* wielded unquestioned authority, the mutual submission of Christian partners must have seemed radical. Indeed, it still is, ruling out, as it does, the extremes of either male chauvinism or radical feminism.

As many scholars have noted, the new pattern of relationship given in Christ was hard to reconcile either with Jewish or Gentile backgrounds. Women who did not follow the social conventions of the day were (and are!) subject to sharp criticism. The larger issue was that the gospel would not be heard if Christian women moved too far beyond the bounds of the social convention of subordination to men, thereby drawing negative attention to the Christian community. Too much freedom for women would create destructive misunderstanding among the Christians' pagan neighbors. (This dynamic is more explicit in the *Haustafel* in 1 Peter than it is here.) Whether or not we moderns like it, this is part of the background of the instructions to wives and husbands.

As in Colossians, wives are addressed first because they were understood to be the subordinate party. The words translated "be subject" do not mention subjection in the Greek. They are literally *tois idiois,* "one's own." The verb for "be subject" (*hypotassomai*) does not appear in v. 22, but is carried over from v. 21. Barth correctly translates the verse literally, "wives to your husbands—as to the Lord." Since it is frequently assumed that the writer of Ephesians used Col 3:18–4:1 as the model for this passage, translators have apparently inserted "be subject" in Eph 5:22, thus bringing it into conformity with Col 3:18. It seems to me that the idea expressed in Eph 5:22 is closer to that of 1 Cor 7:2, which encourages monogamy, than that of Col 3:18, which teaches subjection. ("Subject" does appear with regard to the wife—by implication—in 5:24, and the phrase "in everything," which Colossians applied to the obedience of children and slaves, is here applied to the wife.)

In 5:22–24 the writer assumes that the marital hierarchy of his time parallels an eternal hierarchy. There has been much discussion of the use of "head" (*kephalē*), and the consensus is that it connotes "authority" or "source" rather than "ruler." The writer uses the imagery of Christ as head of the body from 1:22–23, but the use of "savior" here is not the usual Pauline usage and is found similarly only at Phil 3:20. It has been correctly pointed out that the husband's authority finds its origin in the lordship of Christ. Thus, any demands of the husband that are inconsistent with Christ's lordship are outside the scope of this teaching.

Interestingly, the bulk of the instruction in the *Haustafel* is directed to husbands, nine of the total twenty-two verses (vv. 25–33). In a sense, the member of the household who culturally had the most authority has the most serious constraints placed upon him. The clearest statement in the New Testament of the husband's duty is found in 5:25; he is to love his wife as Christ loved the church. Christ freely gave himself for the church; no one forced him to do so. Likewise, the duty of the husband is self-sacrificing love (*agapē*). Surely this is the most startling and difficult principle of action that the writer has set down thus far! It sets a divine standard for human behavior.

Verses 26 and 27 are controlled by an image of baptism. How it applies to Christ and the church is clear. Its application to human marriage is more obscure. It has been suggested that "word" (v. 26) is a reference to the formal claiming of the bride by the bridegroom in a Jewish marriage ceremony, but this hardly clarifies the metaphor. (It was also a Greek marriage custom for the bride to be washed in a stream sacred to a god or goddess before her wedding.) I suspect that from v. 25b through 27 the writer's mind has returned to his earlier thinking about the church and that "she" is the sole referent.

That husbands are to love their wives as their own bodies can be seen as an alarmingly self-serving motivation and one that contradicts the analogy between Christ and the husband, since Christ did not love his body but gave it up. Or the image can be understood to reflect the unity effected by marriage; that is, that the two have, indeed, become one flesh. The word translated "should" (*opheilousin*) implies moral obligation, literally, "owing a debt to someone."

This image of bodily unity continues in vv. 29–31. Because of its voluntary solidarity, marriage is used in the Old Testament to denote solidarity between God and Israel. It is established by God's free act and Israel's response (see, for example, Hosea). Something similar is at work here as the comparison between Christ and the church is extended. In reading v. 29 it should be remembered that Christ literally nourishes the church through his body by means of the eucharist. That "we are members of his body" (v. 30) vividly describes how closely Christians are tied to Christ (cf. Rom 12:5). The quotation from Gen 2:24 reinforces the ideals of closeness and unity, grounds the author's instructions in the order of creation, and refocuses the reader on human marriage.

Verse 32 suggests that the true meaning of the Old Testament passage is only now understood. The implication is that God's true and ideal intention for marriage was not revealed until the coming of the Christ, whose life and death provided the model for it. This is part of "the mystery of his will, according to his purpose which he set forth in Christ" (1:9). To put the matter in Platonic terms, the human institution was not fully known until the heavenly archetype was revealed. (Some commentators have linked "mystery" in v. 32 with 3:4, thus suggesting that the relationship between husbands and wives should reflect that between Jews and Gentiles in the church. But it seems to me that this line of reasoning introduces another analogy that inevitably breaks down.)

But v. 32 also requires that our reading of vv. 25-33 be ambiguous. It leaves us wondering whether the writer had human marriage or Christ and the church uppermost in his mind as he wrote. That he recalls us to the former in v. 33 suggests that he was, in fact, focused on the latter in the passage. In any case, v. 33 serves as a summary of the section on wives and husbands. Husbands are to love their wives as themselves and, correlatively, wives are to respect (*phobetai,* literally, "to fear," although the connotation here is to reverence or to show respect) their husbands.

The Jewish heritage of the writer of Ephesians continues at the fore in his instructions to children and parents in 6:1-4, which relies heavily on the fifth of the Ten Commandments. The phrase "in the Lord" in v. 1 has elicited comment since there is manuscript evidence that it should be omitted. If it did not appear in the original, the writer's thought is that the obedience of children is a natural duty. "Right" (*dikaion*) is used in the sense of "fulfillment of an obligation." The inclusion of the phrase implies that obedience is characteristic of the Lord, and it may also limit which parents children must obey. That is, it may speak to Christian children having pagan parents. If parents are not "in the Lord," children would not necessarily be obligated to obey them, especially if obedience to those earthly parents were in conflict with obedience to the heavenly parent.

The command to "honor your father and mother" (Exod 20:12) is the only command that comes with a promise. It is understood that God rewards obedience (cf. Ps 91:16). The promise of land that occurs in Exodus is omitted by the writer of Ephesians since the reference is now to all people, not just the children of Abraham and Moses. Keeping commandments allows God to fulfill divine promises; long life "on the earth" is promised, not a reward that is deferred until after death.

The writer of Ephesians makes more specific the instruction to fathers given by the writer of Colossians (cf. 6:4 and Col 3:21). Here, the father is not to provoke the children to anger (*parorgizete* implies long-standing and deep-seated anger). Behind the specific relationship stands the general injunction given at 4:31-32. The danger addressed is probably arbitrary exertion of authority for its own sake, authority that the *paterfamilias* certainly had. (A Roman father could expose a newborn, sell his children into slavery, force them to work under any conditions as he saw fit, and even kill them with impunity.) Instead, the father is to "bring them up in the discipline and instruction of the Lord." To "bring up," *ektrephete,* literally means "to nourish and provide for." The emotional connotation of the word is one of tenderness. "Discipline" is *paideia,* the word in Greek meaning "education" and implying training, and thus a long-term view. A process is suggested. All discipline and instruction (*nouthesia,* literally, "admonition") are "of the Lord"; Christ is its model and content. The father is to be the instrument of God's teaching, but God is the real educator.

Ephesians 6:5–9 parallels Col 3:22–25 and, like it, devotes more space to slaves than to masters. As suggested in the comments on the Colossian passage, slavery was an accepted part of the social structure of the ancient world. In Paul's day there may have been some sixty million in the empire. Slaves were part of the ordinary household. They might well be persons of some accomplishment and skill (many teachers and physicians were slaves) who had been taken in military conquest. Debt was also a common cause of slavery. Like racism and sexism today, slavery was so much a part of the fabric of the world, and people were so accustomed to it, that even Christians raised no objection to the practice.

As was the case with wives and husbands, here the writer sees subordination and authority as part of the divine order of things. Slaves are to be obedient to masters (as are wives to husbands) as if the masters were Christ. Literally, the "earthly masters" were their "lords," *hoi kyrioi* (v. 9). (Recall that Paul called himself a "slave of Christ"; cf. 6:6.) As slaves had wholeheartedly, without hypocrisy or ulterior motive, been obedient to Christ, so they were to behave toward their masters.

This obedience must hold not just when the master is looking, but continually (v. 6). The implication is that it gives dignity to all work when it is done for Christ. (The seventeenth-century Carmelite Brother Lawrence carried this point to its logical conclusions in *The Practice of the Presence of God* when he wrote that holiness does "not depend upon changing our works, but in doing that for God's sake which we commonly do for our own." See the translation of his work by Sr. Mary David, S.S.N.D., published by Paulist Press, 1978.) The principle is stated in v. 7; it is the "second-mile principle" of Matt 5:41, which turns compulsion into voluntary service. But as v. 8 makes clear, one reaps what she sows. God rewards as well as judges, and those who do well will be rewarded. (Cf. Matt 6:6; a remarkable portion of the instruction to slaves draws principles from the Sermon on the Mount.)

Although directed to slaves, vv. 5–8 can be seen as general counsel on how Christians are to behave and to work. The passage implies that our motives for action change when we become Christians (even if our particular circumstances do not). We work hard at what we do for the sake of Christ, not for earthly gain or honor or prestige. The Christian's main concern is to honor Christ and to serve him, thereby, in the process, to bring others to him.

The meaning of masters doing "the same to them" (v. 9) is not exactly clear. Presumably the reference is to v. 8 and the principle of reward from the Lord "whether . . . a slave or free." As the writer has made clear, the tongue is a source of danger to the master for he can misuse it to "threaten," *apeilēn*. Threats are not appropriate Christian motivations for action, and the person in authority must realize that there is an authority over him or her. God's authority, not any human authority, is final.

Behind the verse is also the practical problem of favoritism. Not only are the world's grounds for distinctions among persons no longer valid in the Christian community, but "God is no respecter of persons" (Acts 10:34 KJV). Masters are, of course, more in need of this reminder than are slaves.

The principle of reciprocity that governed the Colossian *Haustafel* is also operative here, even though the writer of Ephesians is more explicit in pointing out that everyone is obedient to someone. His list may be more hierarchically ordered, but he insists that all human relations be motivated by reverence for Christ. The word "submission" in 5:21, *hypotassamenoi*, means literally, "to line up under." It was used in a military setting as soldiers lined up and submitted themselves to the authority of their officers. As soldiers give up their own will in obedience to officers, Christians are to give up their rights and wills to Christ. Unfortunately, the call for universal Christian submission to Christ has not been heard clearly, and these texts have been misused to justify the subjugation of women, slaves, and those whose identities would parallel slaves. Perhaps the subjugated can take comfort from 6:8–9. Subjugators have a master in heaven in whose eyes there is no partiality.

M. Barth, *Ephesians* 2: 624–29, 655–62, 668–720.

W. Jaeger, *Early Christianity and Greek Paideia* (Oxford: Oxford University Press, 1961).

A. Malherbe, *Paul and the Thessalonians* (Philadelphia: Fortress, 1987).

A. McKay, *Houses, Villas and Palaces in the Roman World* (London: Thames and Hudson, 1975).

D. Werner, *The Household of God and the Social World of the Pastoral Epistles* (SBLDS 71; Chico, Calif.: Scholars Press, 1983).

Be Strong in the Lord (6:10–20)

At the end of the parenetic section of Ephesians, the author returns, although in a roundabout fashion, to the lordship of Christ and its bearing on the world. Throughout the letter he has assumed the victory of Christ over evil. The main battle has been won; what is left are "mop up actions." Undoubtedly the Jewish heritage of the writer brought to bear the image of God as a defending or avenging warrior, which provides the foundational metaphor in the passage (see especially Isa 59:15b–20).

It has been suggested that 6:10–20 was originally addressed to the newly baptized who were embarking on the Christian life. Behind the teaching here are the blatant evils enumerated in 5:3–20. If the new Christian's inward tasks were those of growing into Christ (4:16) and building up the body (4:12), then the outward task is warfare with cosmic powers. That the enemies are spiritual make them no less real. Heretofore, the writer has addressed the internal matters of Christ's church; now he calls into full view the warfare it must wage without, and the resources it has for battle against nonhuman agents. (Moderns who are uncomfortable with the martial imagery must remember that, in the Christian life, warfare is against spiritual evils, not human beings.) The focus of the letter has moved from the cosmic (1:3–2:22) to the corporate (4:22–6:9) to the individual (6:10–20).

The passage is closely woven together. As did the *Haustafel*, it begins with the principle from which action grows (6:10). The "wiles of the devil" in v. 11 lead the writer to reflect on spiritual powers again in v. 12 (as he has done at 1:3, 10, 20–23; 2:2, 6; 3:10), so that he must repeat the phrase "whole armor of God" in v. 13 to get back on track before he launches into the components of the "armor" (vv. 14–17). As prayer is essential to the arming of Christians, the writer closes with that "weapon," which he asks be employed also on his behalf (vv. 18–20).

The word that the RSV translates "finally" may be either *to loipon* or *tou loipou;* there is good textual evidence for each. Thus "finally" might equally well be translated "from now on," reinforcing the argument of those who see this text as a postbaptismal homily. Or it can be translated "for the remaining time," suggesting that the writer has a limited time frame in mind. The point is that the Christian's strength is derivative; it is from God and from God's "might," from the same power and might that effected the resurrection (cf. 1:19; the writer seems to be returning to his opening prayer for the Ephesians). The present passive imperative verb suggests that the strengthening God provides is continuing.

The Christian needs full battle dress, must put it on (cf. 4:24ff.), because he or she must stand (*stēnai,* a word that could be used in a military sense for "standing watch" or holding a crucial position on the battlefield) against the craftiness of the devil (*diabolou* never appears in the unquestionably authentic writings of Paul). The introduction of "the devil" raises the whole question of "the powers," which appeared earlier in 1:20–2:10.

The cosmological assumptions of the Ephesians were very different from our own. They inhabited a universe in which the unseen world was every bit as real as the material universe. "Heavenly realms" and "spiritual powers" were understood to exert potent influences over human life. In particular, the worship of Artemis was prevalent in Ephesus, with its concomitant practices of magic and astrology, which attempted to manipulate spiritual powers. (It has been pointed out that the spread of astralism in the hellenistic world marked the collapse of popular, anthropomorphic religion.) Even Jews of the diaspora had a lively demonology and employed magic to cope with "the powers," which were an important feature of their visionary literature. The author of Ephesians simply must address spiritual powers again because undoubtedly they were much feared by the new Christians of Ephesus.

The Ephesians already knew that they were "not contending against flesh and blood, but against the principalities, against the powers, against the world rulers of this present darkness, against spiritual hosts of wickedness in the heavenly places" (v. 12). They knew the *kosmokratores* ("world rulers"; cf. John 12:31; 14:30; 2 Cor 4:4), originally an astrological term for the planets, which controlled human destiny. They knew that the "heavenlies" (cf. 1:3, 20; 2:6; 3:10) were not only where Christ sat enthroned, but were also a place filled with competing spiritual forces. Once again, the writer must assert the lordship of Christ over "all things." In Ephesians *ta panta* always refers to Christ's lordship (see 1:10, 11; 3:9; 4:10, 15; 5:13; but especially 1:20–23). The writer believes that Christ has already won the decisive battle and conquered evil. (The most ancient Christian confessions of faith assert that Jesus has defeated and subjected the "powers." See 1 Cor 15:24–25; Heb 10:12–13; 1 Pet 3:22.) That being the case, the Ephesians have already been delivered from its "realm" or control and have as their "secret weapon" the very power of God Almighty. It is to this power that the writer appeals in 6:10, 11, and 13. God, through Jesus the Christ, provides salvation (and freedom) from the powers and all the cosmic forces they represent.

But a foe that knows itself defeated often puts up a fierce, if futile, final resistance. Thus the Christians' need for "battle dress." Because their struggle is against spiritual powers, it is imperative that the Ephesian Christians "take the whole armor of God" (v. 13). "Take" (*analabete*) was used technically in military language for the final stage of preparations before battle began. "Stand" here is from the root *anthistēmi*, which is used in Christian literature of the resurrection. The "whole armor" referred to a Roman soldier's equipment, which included shield, sword, lance, helmet, greaves, breastplate, etc. (For a full description, see Josephus, *Jewish Wars* 3.93ff. The archbishop's palace in Ravenna has an interesting mosaic of Jesus as a medieval crusader or knight in armor, the inspiration for which might well have been drawn from this passage in Ephesians.) The implication of v. 13 is that Christians, having been forewarned, must be forearmed. Knowing warfare is always a possibility, they must make all the necessary preparations beforehand to withstand attack.

The imperative "stand" in v. 14 shares the same root and connotation as the word in v. 11 (cf. Jas 4:7 and 1 Pet 5:9). It introduces the sustained metaphor of vv. 14–17, which catalogues the items of equipment needed. The order of presentation is apparently the order in which the soldier would put them on. (Had Paul, or the writer, frequently watched his captor dress?) Note that each piece is necessary if the Christian is not to be vulnerable at some point. The writer describes the struggle as military combat, but note again that the weapons are described in purely spiritual terms.

One begins by girding the "loins with truth" (RSV) or fastening "the belt of truth around your waist" (NRSV; v. 13). A Roman soldier wore a wide leather belt to protect his lower abdomen and put on a sword belt as one of the final steps in preparation for battle. More commonly, to "gird the loins" was to draw up the flowing outer robe into the belt to prevent tripping during vigorous action. To be girded is the mark of a servant expecting a master's call. Also, the Christian is to be girded with truth (*alētheia*), a virtue also much touted by the Roman moralists. Truth, sincerity, and integrity are the means by which the Christian rids herself of all that is a hindrance in the struggle against evil. To enter spiritual battle without the truth would be like entering it blind or lame. The "powers" cannot be conquered by human theories or fanciful speculations, but only with the truth found in the historic self-disclosure of God in Jesus Christ.

In Roman times the breastplate protected the body between the shoulders and hips. It was usually of the very best metal of which a soldier could avail himself, for it protected his vital organs. The Christian's protection is righteousness, which implied for the Jews all the things that kept one in proper relationship to God, but especially obedience to God's will. Righteousness signaled faithfulness to covenant agreements. (Note that the first two pieces of God's armor are essentially attributes of God, truth and righteousness. The Christian's preparation for spiritual battle is the practice of Godlikeness.)

Paradoxically, the Christian soldier is prepared for battle with the "equipment of the gospel of peace" (v. 15). Battle is begun with a declaration of peace! The shoes in question are some sort of sandal since *hypodēsamenoi* means literally, "to bind under" or "to strap on." The reference may be to the heavy, hobnailed shoe of the Roman soldier. The point of the image is that the gospel of peace makes one surefooted. Being shod with the gospel enables the Christian to stand unmoved against foes. Confidence comes from the good news of a peace which is assured (cf. Isa 52:7, which may well have been in the writer's mind).

A Roman soldier could carry a small round shield or a large rectangular one, roughly 4 x 2.5 feet in size. This latter, whole-body protection seems to be the one the writer has in view. It was generally made of several layers of leather that were soaked in water before battles precisely to "quench all the flaming darts." Faith, confidence in God and openness to God, is the Christian's ultimate protection. 1 John 5:4 implies that faith not only protects the Christian from the "slings and arrows of outrageous fortune," but is the "victory that conquers the world" (NRSV).

The bronze helmet of the Roman legions with its cheek pieces and decorative plumes was famous. Its effect was to make the soldier look bigger and more fierce, but it was also practical, because nothing short of an ax could cut it. The Christian's helmet is salvation. To know the reality of salvation makes it impossible for the Christian to be led astray (cf. Ps 140:7). To anticipate salvation is to have it continually in view as the inspiration to move forward. (Alexander the Great is said to have worn a white helmet so that his soldiers could see it in battle and know that all was well.)

To this point the equipment has all been of a defensive nature. The only offensive weapon in the collection is "the sword of the Spirit, which is the word of God" (v. 17; cf. Jesus' use of Scripture in his temptations in Matt 4:1–10). The writer of Hebrews also used a sword metaphor in connection with the word of God. He describes the word of God as "living and active, sharper than any two-edged sword, piercing until it divides soul from spirit, joints from marrow; it is able to judge the thoughts and intentions of the heart" (4:12). The Christian's only point of attack is God's message declared in the gospel of peace. It, finally, wins the battle (cf. Matt 10:19–20).

Verses 18–20 strongly emphasize prayer. As Arnold has noted, prayer is the essential Christian weapon and is foundational for the deployment of all the others. The prayers for empowerment in 1:15–23 and 3:14–21 reach their zenith here. "Prayer" (*deēsis*) implies a petition for particular benefits arising from a particular situation; "supplication" (*proseuchomenoi*) is a more general word meaning any petition to a divinity. The Spirit forms all truly Christian prayer, which is awareness of God and readiness to respond to God's call whether or not words are spoken.

"Keep alert" (*agrypnountes*) means not just "stay awake" (as on watch), but "be watchful" or "be vigilant." With instructions to "put off," "be subject," and "resist" it forms part of the standard vocabulary of early Christian hortatory material (cf. Mark 14:34, 37, 38). Christians are to remain alert and to persevere in prayer. Persevere (*proskarterēsei*) is used in parallel literature for waiting until one's trial came to court or for being constant in one's work. Constancy in prayer (cf. Rom 12:12; Phil 4:6; Col 4:2; 1 Thess 5:17) is "for all the saints," since the "army" must stand together for its own protection.

The allusion to imprisonment in v. 20 accounts for the inclusion of Ephesians among the prison epistles. The writer wants to be an object of the Ephesians' prayers. He desires greater boldness (forms of *parrēsia* are used in both v. 19 and v. 20) in proclaiming the "mystery of the gospel" (cf. Ps. 51:21). At the outset he declared that the mystery *is* the gospel; now he requires strengthening for further declaration and elucidation of it. He pronounces himself the gospel's "ambassador in chains." An ambassador (*presbeuō*) has the full power to represent a king or government. But, unlike the chain of office that a government official wore, the writer wears the chain of imprisonment, presumably both literal imprisonment by the Romans and thralldom to Christ and his gospel. He does not ask for intercession for his freedom, but for the strength necessary to continue to proclaim the gospel. With that request the body of his epistle draws to a close.

C. Arnold, *Ephesians Power and Magic* (Cambridge: Cambridge University Press, 1989).

N. Baker, "Living the Dream: Ethics in Ephesians," *SWJT* 22 (1979): 39–55.

M. Barth, *Ephesians* 2:766–77 and 793–800.

B. Corley, "The Theology of Ephesians," *SWJT* 22 (1979): 24–38.

M. Goulder, "The Visionaries of Laodicea," *JSNT* 43 (1991): 15–39.

E. Schüssler Fiorenza, *In Memory of Her* (New York: Crossroad, 1983).

T. Matson, "Theology and Ethics in Ephesians," *SWJT* 6 (1963): 60–70.

G. MacGregor, "Principalities and Powers: The Cosmic Background of Paul's Thought," NTS 1 (1954/55): 17–28.

W. Munro, "Col 3:18–4:1 and Eph 5:21–6:9: Evidences of a Late Literary Stratum?" *NTS* 18 (1972): 434–47.

THE CLOSING

Ephesians 6:21-24

The closings of hellenistic letters generally included wishes for the good health of the recipients and greetings to others. The closing formulas of Pauline letters is slightly expanded, including hortatory remarks, greetings, a wish of peace, and a grace or benediction. Obviously, Ephesians' closing departs from Paul's pattern in being much abbreviated. It contains two sections, a personal reference (6:21-22) and a final blessing (6:23-24).

The Personal Reference (6:21-22)

Two aspects of this closing greeting argue against the authenticity of Ephesians. First, if Paul spent an extended time in Ephesus (and the evidence is that he did), would he not have known more people there? And would he not have taken occasion to greet them in this letter? Jerome Murphy-O'Connor takes the absence of greetings as further evidence that Ephesians is a circular letter intended for a variety of communities.

Second, Eph 4:21-22 reproduces nearly verbatim Col 4:7-8. Thirty-two consecutive words in Ephesians are identical with a similar number in the Colossians' passage. Ephesians 6:22 is exactly the same as Col 4:8. It seems that the writer of Ephesians, being familiar with Paul's usual style of closing and having Colossians at hand as a model, simply borrowed the first of several greetings to members of the church at Colossae to close the Ephesian letter.

There is evidence that a person named Tychicus did share the Pauline ministry. As bearer of the Colossian letter, he may well have carried

Philemon as well. He is listed as one of the members of the Asian church who traveled with Trophimus from Greece (And went to Jerusalem at the end of Paul's third missionary journey? See Acts 20:4; 21:29). In Titus 3:12 he or Artemas is to be sent to Titus, and 2 Tim 4:12 reports that he was sent to Ephesus from Rome. Thus, he would have been with Paul during the apostle's final days. Tradition (which is by no means certain) speaks of his work as a bishop later on.

If my supposition that Ephesians is deutero-Pauline is incorrect, then we must take 6:21-22 not as the writer's attempt to conform to the Pauline letter form, but as a reference to a messenger of Paul who was well known to the churches. He would be a man not only dear to Paul, but a faithful minister (*diakonos*), who was able to encourage the Christian communities to which he was sent. (These communities were, undoubtedly, worried by the news of Paul's imprisonment and, if they did not know the state of his mind as reported in Philippians, they would need reassurance.)

The Final Blessing (6:23–24)

The closing of Ephesians is long and somewhat formal. Most of Paul's letters conclude with a single, brief sentence. Ephesians closes with two sentences, either of which could stand alone. The normal sequence "grace and peace" is reversed in Ephesians. That the benediction occurs in the third person again suggests the encyclical nature of the work.

"Peace," the universal opening of the salutations of Paul's letters, frequently also closes them. (Interestingly, it does not occur in Colossians, which in so many other ways served as a model for this letter.) Here peace is offered to the men and women in the Christian community (*adelphois*), along with love and faith, three qualities any pastor would want for the people under her or his care. "Love with faith" (v. 23) is an unusual turn of phrase and might also be translated "together with confidence in God" or "together with trust in Christ." Like the Christian's strength in 6:10-20, peace is derivative; it comes "from God the Father and the Lord Jesus Christ."

The final blessing "grace" (*charis*) occurs in all the letters of the Pauline corpus, and, of course, it was the keynote of this epistle. Here, however, grace is specifically directed to those "who love our Lord Jesus Christ with love undying." This formulation is unique in the New Testament. "Undying" (*aphtharsia*) is difficult to translate since it seems to have different connotations in different places. Although it is not entirely clear to what part of the sentence it is related, in Eph 6:24 the word means "immortal," "imperishable," or "incorruptible," and thus it serves as a final reminder of that ultimate hope over which death has no dominion.

That the letter closes with "grace and peace," a Jewish and a Gentile blessing, reminds the reader again of the unity that God has effected through Jesus Christ. As the note in the Oxford University Press edition of the NRSV suggests, it is "a worthy conclusion" which returns "to the fundamentals of thought of 1:3–14." The letter began with a greeting of grace and peace to the faithful in Ephesus (1:1–2) and it closes in like manner.

R. Bratcher and E. A. Nida, *A Translator's Handbook on Paul's Letter to the Ephesians* (New York: United Bible Societies, 1982).

2 THESSALONIANS

INTRODUCTION

The City of Thessalonica

The city of Thessalonica was located in Macedonia at the head of the Thermaic Gulf. It was founded in 316 B.C.E. by Alexander's general Cassander, who named it in honor of his wife, Thessalonikeia, the daughter of Philip II and half-sister of Alexander. The city rose steeply above the harbor and was built on the site of the village of Therme (which may have been a Corinthian foundation and whose name suggests hot springs in the area) and included thirty-five smaller towns. Few remains of this hellenistic period have been uncovered by archaeologists.

Macedonia became a Roman province, and in 146 B.C.E. Thessalonica was made its capital. As the center of Roman administration, the city was politically important. It supported the victorious Antony and Octavian prior to the Battle of Philippi in 42 B.C.E., which subsequently increased its commercial prosperity. Cicero spent part of his exile there in 58 B.C.E., and Pompey took refuge in the city from Caesar in 49 B.C.E. when it became a sort of "second Rome."

Under Octavian (whose ascendancy is marked by the honors granted him by Thessalonica), the status of "free city" was bestowed on Thessalonica with the accompanying tax concessions and the right to mint its own coins. Extensive coinage indicates the city's prosperity. Thessalonica boasted a Roman forum, stadium, gymnasium and Serapium as part of a larger sacred area. A main station on the Via Egnatia, which ran on an East–West axis from the Balkans to Asia Minor, Thessalonica's strategic importance was increased by its location on North–South trade routes as well.

As were many of the major cities of the empire, Thessalonica was not only religiously vital, but diverse. The cult of Serapis has been attested archaeologically by both a Serapium and a small temple of the Roman period. Inscriptions to Serapis and Isis have been discovered. These cults of Egyptian gods indicate how cosmopolitan Thessalonica was. The cult of Dionysus was in evidence, and archeological finds suggest it was symbolized in the area by the phallus. Dionysian revelry and ecstatic worship certainly would have colored the religious life of the city. Worship of Zeus was important, as was devotion to Aphrodite, Demeter, and Asclepius.

Perhaps the most important religious cult at the time of Paul was that of Cabirus. A mystery religion, the Cabirus cult focused on a martyred hero who was murdered by his brothers, but expected to return to help the lowly and the city of Thessalonica in particular. It was believed that Cabirus promoted fertility and protected sailors. In Samothrace devotees of the cult donned special robes, confessed their sins, and were cleansed by baptism and symbolic immersion in the blood of the gods.

Because of Thessalonica's Roman benefactions, extensive evidence for Roman imperial and civic cults in the city are not surprising. Roma was revered in Thessalonica. In the reign of Augustus a temple of Caesar was built. Thessalonica acclaimed Julius as a god and minted coins that were the first to bear the heads of Romans. The references in the Thessalonian letters to afflictions and persecutions may have resulted from the Christians' inability to participate in these publically important civic cults.

K. Donfried, "The Cults of Thessalonica and the Thessalonian Correspondence," *NTS* 31 (1985): 336–56.
_____. "Thessalonica," *HBD* 1065–66.
H. Hendrix, "Thessalonica," *ABD* 6:523–27.

The Church in Thessalonica

According to Luke, Paul arrived in Thessalonica with Silas and Timothy on his second missionary journey (Acts 15:40–18:22) after being driven out of Philippi (Acts 17:1; 1 Thess 2:1–2). Acts reports that he preached in the synagogue for three sabbaths, but had more success with Gentiles than Jews. Apart from some higher class Gentile women (Acts 17:4), the majority of converts were working class, and Paul practiced his trade alongside them so as not to be a burden to the nascent church. The Jews, apparently jealous of Paul's success, accused him of sedition (Acts 17:7), so Paul and his fellow evangelists had to sneak away by night to Beroea. Their success in that town reached Thessalonica, and they were again driven out. This time Paul went to Athens, and shortly thereafter, to

Corinth (see Acts 17:1–15). It is possible that Paul visited Thessalonica in the journey through Macedonia reported in Acts 20:1–6. In any case, continued opposition to the new Christians after Paul left led him to send Timothy there in order to bring a report on the situation. 1 Thessalonians is considered by some scholars to be his response to that visit (1 Thess 2:6–10).

Paul's usual missionary method was to begin his preaching in the synagogue, and Luke reports that he followed that pattern in Thessalonica. However, it is unlikely that the Christian congregation in Thessalonica was primarily Jewish. In addition to the paucity of references either to Hebrew Scripture or to Jewish Christians in the Thessalonian correspondence, 1 Thessalonians refers to the Christians as having "turned to God from idols" (1 Thess 1:9). Furthermore, Paul worries that the new Christians may live "like heathen who do not know God" (1 Thess 4:5).

The Thessalonian Christians were primarily Gentile in background. They were not of the upper classes, but free artisans or small tradespersons (which, of course, reflected the increasing levels of prosperity of the city as a trading center). Undoubtedly, Paul taught the message of Jesus as he lived and worked among these tradespeople and artisans.

From its inception, the Thessalonian congregation was fervent. The spirit of the hellenistic mysteries must certainly have influenced the spirituality of the church. They had experienced the Holy Spirit in powerful ways (1 Thess 1:5–6) and were anxious for the parousia, which would bring its full outpouring. Thus they were concerned about its arrival (1 Thess 5:1–11; 2 Thess 2:1–12) and alarmed when Christians died before that event (1 Thess 4:13–18). Some felt it so imminent that they quit work and set aside the normal routines of daily life (1 Thess 4:11; 5:14; 2 Thess 3:11–12). The Thessalonian letters address these issues and that of Paul's authority.

M. Goulder, "Silas in Thessalonica," *JSNT* 48 (1992): 87–106.
R. Jewett, *The Thessalonian Correspondence* (Philadelphia: Fortress, 1986), chaps. 6 and 7.
A. Malherbe, *Paul and the Thessalonians* (Philadelphia: Fortress, 1987).

The Question of Authenticity

Ancient sources never question the Pauline authorship of 2 Thessalonians. Apparently J. E. C. Schmidt first raised the issue in 1798 in connection with the differing eschatologies of the letters (the essentials of his argument appear in W. Trilling, *Der Zweite Brief an die Thessalonicher* [Zurich/Neukirchen, 1980]), and the work of W. Wrede in 1903 ushered the question into the critical forefront. In recent years, scholarship, especially German scholarship, frequently argues that Paul did not write the letter. That conclusion is drawn primarily from literary evidence.

Structurally, 2 Thessalonians follows 1 Thessalonians very closely. It also follows 1 Thessalonians in diverging from the typical Pauline pattern (for example, in introducing a thanksgiving in the body of the letter [1 Thess 2:13ff.; 2 Thess 2:13ff.] or a benediction at its close [1 Thess 3:11-13, 2 Thess 2:16]). The phrasing of the superscriptions and addresses is practically verbatim in the two letters, and the greeting is identical. There are remarkable parallels between 1 Thess 2:9 and 2 Thess 3:8. J. Bailey believes there are no other parallels so close in the Pauline correspondence. The question this evidence raises is why Paul would so slavishly follow his own precedent. Why would Paul use his own work so unimaginatively?

The similarities of structure and wording are so close that Wrede drew up a sort of "synoptic parallels" of the two letters. And yet several usages in 2 Thessalonians are problematic if Paul wrote the letter. Why would Paul mention authenticating his own letter in 3:17? Does 2:2 refer to an actual letter from Paul or one purporting to come from him? The *hōs di hēmōn* in the Greek is ambiguous. 2 Thessalonians 3:7 says Paul did not accept money from anyone, a direct contradiction of Phil 4:15ff. 2 Thess 1:12 calls Christ "God," a statement that occurs in no other Pauline letter.

1 and 2 Thessalonians are also very different in tone. 1 Thessalonians is extremely warm and personable. The author of 2 Thessalonians, by comparison, seems short and sharp. 2 Thessalonians is official and formal and contains no personal information like that provided by the writer of the first letter.

Most tellingly, the two letters are very different thematically and theologically. The most obvious difference occurs over the matter of eschatology. In the first letter, the parousia is imminent and will arrive unexpectedly. The issue is raised in connection with the pastoral problem of Christians who have died before Christ's return. In 2 Thessalonians, the author must correct those who believe the parousia has already come by listing the events that will precede it. Its purpose is to condemn false teaching and to support apostolic authority. The two points of view are essentially contradictory. Either the parousia will come suddenly, or it will be preceded by "signs." If the two letters are written close together in time, as proponents of their authenticity usually suggest, is such a quick change of attitude on the part of the writer likely? 2 Thessalonians contains no theme not found in 1 Thessalonians, which seems odd in light of the differing eschatologies.

It has been argued, but not widely held, that these difficulties are resolved if we understand 2 Thessalonians to be written before 1 Thessalonians or understand 2 Thessalonians to be addressed to the leaders of the congregation only and 1 Thessalonians to be addressed to the whole church. On the whole, the intrinsic literary and thematic evidence weighs strongly in favor of the pseudonymity of 2 Thessalonians, that a hand other than Paul's wrote the epistle. Perhaps the clearest defense of Pauline authorship appears in I. H. Marshall's commentary on the Thessalonian correspondence, but the weight of scholarly opinion still tips the scales in favor of non-Pauline authorship, a view assumed in this commentary (although with reservation). Such a position, of course, requires the creation of a setting for 2 Thessalonians, and this has proved to be a difficult task.

J. Bailey, "Who Wrote II Thessalonians?" *NTS* 25 (1978/79): 131–45.
C. Giblin, "The Second Letter to the Thessalonians," *NJBC* 871–75.
I. H. Marshall, *1 and 2 Thessalonians* (NCBC; Grand Rapids: Eerdmans, 1983).
R. Thurston, "The Relationship Between the Thessalonian Epistles," *ExpT* 85 (1973): 52–56.

The Circumstances of the Writing

2 Thessalonians addresses three main issues. First, it addresses the difference between the fate of those who persecute the Christians and of those persecuted faithful. Second, it refutes the teaching that the day of the Lord has already come. Finally, it condemns believers who are living in idleness, refusing to work and living off other members of the Christian community. A number of ingenious theories have sought to account for these concerns.

Several theories about recipients of the letter have been suggested. A. Harnack thought 2 Thessalonians was written at the same time as the first letter, but was addressed to a Jewish-Christian minority in the church. E. Schweizer thought 2 Thessalonians might be the second letter to the Philippian church to which Polycarp made reference. M. Goguel suggested that 2 Thessalonians was originally addressed and sent to the church in Beroea to which Paul fled from Thessalonica. M. Dibelius thought 1 Thessalonians may have been a private letter to church leaders, while 2 Thessalonians was addressed to the whole congregation.

Schmithals has taken another approach. He argues 2 Thessalonians is a composite. Paul's first letter to Thessalonica, he argues, consists of 2 Thess 1:1–12; 3:6–16, which was expanded by the inclusion of a third letter, 2:13–14, 1–12; 2:15–3:3, 17ff. The first letter was written to warn the church to avoid Gnostic fanaticism. In the second, he addressed attacks on himself, and in the third, he took on the Gnostic teaching directly. (Schmithals uses this theory to argue for Pauline authorship.) Bailey, too, believes the letter was written to refute Gnostic teaching, but he considers it pseudonymous and dates it ca. 90–100 C.E.

Wrede sets 2 Thessalonians in the late first century when a group of enthusiasts argued that the day of the Lord had come. An opponent of their position used Paul's name in composing a letter to refute them. Another, similar view, is that 2 Thessalonians was written to discourage belief in the nearness of the parousia.

Although there are a number of different opinions about the exact circumstances from which the letter arose, most scholars who believe it is pseudonymous date it toward the end of the first century. It seems to be the case that 1 and 2 Thessalonians were written in the canonical order and to the same community. 2 Thessalonians may not be written by Paul, but it is related to the Thessalonian situation at the time of Paul. The eschatological passage in 2:1–12 is the primary purpose of the letter (which is why many scholars suggest it refutes Gnostic teaching). In attributing the letter to Paul, the writer attempts to give weight to his position. (Full bibliography for the arguments cited here are found in Bailey and in Marshall; see above, p. 161.)

T. W. Manson, "St. Paul in Greece: The Letters to the Thessalonians," *BJRL* 35 (1952/53): 428–47.

The Structure of the Letter

It has already been noted that in structure and style, 2 Thessalonians is closely related to 1 Thessalonians. Both generally follow the pattern of a hellenistic letter, and both generally follow Pauline conventions. Both arise from a similar life-setting. The author is faced with a situation in which the timing of the parousia is crucial because it raises practical and pastoral questions for the congregation.

R. Jewett has done extensive rhetorical analysis of 2 Thessalonians and believes it to be deliberative rhetoric in which the author seeks to persuade the recipients to take action. The emphasis in deliberative speech on self-interest and future benefits correlates with material in 1:3-12 and 2:13-3:5. The political context of deliberative speech is evident in the writer's commands about the *ataktoi* (the "idle") in 3:5-15.

While some commentators have argued that the error in 2:1-12 is related to the conduct of 3:1-13, B. Kaye discourages this approach because of the absence of *prima facie* lexicographical evidence for the relation of the two passages. None of the eschatological material in 2:1-12 is directly used to correct the problem in 3:6-13, and in any case, the two passages are separated by 3:1-5, which breaks the author's development of thought. The formal phrasing of 2:1 and 3:6 suggests the opening of new sections of material, as, indeed, I think they are.

In this commentary the material will be treated in the following units:

1:1-2	The Opening
1:3-4; 1:11-12	Thanksgiving and Prayer
1:5-10	"The Righteous Judgment of God"
2:1-12	"The Coming of Our Lord Jesus Christ"
2:13-3:5	Thanksgiving and Prayer
3:6-15	"Believers who Are Living in Idleness"
3:16-18	The Closing

B. Kaye, "Eschatology and Ethics in 1 and 2 Thessalonians," *NovT* 17 (1975): 47-57.

R. Jewett, *The Thessalonian Correspondence* (Philadelphia: Fortress, 1986).

THE OPENING

2 Thessalonians 1:1-2

S imple and straightforward, the opening of 2 Thessalonians exhibits
the usual features of a Greco-Roman letter. It introduces the writers,
announces the recipients, and sets forth a greeting.

1 Thessalonians 1:1 and 2 Thessalonians 1:1 are identical. First, each
announces the senders of the letter to be Paul, Silvanus, and Timothy.
Here "Paul" is not described by any of the usual modifiers (for example,
"apostle by the will of God"), which may suggest that his authority has
not been questioned.

Silvanus is the Latin form of Silas. According to Luke, Paul chose Silas
as his companion for the second missionary journey (Acts 15:36-40).
Thus, although not mentioned again in Acts until after his arrival in
Corinth (Acts 18:5), Silas must have been one of the founders of the Thessalonian congregation. (A Silas is also mentioned as the secretary in 1 Pet
5:12.)

Timothy, a Christian from Lystra, is familiar as a frequent companion,
coauthor, and messenger of the apostle Paul. He, too, was present on the
second missionary journey (Acts 16:1-5), although he is not mentioned
by Luke in connection with Thessalonica. According to 1 Thessalonians
3:1-10, however, he made a visit to that church at Paul's request. Luke
reports that Timothy and Silas stayed in Beroea when Paul fled the city
(Acts 17:14-15).

Second, 2 Thessalonians is addressed to the "assembly" or the "church"
(ekklēsia) of the Thessalonians. "The assembly of" would be understood
in a secular, political sense and is given religious meaning only by the
phrase that follows, "in God the Father and the Lord Jesus Christ." In
both Thessalonian epistles the Greek en is instrumental; thus the phrase

means "the church which is brought about by God the Father and the Lord Jesus Christ." That the writer follows Paul's lead in calling God the "Father" of Jesus, and in calling Jesus Christ "the Lord," suggests that he accepts Paul's emerging Christology. The "our" in "God our Father" also serves to unite the writers and recipients. Both are children of the same parent. Clearly, whoever wrote the letter, it is addressed to the community of those who have been called together by their belief in the lordship of Jesus.

With the greeting, the writer diverges from the precedent set in 1 Thessalonians. That letter greets its recipients, "Grace to you and peace," combining the traditional Greek and Hebrew salutations. 2 Thessalonians expands the greeting to include the sources of grace and peace, again, "from God our Father and the Lord Jesus Christ." This makes for a slightly awkward repetition, but a clause with *apo* appears in many Pauline superscriptions in a variety of forms. Here, it emphasizes the personal character of the relationship of God to believers which, in the pagan religious environment of Thessalonica, may be important.

Nothing in the opening two verses alone either confirms or denies the authorship of the letter. However, the close correspondence between the openings of 1 and 2 Thessalonians is noteworthy.

THE THANKSGIVING AND PRAYER

2 Thessalonians 1:3–4 and 1:11–12

In the Greek text, 2 Thess 1:3–10 is one long sentence, and thus technically marks off a unit of text. In terms of development of thought, however, three distinct sections are discernible in this part of chapter 1: vv. 3–4, an epistolary thanksgiving; vv. 5–10, an explanation of "the righteous judgment of God"; and vv. 11–12, a prayer for the recipients of the letter. The two prayer texts will be treated together at this point, and the apocalyptic passage (1:5–10) will be discussed in a separate section.

Although several of Paul's letters claim coauthorship, the plural, "We give thanks," occurs only in Colossians and the Thessalonian correspondence. Here in 2 Thessalonians the unusual phrase "we must always give thanks" or "we are bound to give thanks" (*eucharistein opheilomen*) occurs. The phrase is repeated at 2:13, but does not appear elsewhere in the Pauline corpus. Some commentators have suggested that it sets the cooler tone of 2 Thessalonians, others that it is the writer's response to the Thessalonians' declaration that they are not worthy of the praise given in 1 Thessalonians. However, when coupled with "as is right" or "as is proper" (*kathōs axion*), a more substantive and illuminating reading emerges.

The form of the thanksgiving prayer reflects standard Jewish and Christian conventions of the time. Paul Schubert has noted that it follows a simple thanksgiving "type" which has six elements: (1) we thank; (2) God; (3) always; (4) about/for you; (5) because; (6) so that. The liturgical character of the opening clause has been investigated by R. Aus who points out that it occurs in Jewish prayers in Philo and Josephus. He notes that in a number of prayer texts there is a connection between the propriety of glorifying and thanking God, and suffering. (See, for example, Mishnah *Pesahim* 10:5; *Berakoth* 9:5; and Rev 3:4; 5:9, 12. The texts from the Revelation to John demonstrate that the Greek *axios* was deemed especially suitable in contexts of suffering.) Aus argues persuasively that the author is neither refuting the Thessalonians' unworthiness of praise, nor showing his interest in their physical health, but is expressing a commonplace of piety: the necessity and propriety of thanking God for the reasons given in vv. 3–4 which are within a situation of suffering. The community's suffering prompts the appropriate use of a standard liturgical usage in the thanksgiving.

The Thessalonians' response to and behavior under affliction had made that congregation an example to the churches in Macedonia and Achaia (1 Thess 1:8–9). The author of 2 Thessalonians thanks God for their growing faith, their increasing love, and their continued steadfastness under persecution. In spite of their circumstances, their faith is "growing abundantly" (*hyperauxanei*); the prefix *hyper* on the verb expresses vigorous growth and intensifies the meaning of the word. Furthermore, their inclusive and encompassing love for each other is a mark of their spiritual maturity. *Hypomonēs,* translated by the NRSV as "steadfastness," implies "patient endurance"; according to Reinecker and Rodgers its implication is not grim waiting, but radiant hope, and thus the triad of faith, hope, and love is complete in v. 4. (Compare 1 Thess 1:3 and 3:6. Since, as St. John Chrysostom pointed out, steadfastness implies a time lapse to prove endurance, 2 Thessalonians may not have followed immediately upon the first letter.)

It is for these reasons that the author boasts of the Thessalonians to "the churches of God." (Compare 1 Cor 11:16 for this general phrase. "Boast," *egkauxasthai,* is a compound verb found only here in the New Testament; Paul prefers a simpler form.) Although "persecutions" (*diōgmois*) and "afflictions" (*thlipsesin*) are employed almost synonymously here, the first is frequently used as a term for persecutions that arise externally from enemies of the gospel, and the second more generally connotes any sort of tribulation. The author can boast of the Thessalonians' endurance (*anexesthe,* literally "holding themselves up") because present trials are related to their future resolution. (This idea dominates vv. 5–10, which are discussed in the next section of this commentary.)

The issue of persecutions leads the writer to treat the question of the justice of what was happening. The rather loose transitional phrase "to this end," which begins the prayer of vv. 11–12, refers equally well to the persecutions and afflictions of v. 4 or their justification in vv. 5–10.

The author prays that God will make the Thessalonians worthy of their call and will fulfill their good resolves and works of faith in order that the name of Jesus may be glorified.

Verse 11 makes it clear both that God is the primary actor in the lives of the faithful, and that it takes the power of God to accomplish good resolve and to do works of faith. God calls persons, fills them with Christian aspirations, and empowers them for the work of faith. "Worthy" (*axiōsē*) may connote either "make worthy" or "deem as worthy." The same compound verb is used in v. 5. "Fulfill" (*plērōsē*) here suggests accomplishing, or completing a process already begun. The constant prayer of Christians for one another ("we always pray for you") provides spiritual support in the process of their "completion."

The purpose of a Christian's completion is not for her own benefit or his own glory, but that the name of the Lord Jesus may be glorified (v. 12). The verse seems to allude to Isa 66:5, in which the name of God is glorified. The point is that glory is brought to Jesus by people who live in a way that honors him, who literally "delight in well doing" (*agathōsynēs*, v. 11).

The prayer concludes with the assertion that this process is all "according to the grace of our God and the Lord Jesus Christ," an unusual phrase. As I. H. Marshall points out in his commentary, Paul does not append nouns in the genitive to the word "grace"; and when he uses the two names together, it is not in the configuration found here. Whether this is the result of an error in dictation or of non-Pauline authorship is a matter for debate. The point of the closing, however, is to remind the readers of the source and means of salvation, God and the Lord Jesus Christ respectively.

R. Aus, "The Liturgical Background of the Necessity and Propriety of Giving Thanks according to 2 Thess 1,3," *JBL* 92 (1973): 432–38.

I. H. Marshall, *1 and 2 Thessalonians* (NCBC; Grand Rapids: Eerdmans, 1983).

P. Schubert, *Form and Function of the Pauline Thanksgivings* (BZNW 20; Berlin: Töpelmann, 1939).

"THE RIGHTEOUS JUDGMENT
OF GOD"

2 Thessalonians 1:5–10

As noted in the previous section of this commentary, the thanksgiving and prayer of 2 Thessalonians are interrupted by an emotional digression on the judgment of God. Considering the history and circumstances of the Thessalonian congregation, the writer's fervor was entirely understandable.

The Thessalonian Christians were an example to others in their region because "in spite of persecution you received the word with joy" (1 Thess 1:6). In persecution they were "imitators" of Paul, Silvanus, and Timothy, who "had already suffered and been shamefully mistreated at Philippi" (1 Thess 2:2). Acts 17 does not indicate how long Paul stayed in Thessalonica. It does report that he had to leave quickly when "the Jews became jealous, and with the help of some ruffians in the marketplaces they formed a mob and set the city in an uproar" (Acts 17:5). Paul left for Beroea and subsequently, Athens, but the Thessalonian Christians remained to face the consequences of the disturbance and of their new beliefs. Some, perhaps, were martyred, which would account for the discussion in 1 Thess 4:13–18. Donfried has suggested that 1 Thessalonians was written by Paul to answer criticisms like Dio Chrysostom's of philosophers who "make a hurried exit, anxious lest before they have finished you may raise an outcry and send them packing" (*Oration* 32,11).

Even if Donfried's theory pushes the textual evidence, it is true that the Thessalonian believers would have faced vigorous social pressure when they abandoned Greco-Roman religions and became Christians. They would have incurred the resentment of non-Christians when they declined to participate in the normal social and cultic activities which formerly had been part of life. (In 1 Corinthians, Paul's discussion of the eating of meat sacrificed to idols would give some insight into these difficulties; see 1 Cor 8–10.) Undoubtedly the persecuted Christians would have taken comfort in the idea that God would punish those who had been harassing them. But this passage begins with a very different statement.

2 Thessalonians 1:5 arises from the reference in 1:4 to the persecutions and afflictions that the Christians are suffering. The writer makes the startling assertion, "This is evidence (*endeigma*) of the righteous judgment of God, and is intended to make you worthy of the kingdom of God." How is the innocent suffering of Christians evidence of the righteousness of God?

Explanations of the verse begin with a discussion of the word "evidence." *Endeigma,* which can also be translated "sign," occurs only here in the New Testament. It means "proof by an appeal to facts," or "a token clear for all to see." Commentators have tended to read the verse in connection with Phil 1:27–30 and to argue that the persecution suffered by the Christians is a sign God will count them worthy of salvation. ("For them [opponents] this is evidence [*endeixis*] of their destruction, but of your salvation. And this is God's doing"; Phil 1:28b NRSV.) According to this reading, persecution signals future justice, but suffering is not a present sign.

In a convincing argument, J. Bassler disputes this interpretation and suggests that the sufferings of the church are *per se* a sign of God's righteous judgment. Her interpretation builds on Wolfgang Wichmann's *Die Leidenstheologie* (Stuttgart, 1930). Wichmann's theology of suffering highlights Rabbi Akiba, who taught that God is strict with the righteous on earth in order to be able to lavish blessing on them in heaven. The sufferings of this life are a sign of God's acceptance, a way for the righteous to receive punishment in this life for sins in order to be free to enjoy heaven unencumbered. This theme is found in *Psalms of Solomon* 13:9–10; 2 Macc 6:12–16; and, in the closest parallel to 2 Thessalonians, *2 Bar* 13:3–10 and 78:5.

By the time of the Jewish War, Wichmann argued, the notion of God's strict, retributive justice was widely held. Present suffering was explained in terms of future glory; the righteous were being made worthy of their inheritance. This, of course, was inverted for the godless. Thus the temporal afflictions of the elect are a sign of God's acceptance and justice. Wichmann saw this at work in 2 Thessalonians, but his views were ignored when Pauline authorship was assumed.

Bassler believes that 2 Thess 1:5 is best understood in terms of *Leidenstheologie,* a theology of suffering. The sufferings of the Thessalonian Christians are a sign that they are God's elect, just as Israel's sufferings were signs of its election. But the present sufferings of the elect pale in comparison to the judgment that will come upon their persecutors.

In 2 Thess 1:6-10 the author presents the more common understanding that the wrath of God is directed to those who have afflicted the Christians. In vv. 6 and 7 the *lex talionis,* "eye for eye, tooth for tooth," is clearly at work. The thought is not unlike that in Isa 66:4 in which God afflicts people with what they have caused others to suffer. Although this may sound harsh, it removes punishment or vengeance from human beings who might act out of a spirit of retribution or vindictiveness rather than from motives of divine justice (see Rom 12:17-21).

The avenging God of v. 6 is followed by the comforting God of v. 7. God grants rest to the afflicted. "Rest" or "relief" (*thlibomenois*) in classical Greek referred to the loosening of a bow string, and thus implies the relaxation of tension. The persecuted and afflicted Thessalonian Christians and the author share the fellowship of suffering, and both will share in God's relief or "recreation."

Verses 7b-10 describe the parousia, here called the "revelation" (*apokalypsei*) of the Lord Jesus. From the time of the exodus, the Jewish imagination had been shaped by powerful acts of divine deliverance. The hope for a "day of the Lord," a future deliverance, characterized Judaism in the first century. The New Testament writers incorporated this expectation, and the apocalyptic literary forms that expressed it, into their descriptions of the parousia, literally the "arrival" or "coming" of the Lord Jesus. 1 Thessalonians is the earliest Christian writing to reflect this appropriation, and to demonstrate the eschatological character of primitive Christianity.

Three features of vv. 7-8 are characteristic of the apocalyptic imagery of the time: Jesus comes from heaven, with mighty angels, in flaming fire. That Jesus comes "from heaven" indicates not only his origin, but his authority. Heavenly beings share God's authority (see 1 Thess 4:16). Both Zech. 14:5 and *1 Enoch* 1:9 speak of the angels that will accompany the coming of God. The genitive of quality, "mighty" (*dynameōs*), suggests a class of angels, the powerful ones, and gives force to the picture painted of the might of God. The strange phrase "in flaming fire" (v. 8) is also found in Acts 7:30 in reference to Moses at the burning bush. Fire is a standard feature of biblical theophanies, and so would be appropriate to describe the Lord's return (see also Isa 66:15).

The God who comes with such might and power comes to inflict vengeance (*ekdikēsin,* implying complete punishment) on the unbelieving and disobedient (v. 8b). "Those who do not know God" is used in Hebrew Scripture to describe Gentiles (see Ps 79:6 and Jer 10:24, which was used by Paul in 1 Thess 4:5 and Gal 4:8). Perhaps the writer has in mind that God will first punish Gentiles who are ignorant of God and then Jews who have knowledge and have disobeyed, or who have heard the message of Jesus and not responded.

Both alike will "suffer the punishment" (v. 9). "Suffer" (*tisousin*) means "to pay a penalty" or "to recompense." The word for punishment here, *dikēn,* means "the standard to which a thing should conform," and it came to express the results of a lawsuit. In these terms, the "sentence" is eternal destruction and separation from the presence of the Lord. In conformity with Jewish thought of the time, both Jesus and Paul believed and taught eternal punishment (see 1QS 2:15; 5:13, *Psalms of Solomon* 2:35; 15:11; *4 Macc* 10:15). For the writer, the worst aspect of this punishment was eternal separation from God.

Verse 10 expands on the temporal phrase in v. 7, "when the Lord Jesus is revealed." "That day" refers to the day of Christ's return and is a standard designation for the parousia. The image is of God being worshiped by believers (see Pss 89:7; 68:35). Just as in vv. 6-7 rest follows affliction for the Christians, here in vv. 9-10 glorification and marvel follows punishment. Interestingly, the emphasis is on the manifestation of God's glory and not on that of the vindicated believers. The final phrase, which seems awkward in this context, emphasizes that the manifestation of God's glory is rooted in faithful adherence to apostolic testimony (*martyrion,* "witness"). That the word "testimony" is the one from which the English word "martyr" is derived firmly yokes the importance of preserving true teaching with the situation of persecution in the Thessalonian congregation.

The writer tells the Thessalonians their persecutions reveal that God believes them to be worthy of the kingdom. But the bulk of the passage assures them that their persecutors will not go unpunished. Divine judgment destined the Christians for reward and eternal glory, and the persecutors, the unbelieving and disobedient, for future punishment and eternal destruction. "When the Lord Jesus is revealed from heaven," (v. 7), the balance will be restored and the believers vindicated. Jesus assumes the role played by God in similar Old Testament passages; everything stands under his final authority.

The whole text follows, with some variations, a judgment form discernible in the letters of Paul in which after an introduction, the offense is delineated, the punishment detailed, and a hortatory conclusion is offered. In 2 Thess 1:5-10, the writer introduces God's judgment in v. 5, describes the offenses of the persecutors in vv. 6 and 8 and their punishment in vv. 6 and 9, and closes with a veiled admonition to continue to believe "our testimony to you" (v. 10).

J. M. G. Barclay, "Conflict in Thessalonica," *CBQ* 55 (1993): 512-30.

J. M. Bassler, "The Enigmatic Sign: 2 Thessalonians 1:5," *CBQ* 46 (1984): 496-510.

K. P. Donfried, "The Cults of Thessalonica and the Thessalonian Correspondence," *NTS* 31 (1985): 336-56.

C. Roetzel, "The Judgment Form in Paul's Letters," *JBL* 88 (1969): 305-12.

"THE COMING OF
OUR LORD JESUS CHRIST"

2 Thessalonians 2:1-12

The author's teaching on and admonition about the parousia continues the discussion in 1:7-10, which introduced apocalyptic elements of that event. The primary purpose of this passage is to assure the recipients of the letter that the Day of the Lord (which was described earlier) has not yet arrived. Verse 5 (an anacoluthon or break in the thought) suggests the issue was also a matter of concern when the author was with the Thessalonians.

The text is full of interpretive problems and has been a subject of discussion since the writings of the Apostolic Fathers. The difficulties arise because the author assumes knowledge on the part of the original recipients that subsequent generations do not have. The Thessalonians knew the source and meaning of references that to us are veiled and obscure. In this commentary we may be able to do no more than to outline some of the difficulties and to present some of the suggested solutions.

It has been argued by C. L. Mearns that 2 Thessalonians represents a third stage in Paul's eschatology. From a realized eschatology, Paul moved in 1 Thessalonians to an imminentist Christian apocalyptic. According to Mearns, Caligula's attempt to set up his image in the Temple in 40 C.E. stands behind the third phase of Paul's early eschatological development. The apostle adopted an apocalyptic scheme in which a sequence of signs served as a prelude to the final Day of the Lord. For Mearns, 2 Thessalonians represents this later stage of Paul's apocalyptic development (which comes to maturity in 1 Cor 15).

Whether or not Paul is the author of 2 Thessalonians, it is clear that the letter attempts to correct the false impression among Thessalonian Christians that the parousia had already occurred. Throughout the letter, the writer insists on the accuracy of the tradition and the views he represents (see 1:10b; 2:5, 14, 15; 3:4, 6, 14). The suggestion is strong that false teachers, or at best incorrect interpreters, have challenged it (see 2:2, 3). The writer attacks both the false view and, indirectly, those who hold it (see 3:14–15).

The Problem (2:1–12)

The problem is introduced by an admonition not to be upset by announcements that the parousia has already happened. The danger of deception with regard to apocalyptic expectations is a common theme in the New Testament (see for example Mark 13:5–7). This warning opens with the formula "now concerning," which, in the Pauline corpus introduces questions that congregations had asked Paul in some formal manner (see, for example, 1 Cor 7:1; 8:1; 12:1; 16:1).

"The coming (*parousias*) of our Lord Jesus Christ," which had been introduced in 1:7–10, is here described first in terms of a "gathering together" or assembly (*episynagōgēs*). While some commentators have suggested that this gathering refers to the discussion of the death of Christians in 1 Thess 4:13–18, it is equally likely to refer to the Jewish hope of the gathering of the exiles (cf. Isa 11:12; Zech 2:6); the word is used in 2 Macc 2:7 for a future time when God will gather believers together. Jesus and the early church certainly made reference to the gathering together of the Messiah and his people (see Mark 13:27; Matt 23:37; Luke 13:34). The assembly of God's people was, in short, a standard feature of apocalyptic teaching and expectation.

The writer "begs" (a strong translation of *erōtōmen*) the "brothers and sisters" (NRSV, *adelphoi)* not to be "shaken in mind" (*saleuthēnai,* occurring only here in the Pauline corpus) or "alarmed" (*throeisthai*) by false claims. The aorist tense of "to shake" leads some commentators to suggest that a sudden shock is implied and the present tense of "alarmed," continual agitation following such a shock. Such a disturbing message could come by spirit (a message given by prophetic inspiration or through ecstatic experience), word (a general expression for teaching, sermons, or verbal communication), or letter. The phrase gives a tantalizing but inconclusive glimpse into the modes of authoritative communication in the early church.

The NRSV translation of the qualifying phrase in v. 2, "as though from us," as well as that in the RSV, "purporting to be from us," suggests that there were letters (and perhaps other communications) in circulation falsely attributed to the author. The writer's attitude makes clear that such letters hardly meet the criteria of pseudonymity. (See the earlier chapter in this volume, "Deutero-Pauline Christianity.") "As though from us" means literally "to stand in place of us," and it can be understood to qualify all three modes of communication. Either the Thessalonians have drawn false conclusions from what they were told, or false teachers had begun to present the community with misleading and erroneous ideas, or epistolary forgeries full of false ideas were circulating. The writer wants to make it clear that his view of the matter is the accurate and authoritative one. In order to prove that the Day of the Lord, has not arrived, he outlines the signs that will precede it.

The Prelude to the Parousia (2:3–12)

In vv. 3–12 the author outlines why he knows the Day of the Lord has not yet arrived. The thought provides the primary evidence for those who argue the letter was not written by Paul. As Marshall has pointed out, a major interpretive problem is that the author has not presented his arguments in chronological order; verses 5–7 discuss the period before the Lord's appearance, which is described in vv. 3–4, and vv. 9–12 revert to the period of his appearance before the "lawless one's" destruction, as described in v. 8. Furthermore, the Greek is very irregular. The sentence beginning in v. 3 is left incomplete at the end of v.4. And there is a second anacoluthon in v. 7, which also leaves an incomplete thought.

Three issues have dominated the literature on the passage: the identity of the lawless one (vv. 3, 8, 9), the identity or source of the restraining force (vv. 6–7), and the question of why God would send a delusion (vv. 10–12). These shall be treated in order presently, but the discussion will be enhanced if some possible frames of reference are first introduced.

R. Aus has argued that the writer of 2 Thessalonians has Isa 66 in mind as he writes chapters 1 and 2. The prophet speaks of a time when God will punish the apostate and vindicate true believers. Both the images and language of Isaiah do frequently appear in 2 Thess 1 and 2, and they provide a literary, though not a historical, context.

M. Goulder brings together literary precedent and historical situation in his suggestion that the book of Daniel (especially chapters 9, 11, and 12) and the person of Antiochus IV stand behind this text in Thessalonians. He suggests that the profanation of the Temple by Antiochus

Epiphanes in 168 B.C.E. historically prefigured and provided the language for the Thessalonian author's description of the "lawless one."

Although Pompey's entry into the Holy of Holies in 63 B.C.E. sent shock waves through the Jewish community, Caligula's claim to divine honors and his plan to have a statue of himself placed in the Temple, an episode which occurred in 40 C.E., would have been a more contemporary memory for the author of 2 Thessalonians and would have also brought to mind characteristic elements of apocalyptic, specifically, the powers of evil focused in a persecutor who claimed for himself divinity. The Caligula episode might also have been in the writer's mind.

A variety of scholars have used such historical speculation to provide a *Sitz im Leben,* a setting in life, for 2 Thessalonians. The point here is not to decide for one or the other literary or historical background, but to point out that both apocalyptic expectation and its literary conventions, and the historical memory of the time provided raw material for the author's description of the signs of the end.

What, then, does the text reveal about "the man of lawlessness" (v. 3, *ho anthrōpos tēs anomias;* v. 8, *ho anomos*)? To the original recipients of the letter he was a well-known figure; v. 9 suggests one in whom Satan operated. The term is used in v. 3 in apposition to "the one destined for destruction" (NRSV, or in the RSV, "the son of perdition") and means literally he is the "doomed one." (See 2:8 in which the parousia is described in terms of a cosmic battle in which the rebel will be eliminated. The imagery seems to come from Isa 11:4 in which the messianic king strikes "the earth with the rod of his mouth, and with the breath of his lips he shall kill the wicked." Cf. 1 Cor 15:24–28.) His behavior is described in v. 4. He "opposes" (*antikeimenos,* "lies against"), presumably, God, and "exalts himself above every so-called god or object of worship." (Note the author makes a distinction between God and those mistakenly thought to be gods.) In this, the lawless one bears a marked resemblance to the "king" of Dan 11:36–38. (Recall that lawlessness is a sign of the end times in Jesus' apocalyptic discourse in Matt 24:12.)

If the Temple in v. 4 is the one in Jerusalem (and this is by no means certain), then the "lawless one" could be a historical figure like Antiochus IV, Pompey, or Caligula. If "Temple" is used metaphorically to represent the domain of God, then the lawless one might represent the opposition of evil to God, its attempt to overstep boundaries and enthrone itself. The verse would thus provide a classical description of usurping God's prerogative. That the lawless one "is apparent in the working of Satan, who uses all power, signs, lying wonders, and every kind of wicked deception" (vv. 9–10) suggests that he may be a person-ification of all rebellion against God.

In terms of the writer's purpose here, the man of lawlessness (whether a historical figure or a personification) serves to show that evil must reach a certain intensity before judgment comes. But what, or who, "is now restraining him"? The original recipients of the letter "know" (v. 6). Unfortunately, we can only speculate, and the speculation has given rise to many theories of various degrees of ingenuity.

"What is now restraining him" (v. 6) and "the one who now restrains" (v. 7) share the root verb *katechein,* "to hold down, to restrain," and thus can mean "delay." The fact that in v. 6 the phrase is in the neuter and in v. 7 in the masculine has complicated our understanding of what or of whom the author has in mind. Perhaps he is thinking of something that could be regarded as both a principle and a person.

The general sense of vv. 6–7 is that evil is now at work, though it is held back from its full extent by something/someone. Many "restrain-ers" have been nominated by scholars. Included among them are the Roman Empire as personified in the emperor, as well as the principle of law and order, represented in one view by the empire and in another by the Jewish state. Both Satan and God have been suggested as the restrain-ing force. When viewed in the light of cultic practice in Thessalonica, the author's use of the term can be seen as an allusion to pagan religious practice, especially to prophetic seizure. Another theory is that the restraining factor is proclamation of the gospel since Paul believed that Israel must repent before the end can come.

The common sense assumption that the restraining force is good rather than evil gives the best reading of the passage. As noted above, Aus has pointed out that Isa 66 profoundly affected the writer of 2 Thessalo-nians. The author seemed to know Isaiah in both its Hebrew and Greek forms. *Katechein* in 2 Thess 2:6–7 is, Aus argues, a direct translation of the Hebrew "to restrain," which occurs in Isa 66:9 in which God "shuts up the womb." The writer of 2 Thessalonians knows that the mystery of lawlessness is active because evil has not yet reached its zenith. When it has, God will cease restraining it, and the Messiah will come. God restrains the Day of the Lord because of the plan that the gospel first be brought to all (see 2 Pet 3:9; Rev 14:6–7).

This reading of the text takes seriously the apocalyptic nature of its language and other strands of apocalyptic tradition in the New Testa-ment. It is open to the Pauline origins of its thought (especially as reflected in 1 Thessalonians), and does not contradict *Leidenstheologie,* the theology of suffering that stands behind 2 Thess 1:5–10. Most importantly, it places God squarely at the center of the cosmic conflict (in which, as v. 8 points out, Jesus triumphs) and is consistent with vv. 11–12, in which God is the primary actor.

The final issue in the passage has to do with why God would "send a delusion" leading people to believe falsehoods. The interpretation of vv. 11–12 depends on the final phrase of v. 10, "they refused to love the truth and be saved." Refusal to welcome the truth represents a human decision, an act of will. Even "because" (*anth' hōn*, a conjunction found only here in the Pauline corpus, but used by Luke in the context of judgment; see Luke 1:20; 19:44; Acts 12:23) strengthens the idea that those who perish are responsible for their perdition. Refusal to love truth when it is presented rules out being "saved" or "rescued."

Opening with the phrase, "For this reason," vv. 11 and 12 build on this idea of the necessity for personal response to the offer of salvation. Hebrew Scripture reveals instances when God used evil for God's purposes (see 1 Chron 21; Ezek 14:9). The writer's point is the absolute sovereignty of God; God can use even evil to effect divine purposes. Only on those who have refused the truth does God send "a powerful delusion, leading them to believe what is false." The writer's understanding here is akin to that of Paul's in Rom 1; those who reject the truth become the victims of divinely caused infatuations, and finally, judgment.

Although the syntax of v. 12 is distinctively un-Pauline, the thought is not. Improper belief, or lack of belief, leads to improper conduct, here described as "pleasure in unrighteousness." *Eudokēsantes* can also be translated "delight." The word indicates a circumstance not of momentary or inadvertent lapse, but of active, chosen enjoyment, of flaunting or refusing God's will and way. Those who persist in unbelief, and consequently sin, are responsible for their own destruction. God "gives them up" to the consequences of their own decisions. (Cf. Rom 1:24–32 and 9:14–32.) God is in control even of deceptions, which are more easily accepted by those who have made no commitment to recognizing the truth.

In 2 Thessalonians the writer's central aim is to refute claims that the Day of the Lord has arrived. He admits that the coming of that Day is already apparent in the work of Satan (vv. 9–10). He refutes the argument that it has arrived (i.e., realized eschatology) by noting what must happen first; namely, the rebellion (*apostasia*, literally, "falling away," "revolt," or "apostasy") must come and the lawless one must be revealed

(v. 3). God is holding these events back (until the gospel is more widely declared? vv. 6–7), but eventually will allow them to happen. Then Jesus will destroy the lawless one "with the breath of his mouth" (v. 8; cf. Exod 15:8) and unbelievers will be condemned (v. 12).

R. Aus, "God's Plan and Power: Isaiah 66 and the Restraining Factors of 2 Thess 2:6–7," *JBL* 96 (1977): 537–53.

J. Frame, *The Epistles of St. Paul to the Thessalonians* (ICC; Edinburgh: T. & T. Clark, 1912). (On *katechein,* "to restrain," pp. 258–65; on *anomos,* "lawless," pp. 273–76.)

M. Goulder, "Silas in Thessalonica," *JSNT* 48 (1992): 87–106.

I. H. Marshall, *1 and 2 Thessalonians* (NCBC; Grand Rapids: Eerdmans, 1983).

C. Mearns, "Early Eschatological Development in Paul: The Evidence of I and II Thessalonians," *NTS* 27 (1980/81): 137–57.

THE THANKSGIVING AND PRAYER

2 Thessalonians 2:13–3:5

From the fate of the perishing in 2:9-12 the author turns in 2:13-17 to those who are persevering in their trials and who will be saved. Many commentators have noted that 2:13 sounds like the beginning of a letter, and hellenistic letters do begin with thanksgivings, but to my knowledge few scholars have made strong cases against the integrity of either 1 or 2 Thessalonians. The author may be following the pattern set by 1 Thessalonians which also contains a prayer in the body of the letter (1 Thess 3:11-13) followed by a section beginning "finally" (*loipon,* 1 Thess 4:1; *to loipon,* 2 Thess 3:1). Another deutero-Pauline work, Ephesians, also interrupts the body of the letter with a prayer in which an intercession is followed by a doxology (cf. Eph 3:14-21 and 2 Thess 2:13-17).

As noted, 2:9-12 and 2:13-17 are thematically closely related; the first text describes perdition and the second salvation. It might even be the case that 2:2 and 2:15 form an inclusion signaled by the phrase, "by word . . . or by . . . letter." References to the vehicle of teaching would thereby frame it. R. Jewett also noted the continuity of 2:3-17 and argued that the rhetorical genre of 2 Thessalonians is deliberative so that 2:3-3:5 is the *probatio* section; thus, 2:3-12 is the first proof the parousia has not come and 2:13-3:5 is the second proof.

I agree that 2:13-3:5 forms a discernible unit. All the material in that section is related to prayer. Chapter 2:13-15 is the author's prayer for the Thessalonians; 2:16-17 is a benediction; and 3:1-5 is the author's request for the Thessalonians' prayers on his behalf. Using the genre of prayer as a structural principle, in the commentary which follows these three sections will be discussed.

Called by the Gospel for the Glory (2:13–15)

The phrases that introduce the thanksgivings in 1:3 and 2:13 are nearly identical. At 1:3, 2:1, 2:13, and 3:1 new sections are marked off by directly addressing the faithful Christian believers (*adelphoi*). In 2:13 the author qualifies the address, "brothers and sisters," with the phrase,"beloved by the Lord," because he has demonstrated in 1:5–10 that their sufferings are proof of God's election. (See the previous commentary on that text. Cf. 1 Thess 1:4.) In the first thanksgiving of the letter the author gave thanks for the behavior exhibited by its recipients. Here thanks are rendered for what God is doing for them. God chose them for salvation and called them to obtain glory.

Verse 13, then, sets forth the first reason for thanksgiving: God chose the Thessalonians for salvation "through sanctification by the Spirit and through belief in the truth." A textual variant marks the manner of God's choosing. The Thessalonians are either the "firstfruits" (*aparchēn*), a Pauline word with Jewish theological overtones, or were chosen "from the beginning" (*ap' archēn*), a phrase which Paul does not use, but which signals a Pauline idea, that God's purpose from the beginning of creation was the election of believers. Although "firstfruits" might suggest that the Thessalonians were among the first in Macedonia to be saved, since the author is attempting to comfort the recipients of the letter, the second reading seems more appropriate to the context.

The manner of God's choosing was "through sanctification by the Spirit and through belief in the truth." The first phrase is also found in 1 Pet 1:2, and it marks God's activity through the Holy Spirit which is paralleled by the human response of belief. "Truth" (*alētheias*) here certainly means the truth of the gospel of Jesus Christ, what v. 14 calls "our proclamation of the good news."

God calls believers through the gospel so that they "may obtain the glory of our Lord Jesus Christ" (v. 14; cf. 1 Thess 5:9). As Marshall has noted, the author seems to be following the pattern set in Rom 8, where God's election leads to the calling and ultimate glorification of believers, those who respond to the call. The purpose of the gospel's call is the glorification of believers (see Rom 8:29–30). Since that is the case, the Thessalonian Christians are well advised to "stand firm and hold fast to the tradition that you were taught by us" (v. 15).

"So then" (*eis ho,* v. 14) links the command of the writer closely to the plan of God which he has just outlined. In their dangers and persecutions, the Thessalonian Christians must stand fast (*stēkete*), that is, be stalwart and resolute in trials, and must hold fast (*krateite*) to that which is passed on (*paradōsis*, for a discussion of this term see the commentary on 3:6–12), the teaching of the writer and his colleagues. Although the phrase "hold fast to the traditions" is un-Pauline, the thought is certainly not (see 1 Cor 11:2; 15:1–2; 1 Thess 2:13). But the qualifying phrase "by word of mouth or by our letter" is unusual. Again, the combination of word and letter does not appear in genuinely Pauline letters. Furthermore, when Paul refers to his own teaching, he usually does so in a disciplinary (for example, Gal 6:11 or 1 Cor 16:21) or contractual (Philm 19) context, and not as a sign of his authority. The writer of 2 Thessalonians gives to Paul an authority that he does not need to claim for himself.

The thanksgiving and the benediction that follows it are intended to assuage any uneasiness caused by a claim that the Day of the Lord has come. It reminds the recipients that they are chosen by God and will obtain the glory associated with Jesus' return, so long as they remain steadfast in action and belief.

R. Jewett, *The Thessalonian Correspondence* (Philadelphia: Fortress, 1986).
I. H. Marshall, *1 and 2 Thessalonians* (NCBC; Grand Rapids: Eerdmans, 1983).
P. Perkins, "2 Thessalonians," *HBC* (San Francisco: Harper & Row, 1988).

A Comforting Benediction (2:16–17)

In 1 Thess 3:11–13 a benediction follows a prayer. (In fact, 2:16–17; 3:5; and 3:16 are all benedictions.) As at other points in this epistle, the author seems to be following that precedent. Both benedictions begin with the same transitional phrase, "and now" (*autos de*). Interestingly, both 2 Thess 2:16 and 3:16 appear to introduce closing remarks, raising again a question about the integrity of the letter.

The point of the benediction is to give the recipients of the letter comfort and confidence. The writer accomplishes this by declaring that both "our Lord Jesus Christ" (the full title of Jesus characteristic of the Thessalonian correspondence) and "God our Father" has loved them and through grace given "eternal comfort and good hope" (v. 16). The comfort or encouragement (*paraklēsin*) that God gives is not temporal, but eternal (*aiōnian*). God never forsakes or abandons the faithful. "Good hope" (*elpida agathēn*), a phrase found only here in the New Testament, was a term used by the mystery religions for bliss after death. The language in v. 16 is extremely clever, yoking as it does the Christian assertion that God's gifts are precisely that, divine gifts of grace which are unearned, and familiar phrases which would speak to former pagans of the hope for life after death. Both comfort and hope are "in grace" (*en chariti*), another phrase found only here and in Col 3:16 and 4:6.

The author closes the benediction by praying that God will encourage their hearts and strengthen them "in every good work and word" (v. 17). In the Christian life, inner strengthening is always for outer service. Comfort and assurance in the core of the inner person, the heart (*kardias,* understood to be both the center of emotions and of the will), issues forth in both good deeds (works) and good words, Christian proclamation and teaching. In this context the author undoubtedly thinks of these good words as the tradition of which he is reminding them (see 2:15 and 3:4, 6, 14).

J. Reese, *1 and 2 Thessalonians* (NTM; Wilmington, Del.: Michael Glazier, Inc., 1979).

The Author's Request for Prayer (3:1–5)

Although the NJBC suggests that chapter 3 contains two exhortatory sections each closing with a prayer (3:1–5 and 3:6–16), in 3:1–5 the writer is continuing the prayer mode begun at 2:13. "Finally" can be understood to signal the last prayer thoughts of the writer rather than as introducing the final remarks of the letter. This seems likely since an exhortatory section (3:6–15) does follow.

For the third time in the prayer section, the writer addresses the Thessalonians as "brothers and sisters" (2:13, 15; 3:1), which stresses his connectedness to them and to their sufferings. Having offered prayer for the Thessalonians, he asks for prayer for himself and his fellow workers. (Paul characteristically appeals to his readers for their prayers. See Rom 15:30; 2 Cor 1:11; Phil 1:19.) Here the writer requests petitions for the success of his apostolic work in the midst of serious opposition and for personal deliverance from those who oppose the gospel. The request for prayer for himself shifts at v. 4 to a form of entreaty to the letter's recipients. Apparently the author cannot think of his situation apart from that of his fellow Christians. His task of encouragement in writing the letter is brought again to the fore.

The writer asks the Thessalonian Christians to pray that the gospel will "spread rapidly and be glorified everywhere, just as it is among you" (v. 1). As in many Pauline prayers, the request is not for the writer, but for the success of his message and mission. Here, the author compliments the Thessalonians asking, in effect, that they pray that others will receive the message with the same speed and eagerness with which they did. The LXX used "spread rapidly" (*trechē*) for the runner who carried messages in battle. It was applied to the prophets who, as the authorized messengers of God, were God's "runners" (see also Ps 147:15; Wis 7:24). The word also connotes Greek runners in the games (see 1 Cor 9:24; Gal 2:2; 5:7). The dual reference vocabulary carries the idea of the swift and winning spread of the good news.

The second half of the prayer request is somewhat less Pauline since the apostle usually does not pray for his own needs or safety. The author of 2 Thessalonians, however, hopes that he will be delivered or rescued (*rysthōmen*) from "wicked and evil people" (v. 2). *Tōn* suggests definite adversaries known to the readers. The word translated "wicked" (*atopōn*) is found only here in the New Testament in reference to persons but was used in the papyri for those who behaved inappropriately or in outrageous ways. The author wants to be delivered from the wicked and evil not, admittedly, for his own sake, but so that the gospel can continue to spread (cf. Jer 15:21). Although he understands lack of faith as the reason for the hostility toward him, "for not all have faith" at the end of v. 2 is more an introduction to what follows than an explanation of what preceded it (cf. Rom 10:16).

Not all people have faith, but the Lord is faithful (cf. 2:16). The *estin* should be understood as emphatic. At v. 3 the author's concern shifts once more to the Thessalonians and to the task of reassuring them. God will strengthen them and protect them. "Strengthen" or "make firm" (*stērixei*) may well have been in the author's mind from 2:17. "Guard" (*phylaxei*) is not used by Paul for divine protection (but see Pss 121:7; 141:9). Although "evil" (*tou ponērou*) is neuter here, the NRSV translates it "the evil one," thereby echoing the discussion in 2:1–12, especially the reference to Satan in 2:9. (The same translation issue exists in Matt 6:13. Translating 2 Thess 3:3 "the evil one" would be consistent with 1 Thess 2:18.)

The Thessalonians can be confident that the Lord will strengthen and protect them, and therefore the writer of the letter can be confident about the faithfulness and obedience of the Thessalonians themselves. In both v. 3 and v. 4 the grounds for confidence is Christ's faithfulness. But as in 2:15, 3:6 and 3:14, in 3:4 the writer is anxious that the Thessalonians follow his commands and traditions. "Commands" (*paraggellomen*) was used in 1 Thess 4:11 for ethical and ecclesiastical advice, and it will introduce the next section of the letter (in which the verb appears three times, at 3:6, 10, 12), which warns against idleness.

The section closes in v. 5 with a prayer that the Lord direct their hearts, that is, their very beings, to the love of God and the steadfastness of Christ. "Love of God" (*agapēn tou theou*) can mean either the human's love for God or the love God shows humans. The same translation issue occurs with "the steadfastness of Christ" (*hypomonēn tou Christou*). Since the activity of God and of Christ seems to be held up as an example, the second reading seems preferable. The writer hopes the letter's recipients will exhibit God's love and Christ's steadfastness (cf. Rom 5:5). He wants them to keep on doing what they are known for (see 1:3–4).

After requesting that the Thessalonians pray for the spread of the gospel and the deliverance of its messengers, the writer of the letter returns again to his primary task, that of encouraging the Thessalonian congregation to hold fast to their faith. He assures them that they can do so because of the faithfulness of Christ, which is not only the source of their strength and protection but of his confidence in them. Having faith, the Thessalonians must continue in love and steadfastness, which 3:6–13 will insist be manifested in purposeful action. Having sought their sympathetic concern for himself and having praised them in 3:1–5, the writer is well positioned to admonish the idle in his subsequent remarks.

"BELIEVERS WHO ARE LIVING IN IDLENESS"

2 Thessalonians 3:6–16

The tone and language of 2 Thess 2:1 and 3:6 are formal, in each case suggesting the introduction of a new subject. This passage follows a pattern already established in the letter; a didactic/exhortatory block of material is followed by a "prayer wish" (cf. 2:1–16; 3:1–5; and 3:6–16, noting especially the opening phrases of 2:16; 3:5; and 3:16). This pattern supports a division between vv. 16 and 17 rather than between vv. 15 and 16 as some have suggested, since it shows v. 16 to be the prayer of vv. 6–15 and not part of the general closing remarks of the letter, vv. 17–18.

Within this larger block of material (3:6–16), there are three sections. Verses 6–12 address the issues of idleness and, secondarily, those who have departed from the apostolic teachings. Verses 13–15 are a more general admonition suggesting how to deal with those who are disobedient to "the tradition." And, as noted, v. 16 is the prayer that concludes the section.

The writer is concerned to reinforce a teaching that was apparently common in the early church, that Christians must continue to work for a living. The specific issue of idleness was addressed in 1 Thess 4:11–12 and 5:14, and the necessity for honest labor appears in Eph 4:28. The example for the Thessalonians in the matter of work is the apostles who worked to support themselves while preaching the gospel (see, for example, Acts 18:2–3 and 1 Cor 4:12a). That the Christian apostles worked to support their ministries was especially important since parallel literature is full of examples of peripatetic philosopher-teachers who "sponged" off the persons to whom they lectured. (For a fuller discussion see Charles Talbert, *Reading Corinthians,* in this series.) That behavior was familiar to the recipients of the letter and appears in Christian literature in the *Didache,* which addresses the issue of traveling preachers who refuse to work for their own keep.

> If he who comes is a traveller, help him as much as you can, but he shall not remain with you more than two days, or, if need be, three. And if he wishes to settle among you and has a craft, let him work for his bread. But if he has no craft provide for him according to your understanding, so that no man shall live among you in idleness because he is a Christian. But if he will not do so, he is making traffic of Christ; beware of such. (12:2–5)

After bringing the necessity to continue to work into focus and directly admonishing the idle, the writer of the letter suggests that Christians withdraw fellowship from the troublers in order to encourage them to change their ways and to return to more appropriate activity.

The Problem (3:6–12)

The section of the text that defines the problem is marked off by two verses in which those addressed receive a command (*paraggellomen*) carrying with it the authority of "the Lord Jesus Christ" (vv. 6 and 12). Within these parameters, the example of the writer and his associates is a sub-unit of material indicated by "imitate" (*mimeisthai*) in vv. 7 and 9. The writer first addresses the community generally (vv. 6–10) and then speaks directly to its offending members (vv. 11–12). In the Greek, the writer's reasons for commanding the withdrawal of fellowship from the idle are introduced by *gar* ("for"; vv. 7, 10, 11).

The seriousness of the situation is indicated first by the fact that the writer of the letter "commands" the Thessalonians whom, once again, he addresses as "brothers and sisters." In 3:6 *adelphoi* is rendered by the NRSV and RSV "beloved," a translation that obscures the writer's habit of opening new sections of material by means of this address (see 1:3; 2:1; 2:13; 3:1). Second, his command is issued "in the name of our Lord Jesus Christ," that is, with the authority of the Christ, since "name" (*onomati*) would have signified both the essence and the power of the one invoked. Hellenists, both Jew and pagan, believed that there was actual "power in the name."

The command is "keep away from believers who are living in idleness and not according to the tradition that they received from us" (v. 6). Note first that the offenders are believers, fellow Christians, and in all the instructions that follow they are treated as such, not as the "wicked and evil people" of 3:2, but as erring members of the community. Four important issues are introduced by the command. Two are matters of translation. What are the best renderings of "keep away from" and of "living in idleness"? The other two have to do with the situation of the church in Thessalonica. Why would the Thessalonian Christians have stopped working? And what is the relationship of the "tradition" to idleness?

The Greek for "keep away from" (*stellesthai*) is a rare form in the original. The root word first meant "get ready," and then came to mean "bring together," as, for example, in gathering or tucking together cloth or clothing (i.e., the activity of "girding the loins"). From this sense of "gathering up," the word came to connote flinching or avoiding. Here it means to draw back from those who are "walking in idleness" (*ataktōs peripatountos*). The adverb *ataktōs* is from the same root as its adjectival form in 1 Thess 5:14 and is found in the New Testament only in the Thessalonian correspondence.

Malherbe is correct that rendering the word *ataktōs* "idleness" is an interpretation rather than a translation. Literally, the word means "without rank" or "out of order." It was a military term used for a soldier who was out of step or an army in disarray. From this it came to be used for anything out of order, and it implied unruliness and insubordination. "Idleness," thus, is more than simply refusing to work for a living. It implies general lack of submission to the accepted rules of life, disruptive and disorderly behavior in general. The admonition is against those who on some level were threatening the social order of the Thessalonian congregation.

Why was this disorderliness manifested in giving up purposeful labor? Two possibilities involve misunderstanding of the parousia and are thus related to the discussion in 2:1–12. Most simply, if the parousia is imminent, then work and economic life in general are of little importance. Some Christians may have left off work simply to await the return of Christ. Some may have stopped to engage in something they felt was more important, namely, preaching the gospel. (And they apparently depended on the charity of others to support their evangelism.) On the other hand, if the parousia has already occurred, as some in Thessalonica apparently thought, then the order that God gave humans to work for a living (Gen 3:17–19) was no longer in force. Refusal to work signified acceptance of a completely realized eschatology.

Disorderliness manifested in idleness may also be tied to the hellenistic environment in Thessalonica. Epicurean philosophy taught that happiness derived from a quiet life of retirement from the world. Therefore, some of those who followed Epicureanism abandoned public life and its responsibilities. The writer of 2 Thessalonians may have seen similarities between Epicureanism and the erring Christians' behavior, and to help clarify the situation, he enjoins Christians to be responsible and orderly (i.e., productive) members of society, "to do their work quietly and to earn their own living" (3:13).

For whatever reasons it has arisen, the writer is concerned to correct the problem of improper conduct among the Thessalonian Christians. To do this he appeals to what he has already said to them (vv. 6, 10), to what they themselves know (v.7, recalling the manner of appeal in 1 Thess 2:1; 3:5; 5:2), and to apostolic tradition, "the tradition that you received from us" (v. 6). The language here (*paradosin hēn parelabosan*) is the technical language of the apostle Paul for the transmitting of apostolic materials. Paul uses forms of the verb *paradidōmi*, which means "to pass on what is received" (and which is almost the exact equivalent of the Latin *traditio*, from which we get the English word "tradition"). The correlative verb, *paralambano*, meant "receiving the tradition from those who have passed it on." "Tradition," then would include both doctrinal and ethical material that issues "from the Lord" who authorizes it. The command to hold fast to the received traditions was first introduced at 2:15. Here the same enjoinder makes clear that the people who had received the tradition are now departing from it; thus, the need to remind people how to act, which the writer does by suggesting a model of proper action.

In vv. 7–9 the writer sets himself and his associates as examples to imitate. The infinitive "to imitate" (*mimeisthai*) means, literally, "to mimic by following another's example or teaching." What we now call "modeling" behavior for others was a standard teaching device in the early church (see 1 Thess 1:6–7; 1 Cor 4:16; Eph 5:1; Phil 3:17; Heb 6:12; and 13:7). Christians were taught to follow the pattern set by those who were living their own lives after the example of Christ.

"Imitation" was an especially important mode of teaching in Thessalonica because it followed a technique widely used by hellenistic moral philosophers. Seneca had written "men put more faith in their eyes than in their ears" (*Epistle* 6.5–6). The life of a moral teacher provided a paradigm for his followers; it made his teaching concrete, "incarnate." Thus, when the writer of 2 Thessalonians says, "you ought to imitate us" (v. 7) he was appealing to a widely understood practice in his day.

The behavior to be imitated is that of working for one's own keep (v. 8). The writer reminds the recipients of the letter that neither he nor his associates ate "anyone's bread without paying." "To eat bread" is a Semitism meaning "to make a living" (see Gen 3:19). They worked "night and day" (again, a Semitic way of reckoning time from one evening to the next) not to burden the Thessalonians (cf. 1 Thess 2:9). Although they had the right to accept support for preaching the gospel, they preferred to set an example of hard work (v. 9). (Discussion of rights and forgoing them appears in Paul; see, for example, 1 Cor 9.)

In v. 10 the writer reiterates that he is reminding them of what they already know (cf. v. 7). The command, "no work, no food," was given at a prior time. In form it is similar to the Jewish saying, "if I do not work, I have nothing to eat" (a midrash on Gen 1:2 from *Bereshith Rabba*). Perhaps the writer is quoting a popular proverb. The point is to establish not only the necessity but the dignity of work in the Christian community. Note that it is unwillingness to work when it is available and not lack of opportunity or ability to work that is addressed here. The text is not a general condemnation of the unemployed but a reminder to those who are able and have the opportunity to work that they should do so.

From general remarks to the community in vv. 6–10, the writer addresses himself directly to the idlers in vv. 11–12. Not only are they unoccupied, they are meddling in the affairs of others, hindering the work of those engaged in productive labor (v. 11). "Busybody" (*peri-ergazomenous*) is a pun; the word picture says, literally, "to work around," meaning to waste energy. It is a word used pejoratively at several places in the deutero-Pauline corpus (see, for example, 1 Tim 5:13). Not working themselves, the idlers are becoming a nuisance to other Christians who, presumably, are gainfully employed.

Therefore the writer commands and exhorts (*parakaloumen*) them to "work quietly and to earn their own living," literally, to "eat their own bread" (*ton heautōn arton esthiōsin*; v. 12). At several places in the New Testament epistles the command to live a quiet, well-ordered life appears. The issue not only affects the internal life of the Christian community but the repute of the church in the larger society. In the deutero-Pauline writings, concern for what those outside the Christian community thought of it is evident. A well-ordered, productive church would be more likely to be held in esteem. Here the writer subtly suggests that it will do more to advance the Christian message to work than to be idle, even for the sake of evangelism.

In the Thessalonian context, and the Greek world generally, abandoning work for a belief system was especially damaging to Christianity. Some philosophers, notably Cynic teachers, escaped labor by public preaching. Lucian of Samosata calls them "idle frauds [who] live in unlimited plenty, asking for things in a lordly way, getting them without effort" (*The Runaways,* 17). Making their living by being paid to teach, these philosophers used their message as a pretense for laziness.

If the Thessalonian Christians left their trades to preach in public, they would have been subject to the same criticism Lucian (and Dio Chrysostom) leveled at the Cynics. The writer does not want Christians to be thought of as irresponsible meddlers. And so he offers his life of productive work as a model to be followed. And, as Malherbe has demonstrated, that pattern provided its own mission field, namely the workshops and households of artisans and tradespeople in the hellenistic cities.

The Response (3:13–15)

Having soundly admonished the erring, the writer gives general instructions to the Christian community. The turn in the argument is marked by "but you, brothers and sisters" (*hymeis de adelphoi,* which is not translated in the NRSV). The phrase also serves to include the faithful (those holding fast to the tradition) in fellowship with the author and to exclude the idle. The brethren are to be untiring in doing good, a sentiment that is also found in Gal 6:9. It is easy to understand how the hard-working members of the Christian community might be either tempted to join the idlers or to be uncharitable toward them. Good Christians, the writer notes, "do good" not only in general but in reference to those who may not deserve such treatment, especially fellow Christians with whom there may be disagreements and breaches in fellowship.

This does not mean that the disorderly are to be excused. On the contrary, they are to be carefully disciplined. Verse 6 commanded, "keep away from believers who are living in idleness." Verses 14 and 15 spell out how that command is to be carried out. As in 2:2 and 2:15, letters are seen as vehicles of apostolic authority. The recipients of this letter are to take note of or "designate" (*sēmeiousthe*) the idle and "have nothing to do with them, so that they may be ashamed" (v. 14). Literally, the Thessalonian Christians are to avoid mixing with (*synanamignysthai*) the disobedient (and disorderly) in order to cause them to turn around (*entrapē*). Exclusion is their call to *metanoia* ("conversion").

Avoiding those whose lives show forth unacceptable doctrines is also enjoined in Rom 16:17-20 and suggested in 1 Cor 5:9-11. The point of the solution here proposed is not excommunication but reformation. This is made clear in 2 Thess 3:15. The erring members are not enemies (*exthron*) but brothers and sisters (*adelphon*). As they were included as believers in v. 6, so they are regarded as brethren in v. 15 and are to be warned or corrected. Hostility, anger, or malice might be appropriate in dealing with an enemy but not with a fellow believer. The purpose of the shunning is to restore the erring member to fellowship with the community, and so is implicitly understood as temporary (cf. 1 Thess 5:14-15).

The Prayer (3:16)

If the Thessalonian Christians follow the writer's commands, peace within the community will ensue, even if it faces persecution from without (see 1:3-12). Therefore it is appropriate that this section of the letter close with a prayer for peace. The source of that peace is the Lord. Jesus Christ is Lord not only of the Christian community but of peace itself.

There is a textual question as to whether the wish for peace is "in every way" (*tropō,* as in the NRSV) or "in every place" (*topō*). The latter conforms to Pauline usage in 1 Cor 1:2; 2 Cor 2:14; and 1 Thess 1:8, but the former better fits this context and is strongly supported by good manuscript tradition.

The continuance of peace in all times and in all ways is assured by the presence of the Lord. "The Lord be with you all" (v. 16b) has no exact parallel in the genuine Pauline letters, but the sentiment has Old Testament parallels (see Judg 6:12; cf. Luke 1:28 and 2 Tim 4:22). The prayer for the Lord's presence among them serves to close the body of the letter on an irenic and strongly devotional note. As the letter opened with a wish for peace (1:2), it closes in the same fashion.

H. Barclay, "Conflict in Thessalonica," *CBQ* 55 (1993): 512-30.

B. Kaye, "Eschatology and Ethics in 1 and 2 Thessalonians," *NovT* 17 (1975): 47-57.

A. Malherbe, *Paul and the Thessalonians* (Philadelphia: Fortress, 1987).

M. Menken, "Paradise Regained or Still Lost? Eschatology and Disorderly Behavior in 2 Thessalonians," *NTS* 38 (1992): 271–89.

P. Perkins, "2 Thessalonians," *HBC* (San Francisco: Harper and Row, 1988).

R. Russell, "The Idle in 2 Thess 3:6–12: An Eschatological or a Social Problem?" *NTS* 34 (1988): 105–19.

C. Talbert, *Reading Corinthians* (New York: Crossroad, 1989), esp. 126–28.

THE CLOSING

2 Thessalonians 3:17–18

The main feature of the closing of 2 Thessalonians is its brevity. It contains few of the standard features of Pauline letters; there are no travel plans mentioned and no greetings either in general or to specific individuals in the recipient church. The personal element is absent. Perhaps the author was too worried about the problems in Thessalonica to include pleasantries. If the author were Paul, this would seem odd in view of his experiences in Thessalonica and his previous letter to the church there. Here, the writer of 2 Thessalonians is more concerned to authenticate its message rather than to reproduce the style and content of Paul's personal greetings.

The closing of the letter, then, opens with a reminder of Paul's authority. Verse 17 reflects the common practice of using a secretary or amanuensis to write letters. The sender of the letter would authenticate the letter he had dictated with a closing greeting in his own hand or with his own mark. The "sign" (*sēmeion,* literally, "token") was the author's "mark," the indication of the authenticity of the contents of the letter.

A similar statement appears in 1 Cor 16:21 and Col 4:18 (see the commentary on that verse earlier in this volume; cf. Gal 6:11). In closing his letters, Paul uses the verb "to greet"; here the noun "greeting" is used. It is a small, but telling, departure from precedent. Furthermore, the phrase "This is the mark in every letter of mine," is unique in the Pauline corpus. It has been argued that Paul is pointing to the fact that this is, indeed, his handwriting. But if he wrote the letter and the Thessalonian church had already received an epistle from him, why would this be necessary?

Indeed, if 2 Thessalonians is genuinely Pauline, why is v. 17 necessary at all? If the epistle is pseudonymous (as I am inclined to think it is), then the writer must give his work the stamp of Paul's authority. And, in addition, he is distinguishing his authentic and authoritative letter from those proposing to be but which are not (see 2:2 and 15).

The grace wish of v. 18 is common to the closing of Pauline letters (see, for example, Rom 16:20 or 1 Cor 16:23). No benediction of peace accompanies grace, since the peace wish appeared in the prayer that closed the last unit of material in the letter (3:16). This closing sentence is precisely patterned on 1 Thess 5:28, except for the addition, "all of," which is intended to remind the letter's recipients of the teaching in 3:6–16. All receive the grace of God, not just the obedient but the unruly and idle as well.

Grace is "of our Lord Jesus Christ." The genitive of origin designates Christ as the source of grace. Grace opens the letter (1:2), closes it, and has appeared at the end of each major section of the text (see 1:12; 2:16). The Lord Jesus Christ, the source of grace, will sustain the Thessalonians in persecution and vindicate them when he returns to punish the lawless and reward the obedient and faithful. That same grace will be with them all, since by means of it they are bound together as brothers and sisters.